P9-CDC-892

ASSESSING BASIC ACADEMIC SKILLS IN HIGHER EDUCATION

THE TEXAS APPROACH

Edited by

Richard T. Alpert

William Phillip Gorth

Richard G. Allan

LEA LAWRENCE ERLBAUM ASSOCIATES, PUBLISHERS

1989   Hillsdale, New Jersey   Hove and London

The following documents were reprinted with the permission
of the Texas Higher Education Coordinating Board, the
Texas Education Agency, and National Evaluation Systems,
Inc.: "TASP_{TM} Program Summary" (August version,
copyright © 1988); "TASP Skills" (copyright © 1988);
and "1989 TASP Test Registration Bulletin" (draft version,
copyright © 1988).

"A Generation of Failure: The Case for Remediation and
Testing in Texas Higher Education" (copyright © 1986) was
reprinted with the permission of the Texas Higher Education
Coordinating Board.

"Bias Concerns in Test Development" (copyright © 1988)
was reprinted with the permission of National Evaluation
Systems, Inc.

The Texas Academic Skills Program, TASP_{TM}, and the
TASP logo are trademarks of the Texas Higher Education
Coordinating Board, the Texas Education Agency, and
National Evaluation Systems, Inc.

Copyright © 1989 by Lawrence Erlbaum Associates, Inc.
All rights reserved. No part of this book may be reproduced in
any form, by photostat, microform, retrieval system, or any other
means, without the prior written permission of the publisher.

Lawrence Erlbaum Associates, Inc., Publishers
365 Broadway
Hillsdale, New Jersey 07642

ISBN 0-8058-0336-X

Printed in the United States of America
10   9   8   7   6   5   4   3   2   1

Contents

Contents

(continued)

Part Two
Components of the Texas Approach

Preface

The chapters in the first part of this volume are based primarily on presentations made at the conference "Assessing Basic Skills in Higher Education," sponsored by National Evaluation Systems, Inc., and held in April 1988 in New Orleans. This conference brought together a number of outstanding educators to discuss issues related to basic academic skills assessment in higher education. Much of the conference focused on the development of the Texas Academic Skills Program (TASP).

In the second part of this volume, we have reproduced several documents pre-dating or resulting from the Texas Academic Skills Program. The chapter "Bias Concerns in Test Development" is a reproduction of the manual used throughout the test development process for the TASP Test. This chapter benefited greatly from the comments of educators from various parts of the nation, including members of the staffs of both the Texas Higher Education Coordinating Board and the Texas Education Agency, and the committees of Texas educators involved in the development of the TASP.

Though this book focuses on the Texas approach to assessing basic academic skills in higher education, it also deals with general issues of national concern. It should be of interest to state higher education program administrators and policy-makers, deans and faculty members of colleges, state legislators, and educational professionals working directly in or with institutions of higher education.

This book presents a number of perspectives on a compelling and timely topic and provides insight into the construction of an important testing program. We hope it proves valuable to the reader.

Acknowledgments

This book owes its greatest debt to the writers and presenters who contributed their thoughts on the important issues of basic academic skills assessment in higher education and to the staffs of the Texas Education Agency, the Texas Higher Education Coordinating Board, and National Evaluation Systems, Inc., associated with the creation and development of the Texas Academic Skills Program (TASP).

Getting the ideas of the authors and the components of the TASP into printed form involved the talents of many people at National Evaluation Systems, Inc. Nancy Seely, Emily Silverman, and Edward Murphy copyedited the manuscripts and transcripts from our authors and oversaw the production of the documents that appear in the latter part of this book. Jeanne Brzycki typeset the text. Heather Perry designed the pages and the book cover. Laura Simmons and Lisa Miskimen proofread the galleys.

We also appreciate the help and support of the staff at Lawrence Erlbaum Associates, particularly Art Lizza.

Introduction

A few years ago, National Evaluation Systems, Inc. (NES) sponsored the book entitled *Testing for Teacher Certification*. The introduction included a general discussion of teacher certification testing programs, reflecting the assumption that not many readers would be familiar with the topic. In the past two years, as more and more states constructed teacher assessment programs and as the issues related to teacher testing became familiar to a broader audience, we sponsored two more books: *The Validity Issue: What Should Teacher Certification Tests Measure?* and *Bias Issues in Teacher Certification Testing*.

Turning Our Attention to Another National Issue

In this year's book we turn our attention to a different testing arena: the assessment of basic academic skills in higher education. This topic requires less introduction than teacher certification testing did a few years ago. It has quickly been gaining widespread attention as college faculty and administrators around the country express increased concern about the reading, mathematics, and writing skills of entering freshman-level students.

Many students arrive on our college and university campuses lacking the ability to read and comprehend the material for their courses. Even larger numbers cannot successfully perform fundamental mathematic and algebraic operations. And many are unable to express themselves effectively in writing. In New Jersey, a test of basic skills administered to entering college students since 1978 has consistently produced distressing results about the proficiency levels of those students.

From the perspective of colleges and universities, this degree of underpreparation is a challenging educational fact of life. The notion that every student who comes to college is prepared to do college-level work is simply untenable. Fortunately, state agencies and colleges and universities have generally avoided pointing an accusing finger at other educational institutions and instead have sought an effective solution to the problem. The challenge for many higher education institutions today is to identify their underprepared entering students and to provide developmental education (i.e., remediation) services that will help bring those students' skills to a level that will allow them to perform successfully in college courses. This challenge implies some form of assessment coupled with academic skills development.

Individual campuses are addressing this situation in a variety of ways. It is well beyond the scope of this book to review in detail all of these enterprises. We will instead provide a number of perspectives on the general issues of basic skills assessment in higher education and take the opportunity to focus in depth on activities now under way in Texas.

The Texas Academic Skills Program

Through recent legislation and educational reforms, the state of Texas has made the commitment to deal directly and aggressively with the problem of underpreparation of entering college students. Under the Texas Academic Skills Program (TASP), public colleges and universities will identify students who demonstrate a lack of proficiency in reading, mathematics, or writing and will offer them remediation services. The TASP calls for advisory programs and support for all students who show a need to develop the basic academic skills they should have in order to perform effectively in undergraduate degree programs. Further, the TASP includes a testing component that will serve to identify and provide diagnostic information about the academic skills of each student.

While much attention must focus on the testing component of the program—since it serves as the first step in determining a student's needs—it is important to recognize that the backbone of the TASP is much more than a test and the resulting student scores. One of the most important elements of the program is the ensuing development of instructional and advising programs designed to help students acquire the skills they should have to perform effectively in college-level courses.

The Content of This Book

This volume, *Assessing Basic Academic Skills in Higher Education: The Texas Approach,* is presented in two parts. Most of the papers in Part One, "Access to Quality: The Challenge for Higher Education," are based on presentations made at the conference "Assessing Basic Skills in Higher Education," sponsored by NES in April 1988.

In the first paper, Wilhelmina Delco, a member of the Texas House of Representatives and key author of the legislation that led to the TASP, provides a legislative perspective on the challenge presented to educators and state higher education agencies in Texas.

Next, William Sanford, assistant commissioner of the Texas Higher Education Coordinating Board, offers a brief history on the TASP and underscores the complexity of program goals and issues.

Joan Matthews, a director of the TASP, prepared the third paper exclusively for this book. She provides some details on the efforts being made to prevent bias during the development of TASP items.

The fourth paper, jointly written by Joan Matthews and Richard Alpert, division director of Higher Education Programs at NES, was presented at the Third National Forum on Assessment in Higher Education, sponsored by the American Association for Higher Education in June 1988. They discuss how the TASP is responding to the legislative requirement for extensive participation of faculty. Their presentation includes descriptions of many of the committees and panels involved in the TASP.

Manuel Justiz and Marilyn Kameen, of the University of South Carolina, focus on issues of basic skills assessment for minority populations and emphasize the need to develop testing and remediation programs that do not limit access for minorities.

The next three papers offer perspectives on three areas of basic skills. Timothy Shanahan, of the University of Illinois at Chicago, writes about ways in which developments in reading theory are affecting test design. Charles Pine, of Rutgers University, outlines the results and conclusions of his research based on the the New Jersey Algebra Project. Finally, Edward White, of California State University at San Bernardino, compares two approaches to writing instruction and assessment and recommends a style of writing assessment.

Next, Theodore Marchese, of the American Association for Higher Education, sets the concern for basic academic skills development in the larger context of the assessment and education reform movements.

We end Part One with an edited transcript of the panel discussion that closed the NES conference last spring. Wilhelmina Delco, William Sanford, Pamela Tackett (of the Texas Education Agency), and William Hardesty (former president of Southwest Texas State University) were the panelists.

In Part Two, "Components of the Texas Approach," we reproduce several documents that pre-dated or resulted from the TASP. They include the 1986 report of the Committee on Testing of the Texas Higher Education Coordinating Board; the legislation that led to the creation of the TASP; rules and regulations recently adopted by the Texas Higher Education Coordinating Board; a TASP Test program summary; a document listing the skills on which the TASP Test will be based; the bias-prevention manual used by those involved in test development; and the registration bulletin to be used by students planning to take the TASP Test.

Part One

Access to Quality: The Challenge for Higher Education

Testing from a Legislative Perspective

Wilhelmina Delco

If I were to offer a subtitle for this presentation, it would be "Why are nice people like legislators in the business of dealing with testing?" After I authored the bill requiring basic skills testing in public institutions in the state of Texas, a lot of educators were publicly, and with some degree of hostility, asking the same question. They asked the question because there is a real feeling that legislators and people who form public policy ought to be in the business of appropriating money and should leave the business of educating and decisions about how to spend that money to educators.

If all things were equal in the world, that system probably would work out just fine. The truth is that some of the most critical education policy decisions in the history of our country have been made by people outside of the enterprise we call education. Take, for example, this question: "To whom should education, this wonderful vehicle for upward mobility, be offered?" For years, most educators felt that education belonged to a small, fairly restricted group. W. E. B. DuBois defined them as "the academically talented ten." It was public policy that determined that all people who had the ability to learn ought to have access to the learning process and that public funds ought to be appropriated to support that policy.

Determining Funds for the Enterprise of Education

Every state in the United States has as a constitutional responsibility the charge to educate its people. And today education means much more than just the development of a literate citizenry. Education for many states is truly the cornerstone that spurs economic growth and develops a state's competitive edge among other states and nations. Most states spend up to half, and some spend even more than half

Wilhelmina Delco is a member of the Texas House of Representatives and chair of its Higher Education Committee.

of their state budgets on the enterprise of education. Such appropriations were accepted when state resources were rather plentiful and demands for state money were few. However, because education programs, like all programs that deal with human services and special populations, are being abandoned at the federal level and returned to the states, we are for the first time in many states seeing competition for limited dollars. Legislators, who are trying to determine priorities for limited dollars, must ask why education should get so much money. Even more importantly, they must ask how educators will spend this money, and how the legislature can monitor the expenditures. In other words, we must ask, "Can we take the word of educators that all is well with the enterprise?"

In K–12 education the response was the National Commission on Excellence in Education's 1983 report *A Nation at Risk.* All over the country there was a wave of reform. In the state of Texas there was the perception that there was something wrong with K–12 education and the acknowledgment that we had to spend more money. However, along with the appropriation of funds was a counterconcern for accountability of the money that would be spent.

When the committee on postsecondary education was formed, all the members did not share the same notion about postsecondary education. As a matter of fact, at the opening meeting the governor, lieutenant governor, and speaker of our House of Representatives (who were, by act of the resolution, part of that committee) commented that the enterprise of postsecondary education in Texas was doing well. Most people felt that education in the state was in good hands and just needed fine-tuning. In the minds of a lot of people, that meant we were spending too much money frivolously or unnecessarily and needed to figure out how to tighten the enterprise. We looked at the priorities that had been established essentially by the institutions and the administrators of those institutions. We questioned whether the appropriations that were being allocated for those institutions were right. More importantly, we asked whether postsecondary institutions were really meeting the needs of the students and whether those students were receiving from those institutions what they were led to believe was there for them. From such questions you get the conflict of appropriations and accountability. Legislators asked, "Are we getting our money's worth?"

Legislators, who are ever sensitive to the concerns of warm bodies that can vote, started asking such questions in our state and in all states. It is so easy to ask those questions because in most states the colleges and universities are out there with their budgets naked on a line. And when you have problems balancing a budget, it is very easy, if an institution is not in your district, to draw a line through its appropriations. It is very easy to rationalize a delay tactic: "When times get better. . . . When the need is greater or the fuss is louder or the crisis is felt, we will return the funds. But in the meantime this is not as high a priority as other things are in our state." We see legislators across this country asking questions: "What are we defining as higher education? Who can participate? What do they gain from participation? What is it costing us? What do we get for our money?"

Asking for Accountability through Testing

In Texas, it is with such questions that the issue of testing came in. Testing provides the easy, objective answer in the minds of legislators. Educators are telling us that they, from a professional perspective, expose people in our state, from very young to not so young, to a body of material, and they give them some kind of certification, some kind of diploma, that says they have in fact mastered this material. And they are telling us that such services cost a lot of money. Legislators in turn are saying there ought to be some way to measure whether we in fact have gotten our money's worth, some way to show that people's diplomas are worth what they imply.

Legislators are not picky about how you measure that, and are not terribly responsive to the argument that testing hurts some groups more than others, because that then becomes painful. The point that legislators are making in the increasing hue and cry for testing is that if you say that given enough resources you can educate a person in our state, then there ought to be some way to demonstrate this. There ought to be some way to compare the capabilities of students who have been exposed to a body of material with the capabilities of students who have not. The way to do that is left to the experts.

The message I bring to you is that this process of what you may call legislative meddling is not going to go away. The number of state legislators who have jumped with both feet into the testing business has grown. Over the years the number of states putting demands and strings on funds attached to some kind of accountability has increased. And the rationale for that increase is the perception that what you say you do as educators can and must be measured.

The extent to which the educational vehicle is not developed to the satisfaction of the legislators, and the people who elect those legislators, is the extent to which your dollars are threatened. It is the extent to which alternatives to your institutions are being developed.

This is a critical issue and I would commend it very forcefully to you for your consideration. There are too many other groups with needs in our country today, and they are in line demanding the money that many of our educational institutions receive. There are too many mothers of young children, young mothers of young children, who are saying, "My kids may never get to college. Indeed, I may never get to college." The need is urgent and the need is now. There are not enough resources to provide adequately for all of the needs. We have to establish priorities.

Also consider that in the United States we have an aging population. The number of people who are over 65 exceeds the number of people who are under 18. As people age, they vote more frequently. When they vote they say to their legislators, "We have nothing against public schools. We have nothing against colleges and universities. But if we are to enjoy the fruits of our labors, we want some focus placed on our needs." The college population today is older. It is part time. It is working. It is increasingly female. And so the thrust in most institutions is more utilitarian than educational. It is more "now" oriented than "long-term" oriented. Community colleges are flourishing precisely for that reason.

As people become involved in the political process and see that funds are limited, they are voicing the concerns that legislators reflect in their decisions about funding. And in that vein I want you to understand that this is an important issue. I have no quarrel with the validity of testing. I have no problem with the concept of testing. My problem is with the sole reliance on testing. I do not believe that a test has been devised that can stand as the sole criterion for anything. I say this from having served four years on the board of trustees of the Educational Testing Service, where I became chairwoman of that board. I believe that tests must be coupled with other things. So the charge to you as educators is to develop the best instruments you can and to use those instruments to glean the kind of diagnostic information that you need to do the best job.

Educators and Legislators Together in the Glare of Public Light

You as educators have to be aware that you do not operate in splendid isolation. As long as you use public funds, the eyes of the legislature are on you. And as long as the eyes of the legislature are on you, people are constantly going to say, "Why are we spending this money to do this?" If you as educators are in fact performing a critical public service, and I believe you are, then you have to perform that service in the full glare of public light. What you do is important. Education is critical to the survival of our country and of all the people in our country. But it is no longer the exclusive property of the professionals in education. It is now in the public arena, and every step of the way questions are going to be asked that legislators believe can be answered through the use of testing programs. If questions are raised that we cannot answer, we will turn to you. If you do not make a good effort to answer them, we are going to turn someplace else.

This is a national issue. It is a national priority. And as we talk about turning the corner in economic development and competition in this country, one of the key tools is education. But before we appropriate the money now, we are going to ask for accountability. We are going to ask for some measure of the results that educators say they can produce. We are going to look at the diversity of the populations in our states and we are going to ask questions. We want to know why there are still groups that do not do well on tests and why there are constituencies that are literally afraid of tests. We want to know how much importance we ought to put on tests. If you as educators do not think we should rely so heavily on them, you need to tell us that and why. If we cannot put a lot of faith in testing as an accountability tool, what are the options?

It seems to me that the educators' charge is as serious as that of the legislature. Educators are as much in the arena and the spotlight of public policy as we are. And it is critically important that you keep in mind that the people who appropriate the money are not the villains. They ought to be the partners in this enterprise we call education, because they are essential to the process—and if the process does not work, we are all losers.

TASP:
An Opportunity to
Regain Opportunities Lost

William Sanford

A presentation on the policy issues underlying the development and implementation of the Texas Academic Skills Program (TASP) might best take as its theme a part of a poem by Augustus de Morgan titled "A Budget of Paradoxes."

> Great fleas have little fleas upon their backs to bite 'em.
> And little fleas have lesser fleas, and so ad infinitum.
> The great fleas themselves in turn have greater fleas to go on,
> While these again have greater still, and greater still, and so on.

Public policy develops on the basis of decisions made within a social context. For one to understand the choices we are making in Texas, I must begin with a brief summary of some of the historical, demographic, and economic elements that undergird the nascence and nurturance of the program.

Historical, Demographic, and Economic Elements Behind the TASP

Historians of the Southwest have suggested that the development of Texas can be summarized in this sequence of terms: the horse, the six-shooter, the windmill, the plow, the barbed-wire fence, and the oil well. It is our hope that the terms for tomorrow will be the computer, the satellite, and the test tube. A popular slogan during the last session of the legislature—which focused much of its attention on higher education—was "Brains are the oil and gas of the future."

The state's economic mainstays were first ranching and then farming, until oil was discovered. Until recently, Texas was a rural state. Now, it is in transition.

William Sanford is assistant commissioner of the Texas Higher Education Coordinating Board.

In an environment of cattle and oil wells, the fundamental role of higher education has been "access." Texas is a state in which, from World War II through President Lyndon Johnson's Great Society to the present day, the public has seen higher education, above all else, as a means whereby all citizens have an opportunity to raise themselves from poverty to economic well-being.

This goal has been manifest in the last two decades by a series of actions designed to place an institution of public higher education within 50 miles of every citizen in the state. And this process has been 98 percent successful. One of the products in Texas of the Johnson vice-presidency and presidency was the establishment of 47 junior colleges. In the five-year period between 1968 and 1973, 15 new public senior institutions were created.

During the same period, student enrollment increased 42 percent, compared to an increase of only 16.5 percent in the college-age population. This 42 percent also contrasts with a national average of only 25 percent.

Texas is a large state, but in education it is poor. Some 205 of the 254 counties of the state contain poor school districts; 83 percent of the districts in east Texas and 95 percent of those along the border with Mexico are considered poor. In all, 60 percent of Texas's 2.9 million school children reside in poor districts.

In 1980 approximately 66 percent of the 14 million Texas residents were Anglos, 21 percent Hispanic, 12 percent Black, and 1.3 percent Asian and other. But between 1970 and 1980 the Mexican-origin population increased by 70 percent, compared to 22 percent for Blacks and 15 percent for Anglos. Of all Mexican-born persons in the United States, Texas has one-fourth. (California has one-half.)

During the last decade Hispanics accounted for 63 percent of the one-quarter million student increase in the public schools. Among children under age 15, Anglos will cease being a majority before the turn of the century. During the next 50 years, Hispanic enrollment will rise from less than one million to almost 2.4 million.

In 1985–86 there were more than 3.5 million children between the ages of 3 and 19 enrolled in schools in Texas. By the year 2000 there will be 4.4 million.

More than 70 percent of all Anglos aged 25 or older have completed high school and 20 percent have finished at least four years of college. The respective proportions among Hispanics are 35 percent and 6 percent. Among Blacks, 50 percent have completed high school, but only 9 percent have had four years of college.

In the proportion of residents aged 25 or older who have completed high school, Texas ranks thirty-eighth among all states. In 1983, 27 percent of the half-million children in the state three and four years old were members of families below the federal poverty line. Almost 31 percent of all Black households have no husband present.

Texas spends about 45 percent of all state revenues on education. But it ranks forty-fifth among the 50 states in taxes per $1,000 of income. And in 1987 school children's SAT scores also ranked forty-fifth.

The largest share of Texas's tax income derives from a corporate franchise tax and a rather heavy sales tax. The sales tax accounts for more than one-half of all tax revenues, compared with an average of one-third in other states.

But while service industries are creating 85 percent of the new jobs, revenues in this sector are not taxed for the most part. Service industries contribute less than 10 percent of sales tax revenues, while consumer goods kick in 60 percent and purchases of capital equipment make up another 25 percent.

The last legislature did remove sales tax exemptions from some services, such as those provided by cleaners, janitors, pest controllers, and security guards. But it has yet to touch doctors, lawyers, dentists, architects, engineers, or real estate brokers.

With that as the context for policy development, let's turn now to the Texas Academic Skills Program.

The Policy Development Process

In the policy analysis textbooks, public policy decisions tend to be rational. Decision making is characterized by a problem that is clearly distinguishable, goals and values that are clarified and ranked by importance, consequences that may be investigated and compared, and choices that are based on the preponderance of evidence and preference.

We have not had that luxury in Texas. The testing bill that created the TASP was only one part of an omnibus legislative package affecting virtually all of higher education. Different interest groups continue to have significantly differing views regarding the purpose and value of the test. Lacking a very clear focus, the policy-makers did not fully debate all alternative strategies for achieving the desired goals. The legislature did not, for example, accept a broadly supported recommendation regarding who should bear the cost of the test. The assignments and responsibilities for developing and operating the program were only broadly sketched. Many possible social and educational consequences of the program were only generally anticipated. The costs and management issues of both testing and developing a comprehensive, research-based developmental/remedial program were not fully analyzed or faced. The agencies charged to bring the program into existence were not even provided the resources necessary to guarantee its success.

Because the policy development process was less than "rational" in the textbook definition of the term, we continue today to address major questions and make ends-means adjustments to respond to the intent of the leadership of the state. On many occasions, we continue to find ourselves going back to that leadership and asking what it meant on various fundamental matters.

Recognizing and Addressing the Need

Texas was late in recognizing and addressing the needs of under-prepared students. The first formal awakening came in 1979, when a committee of university English faculty petitioned the Coordinating Board of the Texas College and University System (later named the Texas Higher Education Coordinating Board) to permit limited state support for the teaching of remedial English/reading/writing courses by the public universities. Before this time, only the community/junior colleges were supported for such instruction.

The committee pointed out that studies demonstrated that some students otherwise qualified for admission to senior colleges and universities on the basis of standardized tests and public school grades did not possess reading and writing skills adequate for success in baccalaureate programs and that the universities needed funds to support remedial and developmental instruction. With considerable reluctance the board bowed to the evidence and authorized universities to offer as much as three credit hours of precollegiate, remedial, or developmental English/reading/writing instruction.

The reluctance of some board members was based on the fact that the state already pays twice for this instruction: once in the public schools and again in the community/junior colleges. Providing support for the third segment of the system appeared to many to be throwing good money after bad, as well as reducing the motivation for students to achieve.

The one restriction that was placed on the three credit hours of instruction was that such work could not be counted toward completion of a degree.

Six years later, in 1985, three additional credit hours were authorized to be funded for precollegiate mathematics courses.

Policy Goals Considered by the Committee on Testing

The first Committee on Testing was appointed by Chairman Larry Temple of the Coordinating Board in August 1985. Its charge was to examine the feasibility and desirability of implementing a test for public higher education students in the state. The stated policy objective at the time was to provide a measurement of both the quality of teaching and the quality of learning in the system. The operant question was: "How can we improve the quality of the higher education product unless we know what product is actually being delivered and received?"

By examining this language and other objectives of the program that have been suggested from various sources in the past three years, we can identify at least four policy goals that were initially considered to justify its implementation.

Trimming the Structure through Screening

The first goal considered was to implement a test to screen students, to select the most capable for advancement, to pare the size of the higher education structure of the state, and to reduce the burden that it places on the state budget.

In light of our current economic condition, this is not a stand that was taken lightly. Its problem, however, is that it is in clear conflict with the historic "access" mission of higher education in Texas. The only organized interest group continuing to proffer this as a perceived policy objective of the program is the Mexican American Legal Defense and Educational Fund (MALDEF), but they have other motives—notably, an expressed intention to have the TASP invalidated by the courts. Our current strategy is to ask the Coordinating Board to establish guidelines that will obviate continued rhetoric regarding this point of view.

Public School Accountability

The second policy goal considered was that of forcing new standards of accountability on the public schools of the state. As suggested earlier, it is still argued by some that higher education would not have to deal with the problems of underprepared students if the public schools were effective in doing their job.

This position suffers from several problems. It does not take into account the experiences of other states that have tried to deal with this issue. It does not recognize that public schools have objectives other than preparing students for college entrance. It also ignores a broader social policy objective that has permeated the country's higher education environment for at least three decades—namely, that of democratizing college by making it available to an ever-increasing proportion of society and, by so doing, admitting citizens who inevitably are less well prepared.

Finally, the position is faulty because it not only projects blame for perceived failure, but it also assumes fallacious causal connections. It implies that those who operate the public schools must be incompetent or lazy. Thus it ignores the extraordinarily difficult, perhaps impossible, conditions under which public schools attempt to achieve society's goals.

I elaborate the obvious shortcomings of this argument—that the test should be used to highlight the failings of the public schools—not simply because those shortcomings are so numerous and obvious, but also because this argument still holds a powerful appeal to some persons in the policy-making arena.

Higher Education Accountability

The third goal of the program that has maintained its purchase with an important portion of the policy establishment is that of enforcing greater accountability within the higher education community for the quality of the liberalizing and cultural objectives of the first two years of general studies. The corollaries of this goal take three forms: (1) a swing back to the cultural purpose of the baccalaureate experience, (2) its direct opposite, a protection of the integrity of the specialized and professional training programs in the upper two years of undergraduate study, and (3) an enforcement of accountability on the community/junior college sector, which is seen by some as not preparing students adequately to transfer into senior institutions.

The first corollary—using the test as a tool to improve the quality of the first two years of the college experience—may have some merit. The others, however, suffer from obvious problems. The commitment to protecting the integrity of upper-level programs is simply an alternative form of elitism—a substitute argument for screening students and perpetuating the existing class structure. Also, it is based on the pop-culture thesis that the purpose of college is job training. Although this trend may continue unabated for some time yet, its full implications have not been thoroughly debated by policy-makers.

The final corollary—implementing a testing program to force accountability among the community/junior college sector—suffers from the same shortcomings as the similar goal applied to the high schools. It presumes that the causes of the apparent failure rest in areas that can be readily addressed and solved by those working in that environment. In fact, community colleges today are for the most part serving a different postsecondary clientele than are the four-year schools. Many of their students are poorer and less well prepared for college. A majority are in vocational/technical programs. Only perhaps one-half transfer to universities. Many of the problems are structural and intransigent.

In addition to the many shortcomings of each of the three corollaries, there is an additional problem that all of them share. Each would use a test of students to solve a perceived structural problem only indirectly related to the students themselves. Under each of these goals, students would be required to take, and pay for, a test—and to pass it or fail it—in order for the establishment to gather information that could lead to changes in the instructional delivery system.

Such a policy would invert the priorities of public higher education. It would use students as means to other ends. It would not be a bona fide educational activity; it would be a research project with students as the lab rats.

Assisting the Underprepared

The fourth enunciated policy goal of the TASP, and the vision we have embraced, is that the test should be the first part of a comprehensive instructional program designed to assist underprepared students to remain and succeed in college. It is an educational program, not a testing program. In the words of one faculty member, "It is an opportunity to regain opportunities lost."

The easiest way to understand this goal and its penetration of our thinking and planning is to examine the evolution of the language relating to the program. The first iteration was that of a "rising junior" test. But that concept was quickly abandoned in favor of a postadmissions placement test. The test will be used as a tool to identify areas of reading, writing, or mathematics in which a student may be underprepared and to assist the college or university in placing him or her in remedial/developmental activities that will enhance opportunity for success.

Another pertinent change in language was in the name of the principal developmental oversight committee. It was first called the "Basic Skills Committee." That name evolved, first into the "Council on Learning Excellence," and finally the "Academic Skills Council."

Note also that students are referred to as being "underprepared." There is no suggestion that some may be incapable. They are all products of the system, and the operational presumption is that if the system can be improved in their favor—if students are given a fair opportunity to achieve in college—then they will succeed.

Fundamental Questions Yet to Answer

Turning to other major policy issues, two fundamental questions not clearly addressed in legislation are: "Who must take the test?" and "Who must pass it?" Is it intended, for example, that the test and remediation programs apply to a student taking a single welding course in an occupational program offered by a community college? How do we deal with an adult who returns to college after two decades' absence?

Another unanswered issue is: "Whose test is it?"—or, put another way: "How can support for the program be engendered during the development and implementation stages?"

Of unfathomed import are questions that will arise out of the predictable results of the program—we know there will be a short-term differential success ratio related to economic class and, by corollary, ethnicity. What will be the social and political impacts of this consequence? What will it do to the willingness of the state to carry forward with the program? If differential results are significant and long lasting, what impact will that have on the historical role of higher education in the state, and on the future of the state's economy?

Even ignoring the specter of unfairness and possible political unrest, and focusing only on the economic conditions within the state, will the legislature be willing to provide the new resources necessary to give additional basic academic skills assistance to 30 percent to 50 percent of the three-quarter million students attending public colleges and universities?

Despite these and the many other problems we still have to solve, we believe we have achieved at least a general understanding of what we are trying to accomplish and how we are planning to do it. We are trying to make higher education more accessible for under-prepared students. We seek to help them to be more successful in their lives. We also want to make our public schools, community colleges, and universities more effective in fulfilling their instructional mandates. In a broader frame of reference, we want to save taxpayers money and streamline our educational system by reducing the duplication in instruction in basic academic skills now being carried on among the various sectors of the system.

And in the economic/social context, we hope to develop a more educated work force so we can more effectively emulate the success that has been achieved by other states as they have adjusted to changes in the nation's economic system.

We readily acknowledge that the best place to address the problem of underpreparation in basic academic skills is at the lower grade levels, with methods that engage teachers, counselors, parents, and community leaders. But we have found no single strategy that will solve this problem. And intervention at the lower level will do nothing for the hundreds of thousands of citizens for whom that intervention is already too late.

As one attempts to describe the development of a state-level program to identify and help underprepared students, one inevitably seeks familiar and adequate analogies and metaphors. Intellectually, the exercise is not unlike that of peeling an onion, with each new layer a cluster of new questions and problems. Emotionally it is more akin to the observation of the queen in *Alice in Wonderland.* She shouts to Alice as they race along, "My dear, if you wish to get ahead, you must run twice as fast."

Preventing Test Bias in the Texas Academic Skills Program

Joan M. Matthews

Many years ago at one of our public universities, I counseled a Black nursing student who was bright but having difficulty passing the teacher-made tests in one of her classes. I looked at the items on her last exam. One striking example went something like this:

> Which activity would be appropriate for a patient recovering from kidney surgery within his second post-surgical week?
>
> A.   a game of badminton
> B.   a ten-mile drive in the country
> C.   a card game with three other friends
> D.   none of the above

The student answered D—none of the above—because she understood (and she was quite right) that the principle of a successful recovery requires quiet, sedate activities. So she eliminated badminton because of the running and stretching, driving because of the dangers of sudden swerves or stops, and card games, which was the correct answer, because, she said, they often could get wild. "I know now what my teacher wanted," she said, "but where I come from, card games can be pretty exciting."

This is a clear example of bias in testing.

Defining Problems and Goals

In Texas, with the development of the Texas Academic Skills Program (TASP), bias became everyone's concern. We are a tri-ethnic state where minority citizens are expected to become the majority within very few years. At the beginning of the next century, there will be more Hispanics in Texas than any other group. To complicate the issues, Texas has what we believe to be an unacceptable minority

Joan M. Matthews is a director of the Texas Academic Skills Program of the Texas Higher Education Coordinating Board.

attrition rate in the K–12 years of education. As a result, too few minority students (about 20 percent) are in the public higher education system, a deleterious situation for both students and the state. One of the major purposes of the TASP is to increase successful participation in higher education, not to decrease it and not to create a barrier. From the very beginning, it was obvious that sensitivity to bias prevention must be a paramount concern. In fact, bias prevention became a primary goal of the Texas Academic Skills Program. Since it is our intent to increase participation of all groups in higher education in Texas and to assist those who may be underprepared, it is especially important that biased items do not cloud the results of the tests.

What is test bias? Our TASP Bias Review Panel chose a definition that says it "refers to a person's potential disadvantage in responding to test materials because of his or her gender, race, ethnicity, nationality, religion, age, handicapping condition, or cultural, economic, or geographic background." When a test is biased, inaccurate information is received and inaccurate decisions may be made about the person who took the test. Subgroups of people may be disadvantaged because, due to bias in the testing instrument, they may be unable to represent their skills or knowledge fairly.

When we examined traditional bias prevention strategies, we and our contractor, National Evaluation Systems, Inc. (NES), found them inadequate for the needs of our program. For example, it is typical for a testing company to have one staff member oversee bias review on a test under development. There is also usually a bias review panel that meets once to screen both the items and the test directions. Statistical analyses of bias are routine, of course.

We decided to go much further. In fact, I know of no other large testing program where such extensive bias prevention methods are in place. While no methodology is foolproof, we have every reason to believe that the checks and balances, the careful attention of reviewers, and the appropriate statistical analyses will result in a test that is as bias free as possible.

Measures Taken in Texas

At the outset, the plans drawn up by NES went far beyond ordinary review for bias in many similar testing programs. First of all, NES has its own system of bias checks. As part of regular company policy on bias, they used an equity review panel of external experts who scrutinized all materials before they were presented to any Texas reviewers. This Massachusetts-based group had approximately six meetings while our test was under development. NES also required key staff working on the project to be sensitive to bias concerns.

A Bias-Prevention Manual

To assist Texas educators in their process of reviewing the test, NES produced *Bias Concerns in Test Development,* a manual on bias prevention. They provided many Texas educators with the opportunity to make comments on the manual in draft form and incorporated their views in the final version. This manual was distributed to the Texas Education Agency and Coordinating Board staff, all members of the Texas Academic Skills Council, the Tests and Measurements Advisory Committee, all participants in our nine Regional Forums, the Bias Review Panel, and all three Content Area Advisory Committees—in all, to almost five hundred people. Our goal was to sensitize everyone concerned with the development of the test to the problem of bias.

Advisory and Review Committees and Panels

Those were the tools and procedures brought to bear upon the test development process before any documents reached Texas. From our side, we designed an elaborate review strategy to prevent bias. The context in which it exists is also elaborate. To understand it fully, let me provide a brief overview of our strategy for input into the entire program. In such a large and diverse state where there are almost one hundred public institutions of higher education, we decided that extensive faculty and administrative input was essential. In fact, the law enabling the program specifically calls for "the recommendations of faculty from various institutions of higher education." Given the intricacies of academic politics, we interpreted that mandate liberally. We have about two hundred statewide advisory committees and nine regional panels involved in various aspects of the program.

They include about 950 educators. Thousands more have provided input via a series of surveys related to test development or to the program as a whole. We believe that a process incorporating such wide involvement is valuable in itself in gaining support for the program.

Eighteen of these committees and panels have charges concerned with test development. The Tests and Measurements Advisory Committee advises on anything related to test development and administration. Then there is a review cycle that begins with nine regional panels of about thirty persons each. The documents they review are sent to the Bias Review Panel. The comments of all regional panels as well as of the Bias Review Panel are forwarded to the three Content Area Committees (reading, writing, and mathematics). This cyclic review occurs four times. After these reviews are completed, additional Texas educators serving on Standard Setting Committees will meet (in winter 1989). All committees report to an umbrella advisory group, the Texas Academic Skills Council, whose members chair the most important committees.

External to all, we appointed the TASP Technical Advisory Panel, a group of nationally known experts in testing from other states. They provide oversight and consultation to the state on salient aspects of our test development. Our plans for bias prevention received their imprimatur before we proceeded far into the review cycle. This panel noted that the procedures went far beyond a usual treatment of the issues.

When the commissioner of higher education appointed the 35-member Bias Review Panel, individuals were selected from groups such as the Mexican-American Legal Defense and Educational Fund and the National Association for the Advancement of Colored People as well as from Texas faculty and educators. The committee scrutinized our test development and its own procedures very carefully. They were especially aware that test bias is a reflection of culture, and since our cultures are diverse in Texas, the job of test construction is particularly sensitive. The resulting instrument must communicate equitably to all.

While it is common practice to have a bias review at one or possibly two points in the development of a test, we decided to highlight the prevention of bias throughout the project at the following times:

- when it is decided what skills to measure;
- before and after a validation survey of these skills;
- when item specifications are developed;
- when items are developed;
- when field test results are available; and
- when the standards are set for the test.

There is still another way that we are working to prevent bias. Because some minority groups have received lower scores on tests nationally, we have sought good minority membership on all our committees in the groups of survey respondents and field test participants. Of the higher education faculty in the state, 12.5 percent are minorities. On the TASP committees, 35 percent of the serving members are minorities. These educators have been tireless in their determination that the test will be fair to all students. Their dedication serves all Texas students well.

Summary

Thus, through our contractor's procedures in Massachusetts, the large number of reviews in Texas by educators, the scrutiny by Texas Education Agency and Texas Higher Education Coordinating Board staff, and statistical analyses, we have deliberately made bias prevention the ongoing responsibility of all persons involved in the development of the test.

Balancing State Initiative and Campus Participation in Texas

Joan M. Matthews and Richard T. Alpert

On college campuses across the country, graduation ceremonies are remarkably similar. Despite the great variety of degrees and institutions, the graduates are welcomed into the "company of educated men and women." However, in all too many cases, these words have a hollow ring. Although they are college graduates, many fall short of having even the most fundamental skills that we associate with a college education.

Basic Skills Issues on the National Agenda

The issue of students lacking the basic skills generally associated with college-level work has gained a prominent place on the national educational agenda. We cannot attribute this attention simply to the popularity of such books as Allan Bloom's *The Closing of the American Mind* (1987) or E. D. Hirsch's *Cultural Literacy* (1987). Rather, it grows out of the everyday experiences of more and more faculty in almost every kind of institution in American higher education. Too many students simply lack the reading, mathematics, and writing skills they need in order to perform effectively in college courses. Although a number of factors may contribute to this decline—the impact of television, a decrease in parents' involvement in their children's education, the organization of curricular materials, changes in the populations entering college—colleges and universities must nevertheless face the challenges of educating underprepared students and must try to compensate for the decline.

Joan M. Matthews is a director of the Texas Academic Skills Program of the Texas Higher Education Coordinating Board.

Richard T. Alpert is division director of higher education programs at National Evaluation Systems, Inc.

The New Jersey Experience

New Jersey was one of the first states to address the problem of students with insufficient preparation for college-level work. In 1977 New Jersey developed the College Basic Skills Assessment Program, designed to determine the basic skills proficiencies in reading, mathematics, and writing of students admitted to New Jersey public colleges and universities. The program assesses student basic skills proficiencies through the administration of a test in five areas: writing, reading comprehension, sentence sense, mathematics computation, and elementary algebra. Students lacking proficiency are offered remediation.

Unfortunately, results from the New Jersey program are remarkably consistent. Since 1978 more than five hundred thousand students have taken the test. With little variation since 1978, only 26 percent of the students were proficient in verbal skills; 32 percent were proficient in mathematics computation; and only 12 percent appeared proficient in elementary algebra. In its 1985 report, the New Jersey Basic Skills Council stated that "the proportion of students who are well prepared to begin college work in New Jersey continues to be far below what colleges consider desirable."

New Jersey's experience is mirrored in most other parts of the country. The recent results of the National Assessment of Educational Progress program indicate low levels of mathematics proficiency among 17 year olds. Virtually every testing program echoes the refrain that a very large proportion of students entering college do not have the basic skills—especially in mathematics—to do college-level work.

Identifying Student Needs in Texas

In 1985 the Coordinating Board of the Texas College and University System (later named the Texas Higher Education Coordinating Board) became concerned about high failure rates among students taking the Pre-Professional Skills Test for entrance into teacher education programs. The board's members quickly realized these results were an indication of a broader problem and commissioned a blue-ribbon committee of prominent educators to study it further.

In 1986 this committee, known as the Committee on Testing, submitted its report entitled *A Generation of Failure: The Case for Testing and Remediation*. The committee made its case in direct and urgent language:

> "The exact dimension of the problem in Texas is not known, but the indicators are clear: too many Texas students do not read, communicate, or compute at the college level. We do not know who they are or where they are, but we do know that they represent a generation of failure in our educational system—a failure we can no longer afford to ignore."

Responding with a Testing Program

The response to *A Generation of Failure* came from the Texas legislature in 1987 in the form of House Bill 2182. The bill includes all the recommendations of the committee's report and is striking in its scope and ambition.

Texas will develop a statewide test in reading, mathematics, and writing and will administer it to all students entering Texas public colleges and universities beginning in fall 1989. The following are the requirements and restrictions on which the structure of the testing program is based.

- The test must be diagnostic in nature and provide a comparison of the skill level of the individual student with the skill level the student needs in order to perform effectively in an undergraduate degree program.
- The test may not be used as a condition of admission into an institution.
- Students must take the test before accumulating nine or more semester credit hours.
- Students who do not pass all sections of the test must participate in remediation programs, which must be offered on the institution's home campus.
- Students must pass the test before they can enroll in upper-division courses; students who do not pass the test by the time they have completed 60 credit hours are limited to lower-division courses until they do pass the test.
- Institutions must establish programs to advise students at all levels about their courses and degree options.
- Institutions must report annually on student test results and on the effectiveness of remedial and advising programs.

- Institutions must also report annually to high schools, identifying by name the high school from which each student graduated and whether the student's test performance was above or below standard.

- The recommendations of faculty will be considered in test development.

The new test will also be required for all students seeking admission to a Texas-approved teacher education program, replacing the Pre-Professional Skills Test. In doing so, this project becomes a collaborative venture of two education agencies: the Texas Higher Education Coordinating Board and the Texas Education Agency, which serves public education for grades K–12.

It is important to see this new law in the context of higher education in Texas.

- The state has 68 community colleges, including four technical institutes and 39 senior universities or centers.

- In 1987 the state had a total student body of 780,000 in community colleges and universities. About 200,000 of these students were entering for the first time, with slightly over 50 percent entering community colleges.

- The student population is 82 percent Anglo, 10 percent Hispanic, and 7 percent Black. By the year 2000, the Texas population will be more than 50 percent Hispanic and Black.

In short, Texas has a large, extremely diverse higher education system and student population, a high minority dropout rate in the public schools, and rapidly changing statewide demographics. These factors have added an understandable sense of urgency to the development of our program.

Although considerable attention has been given to the assessment portion of this legislation, the most significant feature is its emphasis on advising and remediation. Our test has a clear subsidiary purpose: to identify students whose skills in reading, mathematics, and writing are inadequate for college-level work so we can provide remedial programs to help them. The challenge of the assessment process is to define those skills, to measure them accurately and reliably, and to provide sufficient information to support effective placement and instruction.

It is placement and instruction that we are emphasizing in order to prepare students for success. The key assumption behind the Texas legislation is that students may lack the skills, not the ability, to do college-level work. To emphasize these elements, we did not choose to give a separate name to the test. Instead, we identified the whole program with a broad title—the Texas Academic Skills Program (TASP). The program is not defined by the test; rather, the test is defined by the program.

Legislative Initiative and Campus Participation

House Bill 2182 creating the Texas Academic Skills Program called for development of a test based on recommendations of faculty. The legislation was specific in calling for faculty participation at all levels. The Texas Higher Education Coordinating Board and the Texas Education Agency have made broad, diverse participation by Texas educators a central feature. Every public institution of higher education will be directly involved.

We wanted a high level of participation for a number of reasons. First, we needed to build legitimacy for the program. The assessment movement has focused on effective links between the usefulness of assessment information and corrective instruction. However, successful educational assessment efforts also have a political component. Legitimacy of the program will be rooted in the intersection between what people consider to be "right" and what they consider to be workable.

The second purpose for broad participation is to ensure that the educational values and goals held by the faculty play a central role in the development and implementation of this program. The program grew out of the public policy process. The state legislature passed a bill, and both education agencies, working with National Evaluation Systems, Inc., have the responsibility for implementing it. However, public policy is never self-implementing. The two agencies realized the need for the widest possible involvement of educators in the development of the program at the outset: participation became the key to effective policy implementation. Balancing public policy concerns and the interests of educators has become one of the major tasks of both agencies.

From the very beginning of the program, the Coordinating Board set up an extensive advisory committee system. The Texas Academic Skills Council takes responsibility for providing policy and procedural advice to the commissioner of higher education. Its members serve as chairs for most of the other committees. The committees and panels under the council's direction include:

- the Tests and Measurements Advisory Committee, which provides oversight for all test development activities and test administration issues;

- the Bias Review Panel, which reviews all test materials;

- three Content Advisory Committees—one each in reading, mathematics, and writing—charged with making recommendations about skills, item specifications, and specific test items;

- the Academic Skills Development Committee, which provides information about existing practices in academic support services and disseminates information about model programs and effective practices;

- the Advisement and Placement Committee, which provides information about existing practices in academic advising and shares information about model programs and practices;

- the English as a Second Language Committee, which advises specifically about policies and procedures relevant to foreign students and ESL students;

- the Evaluation Committee, charged with recommending what information should be collected by institutions and how it should be presented to the Coordinating Board (this committee is also charged with the overall evaluation of the program);

- the Faculty Development Committee, which provides information about procedures and practices for faculty development activities— we anticipate the need to retrain existing faculty to work with underprepared students, and we recognize that many part-time faculty will be hired for remedial courses;

- the Special Committee of Academic Officers, which reviews policies, rules, and interpretations of the law;

- the TASP Technical Advisory Panel, composed of national experts on testing, which provides oversight of special areas within the test development process;

- the Committee on Upper-Level Schools, which deals with requirements specifically for universities serving only juniors, seniors, and graduate students; and

- the Committee on Testing Charges, which advises the Coordinating Board on policies for students on financial aid, veterans, and foreign students.

In addition, panels of selected Texas educators meet in six different regions of the state at each stage of the test development process to review materials and present their views to both the Bias Review Panel and the Content Advisory Committees.

The TASP committees involve almost 700 educators, half from four-year and half from two-year institutions; approximately one-third of the participants are Black or Hispanic. Further, three large standard-setting committees will be appointed in late 1988.

If this committee structure seems unwieldy and cumbersome, the high level of involvement and commitment that has resulted more than compensates. In a state with so many public colleges and universities, a large group is absolutely essential.

Defining the TASP Skills

One of the first tasks of the committees has been to define which basic academic skills to test. Given the diversity in Texas higher education—the large role played by community colleges, the varied types of universities ranging from open institutions to selective major research centers, the heterogeneous student population both in terms of age and ethnicity—would it be possible to gain consensus on the skills to be tested?

We are in an era when one expects more conflict than consensus, but the results of the test development process in defining the basic academic skills required for college-level work have been remarkable. Working with materials that National Evaluation Systems provided, the regional panels, the Bias Review Panel, and each of the content committees developed a set of skills defining what freshmen students should know in order to perform successfully in college. These skills were put into a survey sent to approximately 4,200 faculty teaching in Texas public colleges and universities. Faculty members were asked to review each of the reading, mathematics, and writing skills proposed as the basis for the test and to rate how important each skill is for entering freshman-level students to have in order to perform effectively in an undergraduate degree program in Texas.

Virtually without exception, faculty representing the broad diversity of Texas higher education expressed resounding agreement on the importance of the skills defined by their colleagues on the content committees. What emerged was a broad and strong consensus on what students need to know in order to perform effectively in college. If we sometimes feel shaky about the loose ties that bind us together as a community of educators, we may take some consolation in knowing that at least on the definition of what is basic to college-level work, we do agree. It may not be a very romantic or inspiring standard around which to rally, but educators do stand together in support of a common understanding of what students must know and be able to do in reading, mathematics, and writing in order to do college-level work well. On this, at least, we have a united faculty.

Assessment and Instruction

Throughout the test development process we maintained our focus on the program's overall goals: to provide broad access to both higher education and educational quality. As one of the authors of the legislation stated, "Access without quality is fraud." However, for the test to support both access and quality, it must be closely linked with effective remediation.

If the evidence from similar programs is at all a foreshadowing of what will occur in the Texas program, significant numbers of students will not pass one or more sections of the test. These students will be required to participate in academic skills development programs. Eventually, students who expect to fail the test may not even try to pursue an undergraduate degree—will not try to meet the pressure of both access and quality. Academic skills development will have to play a more central role than it now does in undergraduate education. A ballpark estimate is that 20 percent of entering freshman-level students will fail at least one section of the TASP Test.

Offering remediation to these students will result in a major shift of educational focus and resources from what we consider main-stream educational courses to courses designed to improve basic academic skills. This link between assessment and instruction must be forged. In this process we face great challenges of educational philosophy, pedagogical technique, educational organization, and institutional and individual commitment.

Despite these difficulties, remediation can be successful. Efforts in New Jersey and other states suggest that increases in retention and academic achievement for underprepared students are possible. However, the state, individual colleges and universities, and public schools must work cooperatively to develop programs that are specifically designed to address the needs of these students. Some general principles have emerged from these experiences and from the extensive work in academic skills development that has been under way in Texas community colleges for many years. These principles are currently guiding the remediation planning for the Texas Academic Skills Program. They include:

- the recognition that underpreparation occurs across all ethnic groups and is linked more to socioeconomic status than to ethnic background;

- the understanding that the more comprehensive the advising and remediation activities, the better the results for the students;

- the view that remediation is an integral part of the institution's mission, not a second- or third-class activity, and that efforts will be made, whenever possible, to train regular full-time faculty to teach remedial courses;

- the support by campus leaders for making remediation a central institutional mission.

This is a very exciting time for higher education. After years of languishing in the corridors of professional conventions and obscure journals, higher-education issues have now gained the attention of a broad, popular audience. Two recent books on higher education have had long runs on best-seller lists. A movie about a teacher successfully preparing underprepared students for the College Board college-level, advanced placement calculus test is also very popular.

While Bloom's and Hirsch's books are part of an American tradition of highlighting our purported ignorance, the movie about Jaime Escalante is part of another American tradition—a tradition that links education with hope and progress. It is this link that the Texas Academic Skills Program seeks to forge. It seeks to meet the challenge embodied in the Escalante story and to "stand and deliver" on the hope that through our colleges and universities we can provide opportunity and progress for all segments of our society.

References

Bloom, A. (1987). *The Closing of the American Mind.* New York: Simon and Schuster.

Committee on Testing. (1986). *A Generation of Failure: The case for testing and remediation in Texas higher education.* Austin: Coordinating Board of the Texas College and University System.

Hirsch, E. D. (1987). *Cultural Literacy: What every American needs to know.* Boston: Houghton Mifflin.

New Jersey Basic Skills Council. (1985). *Effectiveness of remedial programs in New Jersey public colleges and universities: Fall 1982–spring 1984.* Newark: Department of Education.

The Assessment Movement: Improving Quality or Limiting Access for Minority Students?

Manuel J. Justiz and Marilyn C. Kameen

Following the release of *A Nation at Risk* by the National Commission on Excellence in Education in 1983 the country turned its attention to the deteriorating condition of education in our elementary and secondary schools. The initiation of a national reform movement in American education signified the public's conviction that education was the cornerstone of a strong and truly representative democracy. The report called on states to increase academic standards and improve quality without compromising the principles of access. State legislatures and policy-makers in all 50 states responded by imposing requirements in the name of "assessment" (e.g., higher graduation requirements, competency testing for high school graduation, standardized tests at various grade levels). More than anything, though, it became clear that the spotlight of national attention would soon be turned on our colleges and universities.

Assessment as a National Issue

The report *Involvement in Learning,* released in 1984 by the Study Group on the Conditions of Excellence in Higher Education, brought higher education into the forefront of the national reform debate. The report cited higher education as being afflicted with some of the same mediocrity found in elementary and secondary schools. Marchese (1987) highlighted these issues when he said that state

Manuel J. Justiz is chaired professor of Educational Leadership and Policies at the University of South Carolina and former director of the National Institute of Education.

Marilyn C. Kameen is associate professor of Educational Leadership and Policies at the University of South Carolina.

policy-makers began asking colleges and universities such questions as "How do you impact student learning? Do your students know and can they do what your degrees imply? How do you assure that? What is the evidence?" (p. 3).

Involvement in Learning challenged higher education institutions to improve quality by strengthening student learning through a model that included: (1) student involvement; (2) high expectations; and (3) assessment with feedback. The Association of American Colleges report *Integrity in the College Curriculum,* released in 1985, supported this learning-assessment linkage by calling on colleges and universities to assess the impact of their teaching. But, as Marchese (1987) indicated, ideas that originated in internal debates about quality have been taken up by external parties and translated into mandates to assess. Concerned that colleges and universities have been slow to implement their own assessment programs, state legislatures have officially addressed assessment as a matter of policy or statute and some are now field testing statewide college assessment programs. These state initiatives range from mandatory admission tests and "rising junior" exams to funding formulas based on student performance. And this is just the tip of the iceberg. U.S. Secretary of Education William Bennett has already reinforced this activist mood by calling on the nation's governors to improve institutional accountability by mandating assessment.

Assessment is not a fad. Concern about the outcomes of higher education and about student achievement will continue to be a major policy issue. But the leadership of the reform movement cannot be left to individuals who have little understanding of the colleges and universities, their faculty, and their students. If it is left to them, states are likely to implement the same model used to reform our elementary and secondary schools. As a result, we could face the disastrous consequences of a national assessment program in higher education where all institutions, no matter how different, would be subject to the same standardized assessment procedures (Hartle, 1985). Colleges and universities must take the lead in implementing assessment programs that meet the public interest while preserving the principles of institutional autonomy and academic governance so important to us.

Involvement in Learning encouraged higher education to do just that. Fortunately, some model assessment programs do exist (e.g., at Alverno College, whose program was partly funded by the National Institute of Education, and at Northeast Missouri State University). The potential for replicating such models at other higher education institutions can only be determined by the leaders of those institutions. In doing so, they must recognize the complexity of the issues and the problems inherent in designing any college assessment program.

Problems Inherent in Assessment

Measuring educational achievement requires more agreement about the outcomes and the processes of higher education than currently exists at most institutions. Defining a general core of liberal learning and then agreeing on assessment methods to ensure that students are both broadly educated and deeply versed in a discipline are not easy tasks (Hartle, 1985). Until recently, "input" measures, such as mean SAT scores of entering freshmen, number of library books, and percentage of faculty with Ph.D.s, have been used to measure institutional quality. But little has been said about the potential of the institution to influence student learning and achievement. To ask questions about "output" requires far more serious and systematic approaches to defining and assessing learning outcomes (Adelman, 1984). In part because of the nebulous way higher education has assessed student knowledge and skills in the past, everyone from Secretary Bennett to the academic community itself has questioned whether a college education is worth the investment.

Many colleges and universities have taken up the challenge prompted by *Involvement in Learning* to define outcomes and design assessment methods consistent with their own institutional missions, their instructional settings, and their student types. As Astin (1985) cautions us, assessing an institution's success in developing the talents of its students requires information on improvement in student performance over time. While many institutions now collect data on students at major transition points in college (e.g., admission tests for placement, comprehensive junior-level exams for progression to upper-division courses, competency tests for graduation), these measures are primarily used for screening and credentialing. As such, they cannot be compared to show change in students' intellectual and personal development over time. Even more critical, such measures can eliminate low performers, typically minority students, who may need additional support to succeed in college.

In designing assessment programs that will assist all students, regardless of ability level and entering characteristics, to meet increased academic standards and persist to graduation, we must also recognize the inherent dangers of cultural bias toward Blacks, Hispanics, and other minority student groups. For example, states are reluctant to follow Florida and Georgia in instituting "rising junior" exams because the considerable evidence of racial and ethnic differences in test performance causes concern about discriminatory access (Ewell, 1987).

The issues of excellence, access, and unbiased assessment are coming to the forefront of the debate in American higher education at a time when significant demographic shifts are changing the very face of our nation. The demographic indicators cited below are, if anything, conservative. Consider the following:

1. By the year 2000 one out of every three Americans will be non-White (Hodgkinson, 1985, p. 3).

2. Today, we are a nation of 14.6 million Hispanics and 26.5 million Blacks. By the year 2020 we will be a nation of 44 million Blacks and 47 million Hispanics—even more if Hispanic immigration rates increase. The total U.S. population in 2020 will be about 265 million people, a very small increase from our current 238 million. More than 91 million of that figure will be minorities, and mostly young people—the group whose fertility rates are highest (Hodgkinson, 1985, p. 5).

3. The composition of elementary and secondary schools is increasingly diverse in race, color, and creed, in addition to socioeconomic and family background characteristics (National Council for Education Information [NCEI], 1987).

4. This nation is no longer, and probably never will be again, as youthful as it once was (Hodgkinson, 1985, p. 3).

5. Similarly, our rapidly aging White middle class will find its retirement income generated by an increasingly non-White work force. The 1980 census revealed that the average White in America was 31 years old, the average Black 25, and the average Hispanic only 22. It should be easy to see that age produces population momentum for minorities: the typical Hispanic female is just moving into the peak childbearing years while the average White female is just moving out of them. By

the year 2020, most of the baby boom generation will be retired, its retirement provided by the much smaller age groups that follow it. By 1992, only *three* workers will provide the funds for each retiree and *one of the three* workers will be a minority (Hodgkinson, 1985, p. 3).

6. During the decade 1976–1986, the proportion of college students who were racial and ethnic minorities rose to 17.9 percent. However, this was largely due to an overall increase in the Asian and Hispanic populations, not to a rise in the college-going rate for minorities (OERI, 1988). According to the Education Commission of the States (ECS), minorities are still underrepresented at all levels of post-secondary education relative to their numbers in the total population; and the underrepresentation becomes even more severe as minorities go on to higher levels of education. For example, Blacks make up 13 percent of the college-age population but only about 9.5 percent of undergraduate enrollment; 5.9 percent of minorities receive bachelor's degrees and 4.8 percent go on to graduate school. The data are similar for Hispanics who make up 7.4 percent of the college-age population but only about 4.6 percent of the undergraduate enrollment; 2.6 percent of the Hispanic population receive bachelor's degrees and 2.2 percent go on to graduate school.

7. The ECS reports that for the traditional 18–24 college-age group, 45 percent of Whites complete at least one year of college but only 36 percent of college-age Blacks and 28 percent of college-age Hispanics complete at least one year.

8. The absence of Black and Hispanic faculty is even more acute. According to the ECS, the number of minority college faculty has only increased from 6.2 percent in 1973 to 9.1 percent in 1980 while the proportion of minorities in the U.S. population has tripled.

9. Minorities are also underrepresented in the country's leadership positions. The ECS reported that in 1987, there were two minorities serving in the U.S. Senate (representing 2 percent of the Senate) and both were Asian/Pacific Americans from Hawaii. Nine percent of the U.S. House of Representatives is minority. And the only governors of minority heritage are the governor of Hawaii, an Asian/Pacific American, and the governor of Florida, a Hispanic.

This dearth of minorities in leadership roles in all sectors of our society is due in part to our inability to recruit, retain, and graduate minorities from our higher education institutions in sufficient numbers. Assessment programs that rely on standardized tests as sole measures of student ability; that "label" or "gatekeep" rather than assist students to acquire the necessary skills to complete their college educations successfully; that do not support the teaching and learning process; and that are otherwise insensitive to bias can and will result in discrimination toward minorities. Such irresponsible action will contribute to the educational disenfranchisement of these cohorts from our colleges and universities and will contribute to the creation of an underclass in our nation—a situation that could certainly threaten the foundations of our democratic system of government.

The research on test bias shows quite clearly that, compared to non-minority students, minority groups score lower on all forms of standardized tests. Rigid adherence to test scores as the single indicator of a student's potential or quality will, therefore, hurt minority students by labeling them failures. Yet, standardized tests are as entrenched as ever in college admission and retention procedures (Bell & Morsink, 1986; Jacobson, 1986; Cole, 1981; McCornack, 1983; Pedrini & Pedrini, 1977).

The research also shows a mismatch between the skills required for successful test performance and the prior learning experiences of lower socioeconomic status students. The same cultural differences that impair test performance are likely to handicap a student's academic performance or job performance (Anastasi, 1968; Cole, 1981). But there is also increasing evidence that effective programming can alter these cultural variables and can improve students' academic performance (Segal & Chipman, 1984). This is not to suggest that standards of program quality should be lowered. It is to suggest that comprehensive college assessment programs must include multiple measures that provide an accurate profile of student performance; they must be sensitive to the fact that motivation cannot be assessed but, if cultivated, can have a positive impact on learning; and they must include diagnostic feedback, remediation, and counseling to help minority students succeed in college.

These recommendations were at the heart of *Involvement in Learning* when it said that assessment can be used to increase student involvement and to clarify expectations if it is designed to measure improvements in performance and if the information gathered is fed back in ways that enhance student learning and lead to improvements in programs and instructional methods (1984, p. 22). Minority student retention and success in college will be directly related to the degree to which colleges and universities design comprehensive assessment programs that have these characteristics.

Recommendations for Assessment

What are the underlying assumptions of assessment programs that are sensitive to cultural bias and that increase the probability of success for all college students, but particularly for minority students? Let us consider some recommendations.

Assessment is Not Synonymous With Testing

Comprehensive assessment programs should yield student profiles that reflect multiple sources of information, enabling the institution to show improvements in student learning over time and to demonstrate the impact of the institution on student development.

- Use admissions tests and other entry assessments to diagnose a student's level of proficiency relative to the demands of particular courses and to advise the student about placement in appropriate courses or remediation programs.

- Assess entering students on the knowledge and skills they are expected to develop in college and use criterion-referenced (not norm referenced) post-tests to assess graduating students on the same dimensions.

- In a student's first year, when the potential for dropping out is highest, use early formative evaluation (e.g., several interim tests and written work prior to exams) to gather baseline data for measuring growth; to communicate clear expectations to students; to diagnose and give feedback about strengths and weaknesses; and to design remediation, study skills, and test preparation programs.

- Administer progression tests or competency tests for graduation *early* in the student's college experience to communicate expectations and to diagnose and remediate learning difficulties.

- Assess in a variety of situations over time and use multiple measures that will allow developmental patterns to emerge and that can compensate for weak performance on standardized tests (e.g., essays, oral presentations, portfolio and performance assessments, simulations, senior seminars that incorporate a wide range of assessment techniques).

- Include unobtrusive measures (e.g., an analysis of course-taking patterns, extracurricular activities, social interactions), especially when these measures can assess student motivation.

Assessment is Learning

Assessment should be used to involve students in their learning and to improve the teaching-learning process.

- Identify specific and measurable learning objectives; communicate clear expectations about intended performance to students long before the actual time of assessment.

- Match learning objectives with appropriate instructional strategies that include opportunities for practice and feedback about student performance.

- Vary instructional strategies to accommodate students' differing learning styles.

- Involve faculty in all phases of assessment—from specifying learning objectives and making appropriate adjustments in teaching approaches to judging performance.

- Provide timely, descriptive, and *positive* feedback that focuses on what students can do to improve. This is especially important in early assessments and with minority students who may have multiple learning deficiencies that overwhelm them. Later assessments can emphasize performance in relation to past work and to ability.

- Design remediation, counseling, and other support services to assist students in overcoming weaknesses identified in the assessment process. Use clubs, organizations, and campus activities to help students apply what was learned in their coursework.

- Tie assessment data to instructional and program improvement; create a college environment where assessment is integral to the curriculum.

Minority Involvement in Assessment

Essential to the success of the measures mentioned above is adequate representation by minorities in faculty pools. Concerted efforts must be made to recruit, retain, and promote minority faculty who can serve as mentors and role models to minority college students and who will be part of the assessment team.

Conclusion

The real challenge to higher education institutions is to design comprehensive assessment programs that result in student profiles that provide multiple sources of information on student abilities, levels of motivation, cultural background, and parental and peer support for learning. Such assessment programs should go beyond standardized tests to provide information on the student's family history, professional goals and aspirations, performance in a job setting, and other indicators of academic success. This assessment information should also be used to develop academic support and remediation services that enhance student learning and to improve the institution's instructional programs.

At the core of all these recommendations is the firm belief that assessment insensitive to the dangers of cultural bias and irresponsibly managed will result in discrimination toward minority college students. Assessment that begins with a clear statement of goals and combines good instruction with feedback and support for improvement will enable minority college students to compete successfully in the academic environment. In this way, our colleges and universities will accomplish the dual goal of expanding access to minority students while improving the quality of the education they receive.

References

Adelman, C. (1984). *Starting with students: Promising approaches in American higher education.* Washington, DC: National Institute of Education and the American Association for Higher Education.

Anastasi, A. (1968). *Psychological testing.* New York: Macmillan.

Association of American Colleges. (1985). *Integrity in the college curriculum: A report to the academic community.* Washington, DC: Association of American Colleges.

Astin, A. (1985). *Achieving educational excellence.* San Francisco: Jossey-Bass.

Bell, M. L., & Morsink, C. V. (1986). Quality and equity in the preparation of black teachers. *Journal of Teacher Education, 37*(2), 10–15.

Cole, N. (1981). Bias in testing. *American Psychologist, 36*(10), 1067–1077.

Ewell, P. (1987, January/February). Assessment: Where are we? *Change,* 23–26.

Hartle, T. (1985, October). *The growing interest in measuring the educational achievement of college students.* Prepared for the American Association for Higher Education under contract to the National Institute of Education for the National Conference on Assessment in Higher Education. Columbia: University of South Carolina.

Hodgkinson, H. L. (1985). *All one system: Demographics of education, kindergarten through graduate school.* Washington, DC: Institute for Educational Leadership.

Jacobson, R. L. (1986). Selective colleges' use of SAT is unshaken by controversies. *Chronicle of Higher Education, 32*(18), p. 1.

Marchese, T. J. (1987). Third down, ten years to go. *AAHE Bulletin, 40*(4), 3–8.

McCornack, R. L. (1983). Bias in the validity of predicted college grades in four ethnic minority groups. *Educational and Psychological Measurement, 43*(2), 517–522.

National Center for Education Information. (October 12, 1987). *NCEI Reports.* Washington, DC: Feistritzer Associates.

National Commission on Excellence in Education. (1983). *A nation at risk: The imperative for education reform.* Washington, DC: U.S. Government Printing Office.

Office of Educational Research and Improvement. (1988). *Trends in minority enrollment in higher education, 1976–1986.* Washington, DC: U.S. Department of Education.

Pedrini, B. C., & Pedrini, D. T. (1977). *The usefulness of ACT scores in predicting achievement and attrition among disadvantaged and regular freshmen: A survey and study.* Omaha: University of Nebraska. (ERIC Document Reproduction Service No. ED 128 429)

Segal, J., & Chipman, S. (1984). Thinking and learning skills: The contributions of NIE. *Educational Leadership, 42*(1), 85–87.

Study Group on the Conditions of Excellence in American Higher Education. (1984). *Involvement in learning: Realizing the potential of American higher education.* Washington, DC: U.S. Government Printing Office.

New Conceptions of Reading for Basic Skills Assessment

Timothy Shanahan

Reading is a basic skill. It has commonly been taught and tested in American public schools and is almost always a focus of concern in basic skills testing at any level, including higher education. The first reading tests were developed early in the twentieth century, and reading tests continue to reflect the design decisions made at that time (Pearson & Valencia, 1987). Despite the fact that reading theory has changed a great deal since then and even the most basic conceptions of what takes place during reading have been altered, our reading tests have not changed much over the past sixty years (Farr & Carey, 1986). We have become prisoners of test design efforts that have been aimed more toward establishing efficient measures with high levels of concurrent validity than toward establishing theoretically sound measures that possess construct validity. With each new test we have attempted to duplicate, in some fashion, the earlier test design efforts in an extensive and elaborate daisy chain that has not necessarily resulted in either a valid or a useful measurement of reading ability (Pikulski & Shanahan, 1980).

The First Reading Tests

Any test is an attempt to describe the whole on the basis of a part. We cannot possibly observe an individual trying to accomplish all reading tasks with all texts, so, instead, we select a significant and representative sample of behaviors on which to evaluate individuals and programs. On the basis of the performance on these samples, we then draw conclusions about how well somebody can read. From these sample test behaviors, we predict how individuals might

Timothy Shanahan is professor of Curriculum and Instruction in the College of Education at the University of Illinois at Chicago.

perform on the entire universe of texts and tasks. Because of the necessity of representing the whole with the parts, the selection of the parts becomes a critical issue of theory. Tests of reading must be based on valid theoretical descriptions of reading.

Initially, reading tests possessed this type of match with theory. Most authorities in the field viewed reading as a behavior used simply to gain objective information from a text; that is, reading was viewed as a simple information transfer process in which the author's ideas were moved from the page to the mind of the reader (Smith, 1965). Consequently, those first reading tests were marvelously straightforward and simple in design (Thorndike, 1917). The tests presented passages for students to read and asked questions about specific information in the passages. Over time, a variety of issues were raised (Johnston, 1984) about the nature of the texts, the question types used, and the relationship of text information to answers to questions, but in general, test design has been seen as a matter of simple modification and matching. Original test designs might be varied in a particular way to satisfy a particular complaint or problem, but the measure of validity was usually based on how well the new test correlated with the previous tests. Thus, reading theory typically has not been addressed directly in most test designs.

Developments in Reading Theory and Test Design

Over the past decade, the amount of research in reading has exploded. Literally thousands of new investigations into the nature of reading and reading development have been undertaken. The field of reading education has experienced a dramatic alteration in its fundamental conceptions of reading (Anderson, Hiebert, Scott, & Wilkinson, 1985). The view of reading mentioned previously—reading as a form of simple knowledge transfer of discrete information—is no longer widely accepted by authorities in the field. Reading is now considered a constructive process highly dependent on the knowledge and strategies of the reader and not just on the information on the page. Information is no longer conceptualized as being objective and discrete, either. This major conceptual, theoretical shift in reading requires the development of a new generation of reading tests that is more consistent with the empirically derived descriptions of the reading process that now exist (Valencia & Pearson, 1987).

Responding to Theory in Test Design

During the last few years, a few dramatically different tests of reading ability have been developed. I have worked with P. David Pearson, Sheila Valencia, and Robert Reeve in an attempt to create a new state assessment test of reading for Illinois (Valencia, Pearson, Reeve, & Shanahan, in press). There is a similar state assessment development project taking place in Michigan under the auspices of Karen Wixson and Charles Peters (Wixson & Peters, 1987). And, the National Assessment of Educational Progress (NAEP) has conducted a major literacy assessment of young adults using a newly developed series of tests (Kirsch & Jungeblut, 1986).

These efforts have focused on developing tests for use with different types of students than those that would normally be tested in a basic skills situation. The two state assessment projects focused on children in grades 3–11, and the adult literacy assessment tested the reading and writing abilities of adults aged 21–25 years. The purposes of these three assessment projects were also quite different from those of the traditional postsecondary basic skills testing program. Each was a large-scale assessment developed either to provide information of an epidemiological nature or to make institution-level decisions. These tests will not provide individual-level diagnostic informa tion, nor will they be used for making decisions about individuals (e.g., minimal competency, access to programs). Finally, these efforts go beyond the measurement of just reading comprehension; they consider writing, students' use of literacy, reading strategies, and students' attitudes.

Nevertheless, these efforts are highly relevant to basic skills testing in higher education because they have attempted to create reading tests that reflect the newer constructivist theoretical positions advanced in cognitive psychology and education during the past decade. These tests are significant because they reflect recent reading theory rather than simply duplicating earlier test designs. The following will describe some of the fundamental issues for basic skills testing in the area of reading theory and will refer to the Illinois, Michigan, and NAEP projects whenever appropriate.

The Role of Reader Knowledge

A basic tenet of constructivist theories of reading comprehension is that the reader uses prior knowledge—knowledge and background information already in possession of the reader before reading—in the reading process (Anderson & Pearson, 1984). Investigations have demonstrated that the interpretation of text can be influenced by reader perspective (Pichert & Anderson, 1977), cultural background (Steffensen, Joag-dev, & Anderson, 1979), and area of study (Anderson, Reynolds, Schallert, & Goetz, 1977). A number of studies have demonstrated the importance of prior knowledge in reading, and there have been many efforts to describe how prior knowledge is used during the reading process. Readers use prior knowledge to eliminate confusion in text (Dooling & Lachman, 1971), to allocate attention (Goetz, Schallert, Reynolds, & Radin, 1983), to reduce the limits of memory (Pichert & Anderson, 1977), to help in memory storage and retrieval (Bransford & Johnson, 1972), and to generate necessary inferences (Whitney, 1987).

The original authors of reading tests were obviously quite concerned with the issue of prior knowledge in reading. They must have discussed in detail the potential bias that could be introduced by the variations in the reader's prior knowledge. It is apparent from the tests they designed that they did not view the use of prior knowledge as a fundamental part of the reading process, but as a source of error that needed to be controlled in some fashion. The solution to what they saw as the problem of reader knowledge was quite ingenious.

To limit the bias due to knowledge differences, reading tests required students to read about a large number of topics. Students might be advantaged on some passages, but they would be penalized on others. These differences would be averaged or balanced across the different passages. A related aspect of test design was the use of collections of passages that focused on information about which none of the readers would be expected to know much. Even today, if you carefully examine reading tests at almost any level, you will find that they are made up of several relatively brief passages on a wide variety of somewhat obscure topics.

What is the result of these attempts to treat knowledge use as a noise factor? First, the use of passages on a large number of topics probably only corrects for error in those peculiar instances in which all students know similar amounts of information about similar numbers of test passages. This, of course, is unreasonable to expect in basic skills testing circumstances given the differences in race, age, sex, ethnic background, school preparation, and life experience usually evident in a beginning college freshman class. What usually occurs is that some individuals know a great deal about many things, and others have very little knowledge of any academic topic. Because of this, the use of many different topics serves only to increase the relationship between reading and IQ (Johnston, 1984). The use of multitopic passages is not enough to limit the influence of knowledge use in reading, but it is enough to improve the performance of high IQ students, and to lower that of low IQ students, on reading tests, no matter what their actual reading ability might be.

And what about the use of reading materials on obscure subjects to limit the amount of reliance on prior knowledge during reading? There are no data on this issue, but I think we need to ask ourselves whether knowledge use is fundamental to the act of reading or is just a noise or error factor. It is only in reading tests that we attempt to divorce the use of what we know from the efforts to gain new information. In almost all other situations, the use of prior knowledge is a necessary and conspicuous component of reading. The notion of examining reading ability by using texts that limit use of knowledge runs the very real risk of describing peculiar rather than typical or representative reading experience.

Using Prior Knowledge

If our intention in reading assessment is to sample from typical reading behaviors, then trying to limit knowledge use in reading tests is clearly unacceptable and a new approach is needed. In Illinois, we have been attempting to measure children's knowledge of texts prior to their reading of those texts. We provide students with a series of statements and ask them to predict the likelihood of that information appearing in a text about a particular topic. Students who know much about a topic are able to predict in a fashion similar to that of adult experts, and those who do not know about the topics perform more randomly. This information can then be used statistically to adjust scores so that we have a clearer idea of what students know as a result of reading the text, but without altering the reading behaviors themselves.

There are other potential solutions to this problem as well, including pre- and post-test designs that would measure the amount of learning due to reading (Carver, 1973), or dynamic assessments (possibly computer-based testing that guarantees that all students must deal with passages drawn from a specified range of familiar subjects on the basis of their individual levels of knowledge). Each method has its own problems, of course, but each is superior to current testing practices in its attempt to describe reading ability while allowing students to use their knowledge as they would in genuine reading situations.

Coherent Texts and the Nature of Information

A second feature of basic skills tests that needs scrutiny concerns the nature of the materials that students are asked to read in reading tests. Most tests include accurate, up-to-date materials from a variety of sources and subject areas. Generally, tests have been reasonably well constructed in this regard, especially when they have sampled passages from the actual texts that make up the universe of interest. If you want to predict how well college freshmen can read beginning college material, you will generally get the most accurate picture by using college freshman material as the source of the texts.

But, again, developments in research and theory would suggest that this is not enough. Not all texts are of equal difficulty. This is a fact that has long been accepted in the field of reading—by both the professional and the layperson. Usually test designers spend a good deal of effort either selecting passages in some normative manner or juggling p-values, or both, in an effort to ensure that equivalent ranges of text difficulties are used. Often some kind of readability formula is used to select passages at appropriate reading levels. Research during the past decade, however, has concerned itself more with the internal dynamics of passage difficulty than with any kind of normative comparison across disparate passages or summary indices of difficulty.

This work indicates that text is more than a series of independent or random sentences. The propositions included in a text must cohere somehow in order to be understood by readers (Kintsch & van Dijk, 1978). This coherence is achieved through the use of linguistic or conceptual links or ties that knit a text together (Halliday & Hasan, 1976). Research has demonstrated that text possesses a structural or hierarchical coherence, too (Kintsch & van Dijk, 1978). This structural coherence is reflected in an author's plan or framework. It provides information about how the ideas are linked in a discourse, and it emphasizes the relevance or importance of some ideas over others. Structural coherence can also communicate important information about author's purpose, causation, temporal ordering, or similar issues.

A major part of reading comprehension is the ability to interpret the structures and linkages that an author has used in order to construct or reconstruct meaning. In fact, an understanding of potential text structures is an important part of the knowledge that readers bring to text. Even in the reading of stories, we find that children learn to expect and search for particular text structures and sequences in the effort to understand (Mandler & Johnson, 1977). There has been a great deal of effort made to describe some of the more common structural elements, such as those evident in fairy tales, and to try to understand how readers use these to enhance their understanding and recall.

The Structural Integrity of Reading Passages

There are really two issues here. One concerns the nature of texts used to test reading, and the other emphasizes the mental operations that individuals perform in order to understand these texts. If a reading test is to sample typical reading behaviors, it seems evident that it must include structurally complete and coherent passages. It is almost impossible to include passages that reflect common structural patterns using texts of the trivial lengths of those commonly included in most reading tests.

The Michigan state assessment effort is particularly important in this regard. The Michigan test attempts to measure reading ability through the use of passages of substantial length (i.e., entire stories or articles) that possess structural integrity and completeness, rather than the snippets and paragraphs common to most published tests. Violations of text structure can have damaging consequences for a reader's understanding (Goetz & Armbruster, 1980), so this test does not interfere with the integrity of the texts used.

Making Use of Text Information

The second part of the coherence issue relates to the reading task itself. Analyses of published reading tests suggest that quite often students are asked questions that require the use of information from only one sentence (Bormuth, Carr, Manning, & Pearson, 1970). Evidence suggests that performance levels can be quite different when questions require the integration or use of several pieces of text information than when only single sentences are emphasized (Shanahan & Kamil, 1982). Individuals, at least in testing situations, will try to carry out their tasks in minimal ways. Since there is no actual reason to understand or even read a text included in a test, the reader often attempts only to answer the questions. If the questions require the use of information from across a text, the reader will attempt to read the entire text; if the questions require the simple use of information from within a single part of the text, the reader will read only that part of the text. It has been demonstrated in studies and in test analyses that "intersentential" questions can be written and that when such questions are used the results are more closely related to recall of text information than when they are not used (Bormuth, Carr, Manning, & Pearson, 1970; Shanahan & Kamil, 1982).

The ability to interpret and interrelate information across a text is a critical reading skill. This skill can be evaluated in a reasonable manner only when there is sufficient information in a text and only when this information is dispersed across a text in a manner that reflects an author's intentional plan to communicate information. Again, this means that a theoretically appropriate assessment of reading ability should use longer, coherent, meaningful texts. In the Michigan assessment, students in the elementary and secondary grades are being asked to read prose passages of approximately 800–1,000 words; about 75–100 percent more text than would be confronted in the most ambitious college tests. These passages, because of their completeness, permit the test designers to observe reading in a manner that is more similar to what would be expected in real (i.e., nontest) reading situations. The Michigan test passages undergo a thorough analysis of the structural qualities of the text, and these analytical maps are then used to help generate questions that require students to use information across the text (Wixson & Peters, 1987).

The Primacy of Text Issues in Questioning

Most reading tests consist of passages followed by a series of multiple-choice questions. Almost an infinite number of questions can be asked of even the briefest passage. A sentence such as "Harry was riding his horse at dawn" raises questions such as "Who was Harry? What was Harry doing? What was Harry riding? What did Harry own? Who owned the horse? When was Harry riding his horse? What is dawn?" and so on. The questions included in a test are not randomly selected. They are almost always constructed according to some form of a question grid. In a test of mathematics, a question grid might be used to guarantee a random sample of each type of problem (40 percent algebra, 20 percent geometry, 10 percent trigonometry, and so on). In reading tests this often means that the definition of reading includes some specification of the nature of question types that can be used. Literal recall, drawing conclusions, vocabulary, main idea, and the like are commonly used question types.

Unfortunately, such specifications often are put forth as if they describe the nature of the information in the text rather than the cognitive operations performed on the text. Test writers, then, will find themselves in the predicament of having to use certain numbers of each type of question, even if such information is not reasonable or relevant in a given passage. In the example of Harry riding his horse, it is almost certain that the test designer will ask about the meaning of "dawn" if required to include a vocabulary item, because that term is the least common in the passage. The test writer is not attempting to focus on the important issues presented by an author. Within traditional test design, vocabulary cannot be ignored just because the passage includes no essential vocabulary word, whose interpretation can help the reader to construct reasonable meanings from the passage.

In the Illinois and Michigan projects, the question grid has not been done away with, but its negative impact has been limited (Valencia, Pearson, Reeve, & Shanahan, in press; Wixson & Peters, 1987). Instead of guaranteeing that each question type will be used for each passage, test designers ask questions on the basis of what is important in a given passage. The test designer considers the nature of the content of the text and the author's plan as revealed in an analysis of text structure. Questions are written on the basis of these considerations, rather than in pursuit of some number of each type of question in the grid. The designer asks, "What would a good reader attempt to understand here? What would the author want the reader to think about? What would a good teacher want students to gain from the passage?" Primary consideration is given to the specific text content and presentation, and this permits the use of important questions, rather than artificial test-like ones.

These tests attempt to ask about information that makes sense in terms of comprehension. This means, for example, that very different types of vocabulary questions will be asked in these tests than would be common in traditional measures of reading comprehension. Vocabulary is important to understanding, but there are uncommon words that are unimportant in a particular passage, and there are common terms whose interpretation is critical to understanding an author's message. Furthermore, vocabulary terms often possess many alternative meanings that must be interpreted and understood on the basis of the particular text. New test efforts attempt to ask about the "important" vocabulary of a passage, as measured by the role the vocabulary plays in the passage, rather than focusing student attention on the most arcane words available in a given passage. Similar efforts are evident with all other question types used.

The Role of Reasoning in Reading

Another concern about reading tests is that they often focus largely, sometimes entirely, on literal or factual recall or recognition of information explicitly stated in passages. Even when basic skills tests require some amount of reasoning on the part of the reader, this is often of a rather circumscribed type and level (Johnston, 1983). Again, this practice probably has its source in historical differences in definitions of reading, and in the fear of introducing biases attributable to variations in prior knowledge.

Possibly the most common type of reasoning evident in reading is the use of inferencing (Whitney, 1987). Inferences are mental operations that allow us to complete those parts of text that an author has not specified. No author can entirely describe any scene or phenomenon. Rather, authors provide enough information to allow readers to recall previously acquired knowledge or experiences relevant to the communication. Even seemingly explicit texts often require a large number of inferences on the part of a reader (Anderson, Hiebert, Scott, & Wilkinson, 1985).

A basic skills test for the graduating senior or college-bound student definitely should be biased toward questions that require the student to go beyond the text—to infer, interpret, and reason. What has been described in the Michigan and Illinois reading tests to this point— the use of materials that would encourage the use of prior knowledge, the use of substantial materials with structural integrity and content completeness, the effort to create questions appropriate to the demands of specific passages—creates a situation that better enables the testing of reasoning during reading.

These test features, however, do not guarantee that reasoning will be measured in a more powerful way than is already common in reading assessments. As Johnston (1983, pp. 35–36) has pointed out, "Multiple-choice items may require more or less reasoning depending on a) the strategy which the reader adopts to answer the alternatives and b) the plausibility of the distractors." The questions might seem to require reading reasoning, but they might actually only elicit test-reasoning (Drum, Calfee, & Cook, 1981). Most tests of reading employ a multiple-choice, single-correct-answer format. Reasoning among choices probably involves the reader in an internal dialogue that might be characterized in the following fashion: "It can't be 'B.' It might be 'C' or 'D,' so I will guess between those." This kind of test reasoning probably improves performance because traditional test formats reward the ability to find the one most acceptable answer. However, test reasoning does not necessarily provide us with the most valid picture of the types of reasoning evident in more genuine reading situations.

The best readers in our society are not those who can find a single most acceptable answer among four clear choices on the basis of a fairly limited passage. The best readers are those who can see the shades of meaning inherent in any communication, and who can consider the multiple possibilities for interpretation that are present in most texts. The best readers are not the single-short-answer geniuses, but the thoughtful, reflective, reasoning individuals who are able to consider many reasonable alternatives (NAEP, 1981).

There is not a single answer to most real questions that are confronted in high schools, or in colleges, or in real life. Possibly the only completely acceptable way to evaluate reasoning in reading is through thoughtful discussion or written responses to text (Petrosky, 1982). However, such formats would be extremely expensive for an assessment, at least in those situations that require the evaluation of large numbers of students. In order to stay within limits of time and economics, the Illinois state test attempts to evaluate reasoning using a more powerful multiple-choice format. That test requires that students select the one, two, or three best answers to questions (Valencia, Pearson, Reeve, & Shanahan, in press). This multiple-choice, multiple-answer format permits the asking of meaningful questions that have a legitimate multiplicity of answers. Such a format does away with traditional test-reasoning strategies to some extent, and it highlights the use of powerful questions that require reasoning more akin to that evident in actual reading.

The Generalizability of Reading

A common assumption is that reading ability is a highly generalizable skill that allows individuals to participate in basic work and communications activities. One of the reasons for stressing basic skills in higher education is to guarantee that all students have the ability to benefit from the educational program provided in a college or university. Another reason is that college students are often in their final preparation for moving into the workplace. Reading tests, because of this basic conception of the generalizability of reading, usually attempt to measure a rather narrow constellation of reading abilities. Best available evidence suggests that reading is not this generalizable, and that reading tests and the interpretation of results from such tests might be highly misleading. Traditional tests are incomplete, for example, in that they usually do not examine an individual's ability to deal with the unique and complex literacy demands of the types common to almost every stratum of the American workplace.

Recently, the NAEP conducted an exemplary analysis of the reading abilities of young adults (Kirsch & Jungeblut, 1986). This test evaluated the abilities of individuals to read a variety of materials and to complete a number of tasks that focused on real world reading activities (including school materials, but also job applications, schedules, newspapers, and so on). These tasks required the answering of traditional and open-ended questions and the use of other appropriate responses (e.g., writing a letter) to the various texts.

This assessment design resulted in the identification of three scales of performance, each of which described distinct aspects of being literate. The scales identified were prose or school literacy, document literacy, and quantitative literacy. Prose literacy refers to the "knowledge and skills needed to understand and use information from texts that include editorials, news stories, poems, and the like." Document literacy refers to the abilities required "to locate and use information contained in job applications, payroll forms, bus schedules, maps, tables, indexes, and so forth." Quantitative literacy refers to the "use of arithmetic operations that are embedded in printed materials such as order forms, checkbook statements, and loan advertisements or applications."

The NAEP effort is notable in that it attempted to identify common underlying skills and knowledge required to carry out real life literacy demands. It is also important in that the scales identified were largely independent of each other. That is, there was very little overlap or connection among the performance levels associated with each of these three scales. A person who was very good at prose literacy might just as likely be good or poor at document literacy or quantitative literacy. Despite the use of highly reliable measures, the highest correlation between any two of the three scales was 0.36; this means that less than 15 percent of the performance on any of the scales was due to the knowledge and abilities tapped by one of the other scales.

Particularly important is the dissociation of prose reading from other forms of reading and writing. The prose scale is the most similar to school reading and writing demands. That it was not highly correlated with the more social or economic uses of literacy suggests that school literacy training, beyond the very lowest levels, probably does little to prepare students to deal with real life literacy demands and that school-based tests probably do little to inform us about these aspects of reading ability. A basic skills test that is too narrowly drawn might not provide the types of information that test users hope to obtain.

Reading tests should include a variety of material types and they should require students to do a variety of tasks. Reading tests have focused on school-like reading materials and on question-answering responses to too great a degree. If our intention is simply to describe how well students can perform on school-like tasks, such a narrow test might be enough (though I doubt it, since even in a school situation there is a greater need to evaluate the ability to summarize, to synthesize or compare multiple texts, to use books in conjunction with other materials, and so on). If our real interest is in developing and evaluating the ability to use literacy to participate in work, scholarship, and communications, then our efforts are damagingly narrow. Historically, test designers have striven for reading tests that capture a single, highly reliable factor. It is time that our efforts focus instead on examining those uncorrelated items that might be the basis of independent scales or those factors that measure valuable literacy abilities. Until our tests begin to consider the reading process in all of its complexity—in the ways that reading is actually done—there will be nothing basic about our basic skills measurements of reading.

Reading tests should not simply attempt to measure some aspect of reading. They should be based on analyses of the actual literacy demands in which we are interested. Such analyses should consider the various types of materials, and the ways that these materials will actually be used, in college programs and in the larger society. The use of traditional test passages and discrete questions militates against the valid description of reading ability.

Summary

Reading test design should attempt to reflect reading theory rather than previous test designs. The theoretical realignment in reading requires the development of dramatically different basic skills tests. Test designs need to be more in accord with modern theory and with the empirical descriptions of reading that proceed from this theory. This paper focused on three ongoing development efforts that have created tests to be used with very different populations and purposes than those common in basic skills programs. Nevertheless, the issues addressed by these innovative projects are *at least* as relevant in basic skills programs. If the purpose of basic skills tests is to describe reading ability in a valid manner, then issues of prior knowledge, reasoning in reading, meaningfulness of questions, textual coherence and quality, and the representativeness of reading tasks are critical and must be addressed. Unless we are willing to make our test designs reflect the nature of reading, we will continue to make decisions on the basis of information that provides neither a useful guide to practice, nor a reasonable description of the abilities of our students.

References

Anderson, R., Hiebert, E., Scott, J., & Wilkinson, I. (1985). *Becoming a nation of readers: The report of the Commission on Reading.* Washington, DC: National Institute of Education.

Anderson, R., Reynolds, R., Schallert, D., & Goetz, E. (1977). Frameworks for comprehending discourse. *American Educational Research Journal, 14,* 367–382.

Bormuth, J., Carr, J., Manning, J., & Pearson, P. D. (1970). Children's comprehension of between- and within-sentence syntactic structure. *Journal of Educational Psychology, 61,* 349–357.

Bransford, J., & Johnson, M. (1972). Contextual prerequisites for understanding: Some investigations of comprehension and recall. *Journal of Verbal Learning and Verbal Behavior, 11,* 717–726.

Carver, R. (1973). Understanding, information processing, and learning from prose materials. *Journal of Educational Psychology, 64,* 76–84.

Dooling, D., & Lachman, R. (1971). Effects of comprehension on retention of prose. *Journal of Experimental Psychology, 88,* 216–222.

Drum, P., Calfee, R., & Cook, L. (1981). The effects of surface structure variables on performance in reading comprehension tests. *Reading Research Quarterly, 16,* 486–514.

Farr, R., & Carey, R. (1986). *Reading: What can be measured?* Newark, DE: International Reading Association.

Goetz, E., & Armbruster, B. (1980). Psychological correlates of text structure. In R. Spiro, B. Bruce, & W. Brewer (Eds.), *Theoretical issues in reading comprehension.* Hillsdale, NJ: Erlbaum.

Goetz, E., Schallert, D., Reynolds, R., & Radin, D. (1983). Reading in perspective: What real cops and pretend burglars look for in a story. *Journal of Educational Psychology, 75,* 500–510.

Halliday, M. A. K., & Hasan, R. (1976). *Cohesion in English.* London: Longman.

Johnston, P. H. (1984). Assessment in reading. In P. D. Pearson (Ed.), *Handbook of reading research.* New York: Longman.

Johnston, P. H. (1983). *Reading comprehension assessment: A cognitive basis.* Newark, DE: International Reading Association.

Kintsch, W., & van Dijk, T. (1978). Toward a model of text comprehension and production. *Psychological Review, 85,* 363–394.

Kirsch, I., & Jungeblut, A. (1986). *Literacy: Profiles of America's young adults.* Princeton, NJ: Educational Testing Service.

Mandler, J., & Johnson, N. (1977). Remembrance of things parsed: Story structure and recall. *Cognitive Psychology, 9,* 111–151.

National Assessment of Educational Progress. (1981). *Reading, thinking and writing.* Denver: Education Commission of the States.

Pearson, P. D., & Valencia, S. Assessment, accountability, and professional prerogative. In J. Readence & S. Baldwin (Eds.). (1987). *Research in literacy: Merging perspectives.* (Thirty-sixth Yearbook of the National Reading Conference). Rochester, NY: National Reading Conference.

Petrosky, A. (1982). From story to essay: Reading and writing. *College Composition and Communication, 33,* 19–36.

Pichert, J., & Anderson, R. (1977). Taking different perspectives on a story. *Journal of Educational Psychology, 69,* 309–315.

Pikulski, J., & Shanahan, T. (1980). A comparison of various approaches to evaluating phonics. *Reading Teacher, 33,* 692–702.

Shanahan, T., & Kamil, M. (1982). The sensitivity of cloze to passage organization. In J. Niles & L. Harris (Eds.), *New inquiries in reading research and instruction.* (Thirty-first Yearbook of the National Reading Association, 204–208). Rochester, NY: National Reading Conference.

Smith, N. B. (1965). *American reading instruction.* Newark, DE: International Reading Association.

Steffensen, M., Joag-dev, C., & Anderson, R. (1979). A cross-cultural perspective on reading comprehension. *Reading Research Quarterly, 15,* 10–29.

Thorndike, E. L. (1917). Reading as reasoning: A study of mistakes in paragraph reading. *Journal of Educational Psychology, 8,* 323–332.

Valencia, S., & Pearson, P. D. (1987). Reading assessment: Time for a change. *The Reading Teacher, 40,* 726–732.

Valencia, S., Pearson, P. D., Reeve, R., & Shanahan, T. (In press). *A new model for reading comprehension assessment.* Champaign, IL: Center for the Study of Reading.

Whitney, P. (1987). Psychological theories of elaborative inferences: Implications for schema-theoretic views of comprehension. *Reading Research Quarterly, 22,* 299–310.

Wixson, K., & Peters, C. (1987). Comprehension assessment: Implementing an interactive view of reading. *Educational Psychologist, 22,* 333–356.

Using Assessment to Improve Instruction: The New Jersey Algebra Project

Charles Pine

Since 1978 approximately 50,000 students entering New Jersey public colleges each year have taken the New Jersey College Basic Skills Placement Tests (NJCBSPT) in Computation and in Elementary Algebra. The test results have consistently indicated that a great many of these freshmen have an inadequate grasp of elementary algebra and have difficulty in doing quantitative reasoning.

Project Background

The New Jersey Basic Skills Council, a group of 12 faculty members and administrators representative of each of New Jersey's college sectors, administers these tests. Each year the Council's Mathematics Advisory Committee, in conjunction with Educational Testing Service of Princeton, New Jersey, develops a new form of the tests.

I served as a member of the Basic Skills Council and also as chairman of the Mathematics Advisory Committee from 1977 to 1986. This provided me the opportunity to use the test results for research studies, which were supported by Rutgers University and by the New Jersey Department of Higher Education. My hope was to be able to deduce from the error patterns on hierarchies of items how algebra instruction at the high school level might be improved and also how best to help entering college students overcome their difficulties with mathematics.

A planning grant from the Ford Foundation in 1982 enabled me to assemble an advisory group of educators. This advisory group examined the standard Algebra I curriculum and textbooks in relation

Charles Pine is professor emeritus of Physics at Rutgers University in Newark, New Jersey, and director of the New Jersey Algebra Project.

to the NJCBSPT data analysis. The group concluded that a more logical ordering of topics as indicated by the data analysis and changes in mode of presentation might substantially enhance student learning. This led to the Algebra Project.

A very capable team of high school and college mathematics teachers worked with me during 1983 and 1984 in formulating the curriculum, writing the text materials, and creating the teacher training program. Pilot implementation of the Algebra Project program took place in the 1984–85 and 1985–86 school years in high schools and middle schools in 18 school districts representing a broad spectrum of urban, suburban, and rural areas. Evaluation of pre- and post-test results for the pilot classes and for matched control classes taught by standard methods with standard textbooks showed that the Algebra Project students were more successful in learning algebra than were the control students. We used the 1982 form of the NJCBSPT Computation test as the pre-test and the 1983 form of the NJCBSPT Elementary Algebra test as the post-test. We also administered a computation post-test (the 1983 form of the NJCBSPT Computation test). These tests, with identification removed, were used with permission of the New Jersey Department of Higher Education.

Now (1987–88) in the fourth year of implementation, the Algebra Project includes 88 teachers in 29 school districts. Though we no longer need to use control classes, we still pre-test and post-test all the Algebra Project classes; the information obtained is very useful, indeed essential, for continuing assessment and improvement of the program.

All the Algebra Project activities described have been and continue to be supported by the New Jersey Department of Higher Education, the New Jersey Department of Education, and Rutgers University. In addition, the AT&T Foundation provided funding for expansion of the project in 1986–87.

We would like now to bring the program to the college level. We feel that we have learned much from our experience in the high schools that will give fresh insight to the teaching of underprepared college students. We hope to run a pilot program in some colleges during the 1988–89 school year.

1980–1986 Proficiency Results

Somewhat more than half of the students who enter New Jersey public colleges each September are recent high school graduates; that is, they graduated from high school in June of that same year. Table 1 (see page 66) gives a summary of the proficiency results for Elementary Algebra and for Computation for recent New Jersey high school graduates over the seven-year period from 1980 through 1986.

The three proficiency categories have the following meanings.

Lack Proficiency: Students in this category may have some smatterings of knowledge or understanding but definitely need considerable help. They need "remediation."

Appear Proficient in Some Areas: This represents a continuum from very weak to relatively strong. Most students in this category likely need some additional instruction. The Basic Skills Council urges colleges to take into account other indicators besides the basic skills test score when doing placement. This advice is particularly pertinent in the case of this middle category.

Appear to Be Proficient: The caveat "appear to be" is here because the test items do not extend far enough in difficulty level to justify a flat statement that a student in this test score range is indeed proficient.

The proficiency results are distressing. Also, they are quite consistent, varying very little for each course category from year to year. Students with fewer than three years of mathematics in high school almost certainly have little understanding of algebra and also generally are weak in computation. Particularly distressing are the results for course category 5, students with three years of high school mathematics. What were they learning in the three years of course work?

The appellation for course category 6, "Pre-Calculus," is a catchall for students who have taken four years of mathematics but not calculus. Their fourth year courses might include trigonometry or senior mathematics or both.

The very abrupt change between category 5 and categories 6 and 7 in our opinion reflects more likely that students who elect to take a fourth year of mathematics feel comfortable with mathematics than

TABLE 1

Relationship Between Mathematics Courses Completed in High School and the Elementary Algebra and Computation Proficiencies[1] of the Students Tested with the New Jersey College Basic Skills Placement Tests: 1980 through 1986, Recent New Jersey High School Graduates Only.[2]

Course Category[3]	Total Number	ELEMENTARY ALGEBRA						COMPUTATION					
		Lack Proficiency		Appear Proficient in Some Areas		Appear to Be Proficient		Lack Proficiency		Appear Proficient in Some Areas		Appear to Be Proficient	
		N	%	N	%	N	%	N	%	N	%	N	%
1. Business Math or General Math	11,771	11,663	98.8	131	1.1	7	0.06	10,421	88.5	1,138	9.7	212	1.8
2. Algebra I	11,945	11,356	95.1	583	4.9	6	0.05	9,099	76.2	2,203	18.4	643	5.4
3. Algebra I & Geometry	21,031	18,832	89.5	2,157	10.3	42	0.2	13,520	64.3	5,466	26.0	2,045	9.7
4. Algebra I & Algebra II	6,616	4,711	71.2	1,819	27.5	86	1.3	4,065	61.4	1,766	26.7	785	11.9
5. Algebra I, Geometry, & Algebra II	46,854	23,415	50.0	21,720	46.4	1,719	3.7	17,789	38.0	16,495	35.2	12,570	26.8
6. Pre-Calculus	46,739	8,133	17.4	26,408	56.5	12,198	26.1	6,348	13.6	12,518	26.8	27,873	59.6
7. Calculus	18,233	553	3.0	5,416	29.7	12,264	67.3	549	3.0	2,092	11.5	15,592	85.5
Total Tested	163,189												

[1] The proficiency categories are content-referenced, scaled score ranges defined by the New Jersey Basic Skills Council. The raw score equivalents have varied only slightly over the seven-year period, and for each of the 30-item tests the raw score ranges were typically:

	Lack Proficiency	Appear Proficient in Some Areas	Appear to Be Proficient
Elementary Algebra	0–14 correct	15–25 correct	26–30 correct
Computation	0–19 correct	20–24 correct	25–30 correct

[2] Recent high school graduates are those who graduated the spring prior to their enrollment in college. Limited-English–Proficient students are excluded.

[3] The courses given for the course categories represent the highest-level mathematics courses completed in high school by the students falling in each category.

that their learning greatly increases in the fourth year. Nor do we think that students who stop taking mathematics courses after the junior year "forget everything" during the senior year.

The Elementary Algebra Test

A hierarchy of linear equations similar to the one shown in Table 2a (see page 68) appears in every form of the test because we feel that it gives so much information about examinees' ability to do sequential thinking. Three different kinds of information appear in this table. The rank order of "easiness" column gives a sense of the difficulty level of the algebra test. If solving the equation $ax = c - bx$ is the most difficult task on the test, then it is not a very hard test for anyone who understands algebra.

The raw score proficiency ranges for the 1983 form of the Elementary Algebra test were 0–13, 14–25, 26–30. Thus the "Percent Correct by Total Test Score" columns give a sense of what students who score at the boundaries between the proficiency ranges can do. It is readily apparent that students who achieve a test score of 14 have pronounced weaknesses in elementary algebra.

In the "Percent Correct by Course Category" subtable, the course categories are those named in Table 1. The results for category 5 give a feeling for why the proficiency results for this category are so poor in Table 1. This is one of the things that shocked us the most in 1980 when we first began to break down the results by course category.

Should not a student with three years of study in mathematics realize that the first thing to do with an equation such as the one in Item 30 is to multiply both sides of the equation by 10? For that matter, the students in category 6 do not perform very much better on this item.

Pilot/Control Algebra Post-Test Results

In each of the two years of pilot implementation of the Algebra Project, we conducted a study to evaluate the effectiveness of the program in enabling students to learn algebra. Through the cooperation of school districts that agreed to serve as controls, we were able to compare the year-end performance of students taught by the Algebra Project methods (the pilot students) with that of students taught by the standard methods (the control students).

TABLE 2

Table 2a: Results for Selected Items on the 1983 Form of the New Jersey College Basic Skills Placement Test in Elementary Algebra. These results pertain to the recent New Jersey high school graduates (N = 23,112) who entered New Jersey colleges in September 1983.

The sample items below are similar to the actual test items.

Rank Order of "Easiness"	Item		Percent Correct by Course Category			Percent Correct by Total Test Score	
			5	6	7	test score: 14	26
4th	5	If $7x - 3 = 2$, then $x = ?$	66	87	96	73	98
12th	9	If $9x - 2 = 11 + 4x$, then $x = ?$	55	75	91	57	94
28th	30	If $\frac{4x}{5} = 3 - \frac{x}{2}$, then $x = ?$	23	43	71	20	66
30th	29	If $ax = c - bx$, then $x = ?$	17	33	71	14	55
	number of students:		6,669	6,951	2,837	769	704

Table 2b: Algebra Project Pilot/Control Results for 1984–85 and 1985–86 for Selected Items on the Algebra Post-Test. The test used was the 1983 form of the New Jersey College Basic Skills Placement Test in Elementary Algebra.

Percent Correct by Pre-Test Score Range

Item			– – – – – Pilots – – – – –				– – – – Controls – – – –			
		range:	25-30	21-24	16-20	0-15	25-30	21-24	16-20	0-15
5	If $7x - 3 = 2$, then $x = ?$		97	90	83	68	87	80	71	53
9	If $9x - 2 = 11 + 4x$, then $x = ?$		92	81	74	61	77	69	57	44
30	If $\frac{4x}{5} = 3 - \frac{x}{2}$, then $x = ?$		74	59	47	38	36	25	22	18
29	If $ax = c - bx$, then $x = ?$		80	65	55	37	22	18	19	19
	number of students:		671	727	869	768	439	496	538	358

The combined results for 1984–85 and 1985–86 for totals of 3035 pilot students and 1831 control students are given in Tables 3a and 3b (see page 70). The left-hand column in the two tables contains the four score ranges which we use for the computation pre-test. Across the top of each table are the four score ranges which we use for the algebra post-test. The number shown in each box is the number of students in a particular pre-test score range and a particular algebra post-test score range. For example, there were 671 pilot students in the 25–30 score range on the pre-test. Of these 671 pilots, 318 (47.4 percent of 671) achieved an algebra post-test score in the 26–30 range, 210 (31.3 percent) in the 21–25 range, 93 (13.9 percent) in the 16–20 range, and 50 (7.5 percent) in the 0–15 range.

In Table 3b, of the 439 control students in the 25–30 score range on the computation pre-test, 37 (8.4 percent of 439) achieved an algebra post-test score in the 26–30 range and 140 (31.9 percent) had an algebra score in the 0–15 range.

Overall, 478 pilots (15.7 percent of 3,035) scored in the highest algebra range while 47 controls (2.6 percent of 1,831) scored in that same range.

Clearly the pilots perform considerably better than the controls for every corresponding pre-test score range comparison (except for the 0–15 pre-test range, where the results are poor for both groups). But, while the results are quite good for the ostensibly well-prepared pilots (the 25–30 group)—especially when one considers the results in Table 1 for students entering college—they drop off much too rapidly for the pilots in lower pre-test ranges. Evidently, the ability to learn algebra well strongly depends on what happens to the student in lower grades. We have done a longitudinal analysis of the results for the first three years of implementation in an attempt to identify the factors involved. We think that number sense, including a good understanding of our decimal place value system, is one of these factors. This year (1987–88), we included material in the program that we hope will help this situation.

When one studies the results for the controls, it is evident that the standard curriculum does not work well. So many students, even the best prepared ones, are receiving a poor education in algebra. Table 3b, unfortunately, provides an explanation for the incredible

TABLE 3

ALGEBRA PROJECT

Two-Year Results: 1984–85 and 1985–86

Frequency Tables

Algebra Post-Test Scores vs. Computation Pre-Test Scores

Table 3a

PRE-TEST		– – – – – PILOTS ONLY – – – – –				
		POST-TEST				
FREQUENCY ROW PCT	26–30	21–25	16–20	0–15	TOTAL	
25–30	318 47.4%	210 31.3%	93 13.9%	50 7.5%	671	
21–24	104 14.3%	220 30.3%	189 26.0%	214 29.4%	727	
16–20	50 5.8%	147 16.9%	236 27.2%	436 50.2%	869	
0–15	6 0.8%	50 6.5%	127 16.5%	585 76.2%	768	
TOTAL	478 15.7%	627 20.7%	645 21.3%	1,285 42.3%	3,035	

Table 3b

PRE-TEST		– – – – – CONTROLS ONLY – – – – –				
		POST-TEST				
FREQUENCY ROW PCT	26–30	21–25	16–20	0–15	TOTAL	
25–30	37 8.4%	122 27.8%	140 31.9%	140 31.9%	439	
21–24	5 1.0%	68 13.7%	138 27.8%	285 57.5%	496	
16–20	4 0.7%	33 6.1%	91 16.9%	410 76.2%	538	
0–15	1 0.3%	5 1.4%	29 8.1%	323 90.2%	358	
TOTAL	47 2.6%	228 12.5%	398 21.7%	1,158 63.2%	1,831	

results in Table 1 and Table 2b. It is not that students forget algebra and how to solve equations. They never really understood it in the first place.

Pilot/Control Results for the Linear Equation Hierarchy

Table 2b speaks for itself. Comparison with the course category subtable in Table 2a is interesting also. The Algebra Project is (comparatively) very successful in having students learn how to solve equations. This has to do with a more logical ordering of the material. We handle all linear equations in one chapter instead of having them scattered throughout the book. But before students get to this chapter they learn sequential thinking through extensive work with the step-by-step approach we use for the simplification of complex fractions.

Conclusion

As a review of the New Jersey Algebra Project has shown, the problem is not one of discrete skills that an individual student may lack and can be "remediated" for. This is patchwork and will not be effective in the long term. The real problem is with quantitative reasoning.

Too often people think of basic skills as low-level skills or minimum skills—they are not. We should think of basic skills as essential skills. What then are the basic skills needed for quantitative work in college and elsewhere? What proficiencies in math do we really want students to have?

There are three major skills, really abilities, involved. The first is the ability to analyze a situation or a problem and decide what needs to be found, then to verbalize an approach, which very often will be an equality, and finally, to translate from verbal form to symbolic form—that is, to set up an equation or equations. The second is the ability to solve the equation or equations—this involves various algorithmic skills, and these depend primarily on the capability for doing sequential thinking. And the final one is the ability to interpret and assess the solution to the equation—to determine whether the result answers the original question and is indeed a reasonable answer.

Measuring Writing Skills Using the Process Model

Edward White

When writing researchers, textbook writers, and teacher trainers talk about writing instruction these days, someone is sure to come up with the latest catch phrase: Writing is a *process* not a *product*. Since this slogan, like all slogans, embodies an entire complex of attitudes and approaches, I will be using it as the underlying idea of this presentation. I intend first to examine what writing teachers and researchers mean when they say that writing is a *process* and then to consider the implications of that meaning for the measurement of writing ability. I will be concerned with the relationship of measurement to teaching and with the ways changes in teaching must affect concepts of measurement.

The Shift in Approach

In the first place, it is important to notice that a major change in writing research and writing instruction has occurred during the last generation. Numbers of scholars, describing this change, have turned to Thomas Kuhn's metaphor for scientific revolutions and called it a "paradigm shift," though other scholars have argued that the change is so based in the rhetorical tradition that such elaborate terminology is unseemly. The product/process distinction surely overstates the opposition that is involved in the change, but nonetheless puts the issue in stark relief. Briefly put, this change has shifted the teaching of writing into the same context as the teaching of critical thinking and problem solving and somewhat diminished the role of writing as an agent of social stratification. I will not take time to trace the causes of this change here, but I will mention a few contributing factors: the onset of open enrollment in the City University of New York in 1970, research in sociolinguistics and dialectology demonstrating the value of variant dialects, heightened concern for racial

Edward White is professor of English at California State University at San Bernardino and author of *Teaching and Assessing Writing,* published in 1985.

bias in instruction and measurement as part of the drive toward a more racially open society, increasing worries about the place of creative thought in a weakened school curriculum, fuller understanding by writing researchers of how writers actually produce texts, and so on. All of these issues have asked us to define writing as more than a mere product to be graded for correctness.

Now, of course, the slogan oversimplifies the issue: every sensible person knows that writing is, or can be, both a process *and* a product.

Objections to the Product Model

The objection to writing as product too easily ignores the fact that a term paper, a letter of inquiry, a job application, an essay on a test, an article for publication, or a presentation such as this one is a product offered for evaluation and consumption. But the objection is nonetheless sound, for almost all school writing is not inherently valuable or meaningful as product; in a world of wastepaper, what is less likely to be published or even saved than old exams or essay assignments? We do not assign writing to students because they will turn out work that will inform us or anyone else; even doting parents, treasuring diaries and letters, have no use for term papers. We do need to collect and grade occasional presentation copies of student work to be sure that they can, when needed, turn out presentable products. But we assign writing to students not so that they will give us valuable documents but so that they will learn something valuable while producing their usual mediocre documents. That is, school writing is necessary for instruction because it is an important, probably the single most important, way to learn.

I am not telling you anything new by saying this—everyone who writes and teaches knows it—but the implications for teachers (and thus for tests) are quite new. The teacher who basically considers school writing as a *product* will serve basically as a more or less negative evaluator, red-marking errors on the page (generally to little or no effect, but that is another subject altogether). Traditionally, English teachers spend endless hours grading papers, which, in fact, usually means editing them for perceived violations of the rules. Teachers outside of the field of English have normally done the same thing, or, to be more realistic, have resisted using much writing in their teaching because they have not wanted to do the same thing. Writing, when defined as a product, demands a high level of careful editing for correctness and neatness, both of which (according to fairly accurate student belief) count more than such risky matters as originality, a personal voice, or even a developed idea. Teachers and tests, according to the product model, serve as society's gatekeepers, screening out those students whose written products do not measure up to the standards of school correctness and the school dialect.

The quaint faith in rules for writing—the belief that if one is sufficiently correct one will write well—is not only pervasive among old-fashioned teachers and test makers, but also is firmly held by most students. Survey any group of college students and you will find that in their heart of hearts they believe that there are a handful of rules (which could be learned by sufficient drill) that would transform ordinary students into good writers. They, of course, do not know what these rules are, but English teachers are supposed to have the inside information and they are not telling. If students could only learn these rules, they believe, they could then turn out perfect first drafts, which they believe good writers invariably do. In fact, every student has picked up and clings to one or two of these rules: never use the word "I," avoid all contractions, use lots of Latin terms such as "ibid.," and so on. The fact that the supposed rules are wrong or ridiculous in no way diminishes the fervor with which they are held, and the belief that a few more rules will make them good writers forever never dies. Furthermore, they imagine that Miss Grundy handed out these rules in the fifth grade on the day they were sick; thus, everyone else *does* know all the rules, a belief fraught with a subjective sense of frustrated inferiority in the face of now inaccessible knowledge.

I trace this painful perplex, identifying good writing with supposed rules of correctness, to all the misplaced "grammar" instruction and multiple-choice usage testing that students, particularly good students, receive on their way through school. While that instruction and testing hinders rather than helps their writing, it fills them with a belief in simple right answers about writing and the conviction that memorization rather than discovery is at the heart of writing. As long as writing is defined as a finished product to be edited and corrected, writing remains a matter of guessing about the rules that govern correctness as defined by those in power. Such a definition is perfectly enforced by the usual multiple-choice editing test.

Arguments for the Process Model

Thus there is a hint of the social revolutionary behind the product/ process slogan. It not only asks the teacher to teach all students to write, even those whose home dialects may be different from the teacher's, but it argues for complex judgments based on more than the correctness of the product. The process model sees writing as a series of overlapping activities, all of which have to do with critical thinking and imagining: inventing and prewriting, drafting, refining and rethinking, connecting, revising, and (finally) editing. The role of the teacher according to this model is very active: deviser and prompter of writing tasks, writing coach, sponsor of peer evaluations, sympathetic but questioning reader of drafts, merciless taskmaster asking for critical rethinking and revision, and (finally) evaluator. Conservatives suspect that this means abandoning standards, but proponents of the process model argue that it moves standards from a rule book into a real world: this is writing seen as part of thinking, responding, evaluating, selecting, and connecting ideas. Good grades become less a matter of the dialect spoken in the home (traditionally, the nearer the home dialect to the school dialect the better the student's grade) than a measure of the thinking process of the student. The process model, by redefining writing, does not abandon standards but tries to redefine standards more substantially and more fairly. No sensible teacher using the process model abandons the requirement for a well-edited presentation copy of student work, but the edited final draft is now just one part of the job, rather than the only thing that matters.

Social Issues Behind the Debate

The social issue in the product/process debate is far from trivial. The process model in part takes issue with an inescapable aspect of education in all societies: socializing students to fit into their world. This is a responsibility no writing teacher can avoid. In a highly verbal society, an essential part of this socialization has to do with learning the conventional rules of verbal behavior. An absolutely necessary part of learning to write has to do with learning linguistic etiquette, memorizing the way things are done in the school dialect, internalizing the writing patterns of those in power. We do not want original approaches to spelling, punctuation, or sentence structure (though we often get them); rather, we say students should learn the rules on such matters and conform. But the process model urges us to be cautious about the place of such matters in the definition of writing skill.

Take spelling, for instance, the archetypal socializing study, the darling of those who in the name of "standards" want education to focus on rote drill. The fact that Shakespeare spelled his name in an engaging variety of ways did not mean he was a bad speller; there was no such thing as a bad speller until much later when spelling began to matter. When printers began to normalize spelling, for their convenience, and when the written and spoken language diverged to the degree that simple phonetic spelling became impossible, spelling became (as it now is) an important social skill, comparable to knowing how to use knives and forks at the table. Spelling is important because manners are important for social mobility, and good spelling suggests good linguistic upbringing. Spelling is important not because it makes sense, or because it is good mental discipline, or because it has anything at all to do with thinking; spelling is important solely because people will think you are stupid if you fail to spell words the way everyone else spells words.

But education in a democratic society cannot rest content with teaching conformity and good manners, useful though they are for the society and for the students eager to fit into that society. Thomas Jefferson and his colleagues (five of whom founded universities) spoke of the need for public education not because they were concerned about spelling, or job skills, or even competing with the Japanese for world markets. They spoke of it because they were concerned about maintaining a government whose powers derived from the consent of the governed. The problem for democratic political theory is that an uninformed consent is not consent at all. Behind all the volumes talking about school curriculum lies that simple fact: education in a democracy must prepare an informed and independent electorate. Despite the necessary conformity and socialization that must go on in school, any school, we have the particular obligation to foster critical thinking, questioning, creativity. And writing, as defined by the process model, turns out to be the single most effective way to develop *these* most essential basic skills, at all levels. Any definition of basic skills in writing that leaves out thinking is undemocratic and insubstantial.

Addressing the Conflict in Other Basic Skills Areas

Before I turn to the ways in which writing tests have responded to the concerns I have been summarizing, let me just note in passing that many other fields have also been dealing with a similar process/product conflict in definition. Reading theories these days point out that readers are not merely passive recipients of a given text but rather active participants in the creation of the meaning of that text; reading and writing are similar meaning-making activities. And mathematical reasoning is clearly more important than the calculation of formulas that may lead to the right answers. In every case, the product definition, based on rules for correctness, leads to easy test-making but also to a simplified curriculum unsuited to free men and women.

Styles of Measurement

The implications of the process/product issue for tests of writing skills are profound. I will consider them briefly according to the three kinds of measurement now in use: multiple-choice usage tests, essay tests, and portfolio evaluations.

Multiple-Choice Testing

The familiar multiple-choice usage tests are, of course, based on the definition of writing as product. The assumptions are plain: (1) there are clear right and wrong answers to problems in the editing of texts, (2) the brief fragments of writing given on a test can elicit a student's knowledge of those answers, and (3) the student's ability to write (vaguely defined) will correlate highly with his or her ability to edit correctly the prose on the test. Unfortunately for those committed to this set of assumptions, the process model of writing disputes each of them.

The advantages of this kind of test are familiar to everyone and result from the established traditional methods of devising a reliable norm-referenced test. Once the very high development costs (higher than ever under truth-in-testing laws) are covered, the test can be easily administered and scored at low cost by computer. Once an appropriate norm group has been established, the norms can be published and score comparisons can be made. The statistics are impressive and scoring reliability is essentially perfect. Best of all, professional educators love these tests and the data produced by them, and the tests have a resounding appearance of objectivity (some even call them "objective tests" as if they had been constructed by the same computers that score them).

These are powerful advantages of multiple-choice usage tests, powerful enough for them to survive and even to thrive despite the attacks of those who define writing by the process model. But we do need to state the disadvantages of those tests. The very narrow definition of writing as editing puts their validity in serious question despite their reliability. The validity issue becomes even more serious as evidence accumulates that the supposed correlation of scores on those tests with measures of actual writing is much higher for students who call themselves "White" than for those who are part of racial or ethnic minorities. As long as the validity of the multiple-choice tests of writing is so suspect, none of the other advantages should carry the weight they now do.

Essay Testing

In response to the validity problem, we have seen major advances in essay testing over the last generation. Asking students to write on a writing test solves many, but by no means all, of the problems I have just alluded to. Writing is still defined as a product to be measured, so the process model is still unsatisfied by such a test, but at least these tests measure a much wider range of writing activity than mere editing. Students need to demonstrate the ability to generate prose and to develop thought in prose, and so the measurement can respond to these parts of the writing process, as well as to editing in a more natural setting. Of course, such a test is still an artificial situation for writing and still a small sample of the universe of writing, so we cannot consider the writing produced to be "real writing," as some uncritical proponents of essay testing put it; nonetheless, such writing tests have become more and more widely used nationally in recent years. They have become standard on college placement tests, for example, and on teacher certification skills tests, though they are often combined with multiple-choice components to increase reliability. Most such tests are carefully developed, using recognized procedures calling for test criteria and pre-testing of topics; rating reliabilities and costs (always the twin problems for writing tests) have become manageable using controlled holistic scoring.

The advantages of essay tests are clear: their increased validity, adequate reliability, and nearness to the process model of teaching have earned them support from teachers and many administrators. The evidence of relative freedom from racial bias has been impressive. Furthermore, the necessary teacher involvement in creation and scoring has led to substantial in-service training of teachers as a useful byproduct of the testing.

But the disadvantages of essay tests are also obvious: even though development costs are much lower than for multiple-choice tests, scoring costs are higher. Although it has become more and more customary to achieve very high interrater score correlations, it is difficult to achieve high overall test reliability with a single essay. If test reliabilities above 0.5 are needed, more than one writing sample must be obtained and scored, or a multiple-choice test of some sort, perhaps a reading test, must be added. And test development is a never-ending process. Testing with essay writing always involves a series of compromises, and partisans of the process model are never altogether comfortable with tests that exclude revision, for them the most essential part of the writing process.

Portfolio Assessment

In response to these problems, portfolio evaluation has recently been adopted from the fine arts for writing measurement. For example, the University of Minnesota has announced that it will evaluate writing portfolios as the test for entry into freshman English, the State University of New York at Stony Brook has begun using port-folios to measure upper-division writing proficiency, and even the Educational Testing Service has continued to support and publicize a writing portfolio research project. Portfolio assessment is the most responsive of all assessments to the process model of writing. Whether it can solve the problems of reliability and cost, as essay testing has, remains an open question. At present, portfolios are an intriguing but experimental approach to writing assessment. I suspect that this approach will not work for large-scale assessment, but that's what specialists were saying about essay testing a generation ago, and they turned out to be dead wrong.

Conclusion

The measurement of writing ability should understand and support the best goals of writing instruction. This means that the measurement as well as the teaching of basic skills must include critical thinking and creativity in the definition of these basic skills. It also means that the processes of thinking and writing as well as their products need to appear somehow in the measurement of writing ability. We are clearly a long way from realizing that goal, both in the testing and the teaching of writing. A community college teacher once told me of a one-sentence "essay" she received from a remedial level student, responding to the topic "Why Write?" "They make you write," the student wrote, "so they can *getcha*." For this student, not only the test but all school writing was a trap; our task and our challenge is to help such students see the opportunity as well as the dangers that writing offers to them.

The Role of Basic Academic Skills Development in the Reform of Education

Theodore J. Marchese

My goal in this presentation is to set the concern for basic skills development in the larger context of the assessment movement and the movement to reform and empower American education. First let me say that the assessment movement is alive and may be all too well. By our count at the American Association for Higher Education (AAHE), about forty states are now working on something called assessment. As well, about ten states are implementing formal mandates, and at least thirty other states will soon be doing so. The most recent activity is in New York, which has been one of the holdouts until now. I am also happy to say that in the last two or three years hundreds of institutions have gotten into the assessment movement. We now enjoy a certain amount of institutional experience with assessment issues that we did not have back in 1985 when this all started.

As far as the larger educational reform movement is concerned, most of the action in that, as in assessment, is not going on in Washington; it is going on in statehouses. An incredible number of things are happening now in state after state.

My focus here, though, is on the basic skills development effort. And my text is inspired by the presentation of Dr. Charles Pine (see page 63) on the New Jersey Algebra Project. I think that Charles Pine is an authentic American hero. If we had a thousand Charles Pines we would have far fewer problems in education. He gets in there, makes a commitment, and does something about it. He is sort of the John Madden of American higher education. Dr. Pine's work leads me to the following comments.

Theodore J. Marchese is vice president of the American Association for Higher Education and executive editor of *Change* magazine.

A Pattern of Underpreparation

The absolute levels of student achievement at college entry in the United States today are appallingly low. That is especially true in mathematics, as indicated by the example of the New Jersey Algebra Project. It is also true, as any teacher knows, that the levels of basic communication skills—reading, writing, and listening—are very low. We have a broad, deep pattern of underpreparation—a phenomenon of underpreparation—at entry into American colleges. As we see more assessment, such as what we have seen in New Jersey and are going to see in Texas, the dimensions of this problem are going to become clearer and clearer to the public and to policymakers. That, in turn, will fuel greater demands that we educators do something about the problem. Student underpreparation has been a hidden problem, especially at the college level, but that situation is likely to change.

The Damaging Effects of Student Underpreparation

Basic skills underachievement, that phenomenon of our college entrants, is a very serious problem. When underachievement occurs in two or more areas, the chances of degree attainment fall to near zero. Moreover, an estimated 60 percent of all undergraduate majors require math competence at the college algebra level, and some fields require calculus. That is a status, according to the New Jersey data, that only a small fraction of our entering students have attained. This means that broad, important areas of study and eventual career paths are effectively closed to large portions of our student populations. It also means that there are meager talent pools for fields of critical importance to the nation's future.

Addressing the Problem of Underpreparation

There are two kinds of problems in the world—problems you decide you can live with, and those you know you have to do something about. I believe we need to move the whole business of student underpreparation and basic skills development, from kindergarten through college, onto the side that says: "We have got to do something about this problem." Eighty percent of the jobs we hope to create in this country by the year 2000 will require some form of postsecondary preparation. As a society we do not have the option of imposing new barriers or gateways for progression. We need greater numbers of people in postsecondary education, and we need to educate people effectively to provide the labor force for a competitive economy. We are going to need larger and larger cohorts, effectively educated and productively employed, to support the huge number of people who will be in retirement at the start of the twenty-first century. Now, as never before, we need to give every young person in this country the best possible education for productive employment and citizenship. We cannot afford to waste anyone.

Arriving at Solutions

The problem of underpreparation cannot be solved at the college level. By the freshman year, some repair and catchup is possible, but underpreparation to the extent that we currently confront means that many important options for the individual are already excluded. There is only so much, and no more, that a college can do. College time on basic skills tasks is time no longer available for higher-order tasks. The solution lies back in the schools. That solution lies partly with us in higher education because we set the expectations for what is supposed to happen in the schools. We prepare the teachers. We shape the climate. We are implicated in poor school performance in a dozen ways. That is not something that occurs "over there"; it is something that we allow. Dr. Pine saw that point, and his efforts, which now reach over fifty high schools, need to be extended a thousandfold.

I am glad to say that there are new linkages across that great divide between K–12 and the postsecondary levels. We see, for example, the work of Claire Gaudiani, a teacher of French at the University of Pennsylvania, who is another American hero. Over the last five years, through personal effort, she has strung together over five thousand high school and college teachers, by discipline, in so-called academic alliances that include all the teachers of, for example, French or physics, in Lake County, Illinois. These teachers will get together and work for the advancement of their disciplines.

The alliance of high school and college faculty is a very important development. There are over 250 alliances now in 11 disciplines. We see in the school-college collaboration directory, recently published by the AAHE with the National Association of Secondary School Principals, that there are over a thousand formal linkages—aiming to improve communications and results—between high schools and colleges. In fall 1987, 37 college presidents, led by Donald Kennedy of Stanford and Dennis O'Brien of the University of Rochester, committed themselves to a major effort to break down the barriers in school-college relationships.

A lot more is going on in that arena, but I want to emphasize that a commitment must be made by educators at the university and K–12 levels to attack the problem of improving school and student performance. It is important, for example, that results from the Texas Academic Skills Program be used by college people not to excuse themselves or point fingers at other parties, but to awaken the state to a problem that needs broad and immediate address.

The problem of underpreparation has to be addressed as best it can at the college level, too. This means a full-court press on basic skills development. We cannot scapegoat or write off a generation of students that did not have the education it needed. We need them. Rather than treat basic skills instruction as a stepchild or orphan, we need to marshal our best people in research and organizational efforts to make that function more effective. I also suspect that we may need new delivery forms to achieve heightened effect—delivery forms that break away from the Monday-Wednesday-Friday class from 9:00 to 9:50, 15 weeks a semester. We need new delivery forms that are more likely to be short term, intensive, maybe full time, maybe residential, and funded on a totally different basis—on the basis of results, such as the way the Department of Labor funds its training programs for at-risk youth.

Instruction and Assessment

Assessment is not in essence about student placement. It is about learning outcomes. It is about quality measured in terms of results. So the effectiveness of the basic skills instruction we do is sure to follow as the next issue, as it has already in New Jersey. That is, the real crux of the trilogy—testing, placement, instruction—is that third element, the instruction. Assessment and placement are means, but the end is student learning and the attainment of goals. That and the effectiveness of instruction in achieving student learning is going to be much more of an issue than the placement of students.

You come right to the problem, then. Do we fit students to instruction, or fit the instruction to the students? I think the problem is going to be the latter. And, in the experience of institutions that have gotten into this recently, the effectiveness of basic skills instruction as measured by the outcome of student learning is the criterion that institutions will be held to. So, when you start entry testing, be ready; the other shoe is going to drop. People are going to want to know: How effective is the instruction?

Effective instruction will not necessarily follow assessment. It will come from coherent curricula, imaginative teaching, high expectations, and student involvement, but no improvement is going to come from assessment per se. In New Jersey, for example, where they have had assessment for ten years, there was not a unit of improvement in high school results between 1980 and 1986, even with the test and with widely publicized results. Improvement came when one person stepped forward, and then a group of people stepped forward and said, "We are going to make a difference." How did those people make a difference? They started to talk about changing the character of the instruction. They worked on the curriculum, the expectations, the level of student involvement. I might even paraphrase the trinity of the National Institute of Education report: After 25 years of research on effectiveness in learning, set high expectations, involve students in their learning, assess and provide feedback. The involvement and expectations are really going to make the difference to student learning in the long run.

Yet, assessment is an essential part. An analogy, though an imperfect one, is in how you lose weight. A bathroom scale does not cause you to lose weight; dieting and exercise cause you to lose weight. The bathroom scale is a very important device for monitoring weight loss and providing feedback on your efforts, but it does not cause weight loss. If we care about the effectiveness of our basic skills instruction, we must pay a lot more attention to basic educational issues and not quite so much to psychometric issues.

Conclusion

I am often asked at the AAHE Assessment Forum, "What kind of assessment should we do?" My response to that almost always is, "What do you want to accomplish, and what is your strategy for doing so?" Then we can talk about forms of assessment in support of that strategy. The Texas Academic Skills Program will be impressive if, instead of focusing on a test as the event, it focuses on a commitment to define and attack the problem. The test, then, will play a significant but small role. It is the larger sense of the goal and the strategy, not psychometrics, that needs to drive programs like this.

Assessment alone will not induce improvement or change. People bring about change, and I submit the New Jersey project as an example. Charles Pine has brought together eighty-eight teachers from fifty high schools. There are now four thousand students involved, and you see a dramatic improvement in the results for significant numbers of them. My point is that we need a people apparatus—a network of educators committed to achieving better results. I hope that five years from now you will count me among the committed, and that we will all have reason for pride in what we have achieved.

A Panel
Discussion
on the TASP

The following panel discussion took place at the end of the conference "Assessing Basic Skills in Higher Education," sponsored by National Evaluation Systems, Inc. (NES) and held in New Orleans in April 1988. Richard G. Allan, vice-president for instructional development at NES, served as moderator. Wilhelmina Delco, a member of the Texas House of Representatives; Robert Hardesty, then president of Southwest Texas State University; William Sanford, assistant commissioner of the Texas Higher Education Coordinating Board; and Pamela Tackett, a program director for the Texas Education Agency, were the panelists. Joan Matthews, a director of the Texas Academic Skills Program of the Texas Higher Education Coordinating Board, was asked to join the panelists during the question-and-answer session that followed the short presentations made by the panelists. Many of the comments made during the panel discussion reflected on more formal presentations given earlier in the conference. Those formal presentations served as the basis for the other chapters in Part One of this book.

ALLAN:

Up until this point in the conference, most of the speakers have been presenting issues of broad concern, broad issues from a national perspective. What we are intending to do with the panel this after-noon is to take what has been pursued at the national level and talk about how these issues, concerns, and problems have been or are in the process of being translated into a particular basic skills entry-level testing program in Texas. Wilhelmina Delco will talk from a legislative standpoint of the specific piece of legislation that she wrote, why she wrote it, and what it is intended to do. She talked this morning on a more broad level. This afternoon she will be talking specifically about Texas. I would then like to have Bob Hardesty, who headed the Committee on Testing of the Texas Higher Education Coordinating Board and basically did the research in Texas, speak on the form this program should take. He will talk to us about what kind of research they did, what they found, and what their recom-mendations were. In essence, this forms the bridge between what the legislation did and what the Higher Education Coordinating

Board is going to implement. I will then ask Bill Sanford to describe from the standpoint of the Higher Education Coordinating Board what this program is going to look like in some more detail. Finally, Pam Tackett is going to speak from the perspective of the Texas Education Agency (TEA). Pam has been actively involved for the last four years in developing and implementing teacher certification tests. One of the programs that they have had since 1984 is a basic skills test taken at the end of the sophomore year by all students going into the teacher preparation programs. In essence, that program will be subsumed by the broader-range program for all entering freshmen, and she is going to talk a bit about why TEA is comfortable in moving from what they have been doing to this new program.

As each speaker talks about this program and how it was implemented, I think it is important to remember what Manuel Justiz pointed out this morning. Assessment that serves only as a gatekeeper, rather than as assistance to students in overcoming any deficiencies or lack of preparation, is doing a disservice to the enterprise. The Texas Academic Skills Program has a strong instructional focus. When Bill Sanford was describing policy issues this morning, he mentioned the various permutations the program has gone through. When we, as a testing agency, first got together with the Higher Education Coordinating Board and Texas Education Agency, the first point that we all agreed on is that we are not developing a test. What we are doing is developing an instructional program where the test is just one feature, one aspect, albeit a very important one, but only one aspect of the entire endeavor.

At this point I will ask Wilhelmina Delco if she could describe from a legislative standpoint why this piece of legislation was engendered in Texas, and what specifically she intended to accomplish with it.

DELCO:

I talked in the morning session about the philosophy behind the organization of the Select Committee on Higher Education. What you need to know is that there was a deliberate effort on the part of the legislature in structuring that committee to make sure that there was a minimum of both legislative and professional educator input. The intent was to saturate the Select Committee with businesspeople because they were supposed to provide a hardheaded, objective look at the enterprise. Following up on the concept of trying to cut out the perceived fat in higher education, the first thing that they wanted to do was authorize a major accounting firm to look at the administrative aspect of education and to determine from that whether, at least on the administrative side, there might be some problems. The Select Committee broke down into three groups. One group was to look at what all of us thought were the philosophical points of legislative involvement in education, the very real questions of quality and access. Another was to look at the economic implications of education. What did businesspeople see in the education enterprise? They were investing a lot in taxes. What did they expect to get out of it? How could they be cooperating partners? And the third group provided the hardheaded business of how the enterprise ought to justify its existence in terms of the appropriations of tax dollars.

I served on the section that dealt with quality and access and basically that was the heart of the issue as far as I was concerned. We, in Texas, as in the rest of the United States, bent over backwards in the years following the Second World War and the GI Bill and the Affirmative Action thrust. We tried to make access to education a reality for everybody who could benefit from it. But we were beginning to feel, with the shortage of dollars, that some questions were being raised both outside and inside the enterprise of education about what we were buying in the name of access, what we were sacrificing in the name of access. There was a perception pretty far out there that you were letting everybody in, but somehow you were diluting the process and the product to the least among the students rather than the best. And so the old concept that says we are trading quality for access was a very real one. We did not want to, in that process, trade one for the other. We honestly felt that access without quality was fraud. And quality without access was the worst kind of elitism. So we were determined to combine the two, and one of the ways we could do that was to acknowledge publicly that some students come to the university without the educational tools that students from better schools have acquired. Instead of the institutions facing that issue head on, what they were doing was saying to those students "Oh, we know you can't do it." So what they would do would be either to give them a diluted degree or to say to them, "We're going to give you endless remediation until you either get a degree that is worthless, or get turned off."

So what we said, in effect, through this legislation was: okay, institutions, all the way from community colleges to our flagship institutions, whatever normal admissions standards you apply, apply them. But once you admit those students by your standards, no matter what they are, all students will be tested and they will be tested for a mastery of basic skills. And the result of that testing will be that the institution, now, must offer some kind of remediation to address those deficiencies if, in fact, they do exist.

We said to the students, that's what the institutions have to do. Students, if you feel that you don't need the remediation or that the test wasn't reflective of your abilities, there are some exceptions. But for the most part then, you will be restricted from entering an upper-division curriculum in an institution. You cannot go past the sixtieth semester credit hour. And the reason is that there must be a point at which you do college-level work. And if you have demonstrated through this process—and as I said, there are exceptions to using the test as the sole criterion—that you do not demonstrate a mastery of these basic skills, then we are saying that you are not going to be a college graduate. Now we received a lot of concerns when we made that effort. The minority students, Black and Hispanic, who had always feared the test, said this is just another impediment, this is just another way of keeping us out. Well, my personal reaction to that was, "Is it better to be logically confronted with your deficiencies and a commitment on the part of this state to address those deficiencies, or to be patted on the head and pushed through a system where you come out with literally a worthless, meaningless piece of paper?" And the resistance from that standpoint diminished. It didn't go away, but it diminished.

There was also a concern on the part of the institutions because the institutions felt that here we were loading on another layer for them. And of course the flagship institutions said, "We don't understand why we have do this because we don't admit those kinds of students. Our students don't need remediation." And the response was quite simply, "Well, if they don't need it, you got a piece of cake! You don't have to offer it to anybody who doesn't need it. If they pass the test, no problem." What we were convinced of then and we are still convinced of now is that the only way we are going to know the dimension of the problem is by testing to see what is there. And the only way we can deal with what is there is mandating that the institutions address what is there.

There is one other concern that has developed since National Evaluation Systems (NES) was awarded the contract to develop the test and to administer the test. NES is very concerned about making sure that the test is secure, and I applaud that. But I am unalterably committed to access, and as we look in Texas—I guess it is reflective of other states as well—we see that our average student age is twenty-seven. Our average student is part time. Our average student works to pay his or her way through school. And our average student is taking longer and longer to get through, dropping in and out of college. I am determined, as author of that bill, that we will not sacrifice access for security, that if colleges are in the business of giving tests, and they really are, they ought to be able to provide security. And I want to wave that as a flag of caution. I do not want that test to be yet another impediment to that student. In Texas, one out of every three students in our colleges in the next five or ten years ought to be Black or Brown. That is where the babies are, that is where the birth rate is. In Texas, twenty-seven percent of our Anglo students drop out before they finish high school, thirty-five percent of our Black students drop out before they finish high school, and forty-five percent of our Hispanic students drop out before they finish high school. We cannot afford that brain drain. Our only survival resource is the minds of our people; we cannot sacrifice one out of three. Any instrument that will help us to identify and to build on the brain base that we are born with in Texas is worth pursuing.

When I went to a historically Black college a long, long time ago, it was a given that when we went to college we were tested. It was not a feared process because it was promoted to us as a way of determining where we were in order to help us to go where we wanted to be. And I would submit that that is the attitude that we must adopt if we are going to maximize the potential of all of our people and maximize the resources that we have in the minds of our people. I see testing as a way to do that, and I am determined that we will not sacrifice the reality of testing both as an accountability tool and as a way of ensuring quality by creating an impediment to

DELCO (CONTINUED):

access. I believe it can be done and I believe in Texas. We have taken a giant step toward making it possible to do it with this generation of students.

ALLAN:

Thank you, Wilhelmina. Our next presenter this afternoon is Bob Hardesty, president of Southwest Texas State University. With his presentation, there is a progression that I think is important to keep in mind. Wilhelmina has talked about, from a legislative standpoint, why this piece of legislation exists. Bob headed up the Committee on Testing of the Texas Higher Education Coordinating Board. They did research into what a testing program for high school students should be. They went all around the country and came to conclusions, and these conclusions formed the basis of this legislation and then what the testing program is going to be. Bob, if you could spend a few minutes describing what this endeavor was and what your conclusions are, I think that would be in order.

HARDESTY:

In summer 1985 Larry Temple, then chairman of the Texas Higher Education Coordinating Board, asked me to chair a special committee on basic skills testing. Our mandate was to investigate the advisability of administering some kind of achievement or progress test to undergraduate students to make certain that they are, indeed, learning the basic skills of an educated person.

My selection as chairman was the result, I believe, of a unique perspective on basic skills that I had developed as president of Southwest Texas State University—where we were in the process of developing rising junior exams in English and math, and where the English exam is now in place.

There were twelve of us serving on the committee: a regent . . . a student . . . a professor . . . two testing experts . . . six college and university presidents . . . and one public school superintendent. They were dedicated, committed, and hard working, and infused with an incredible spirit of cooperation.

We first met on August 27, 1985. Over the next ten months, we held nine meetings, attended a national testing conference in Columbia, South Carolina, visited model testing programs in Florida and New Jersey, and conducted five public hearings throughout

Texas to obtain testimony from more than fifty educators, students, concerned citizens, and policy-makers on the proposed testing program. In May 1986 we held our final meeting, at which we shaped our recommendations. It should be noted that we were unanimous on each of our seven recommendations. There wasn't a single dissenting vote on a single major issue. I say this to emphasize the seriousness that we attached to the basic skills crisis in Texas. Not one member of our committee believed we could afford to ignore this problem for another generation, or another decade, or another year. Every year, more than 110,000 freshmen enter Texas public colleges and universities. Of these, at least 30,000 cannot read, communicate, or compute at levels needed to perform effectively in higher education.

Our committee started with a serious handicap. We knew there was a problem, but we didn't know its extent—and we had no quick way of measuring it. The one measurement we did have was not at all encouraging: the Pre-Professional Skills Test (PPST), which we have been giving since 1984 to test sophomores throughout Texas who are planning to become teachers. That test measures skills and knowledge that students have had an opportunity to learn by the tenth grade. In the seven times the test had been administered up to that time, an average of 28.2 percent of the Texas students who aspired to be teachers were deficient, according to these tests, in the basic skills of reading, writing, or math.

The public generally assumed that those PPST scores were symptomatic of poor teacher education programs, or of the quality of the young people going into teacher education. But that did not turn out to be the case. What the news stories neglected to say was that students take the test before they enter the teacher education program, so the schools of education can hardly be blamed for their deficiencies.

As to the quality of the students, we did a study at Southwest Texas and discovered that the average SAT and ACT scores of the teacher candidates were virtually the same as the average test scores of the student body as a whole.

Our committee concluded that if the PPST were given to all students, statewide, the pass/fail rate would be about the same as it is for those planning to enter teacher education. In other words, about thirty percent of the sophomores at Texas public colleges and universities would fail at least one part of a tenth-grade-level basic skills test. So the committee asked, "What would happen if freshmen—not sophomores—were given an examination measuring not tenth-grade-level but college-level skills?"

Frankly, we had no way of knowing exactly, but the indicators were clear: too many Texas students do not read, communicate, or compute at the college level. We did not know who they were or where they were, but we did know that they represented a generation of failure in our educational system—a failure we could no longer afford to ignore.

At the outset, we thought we were looking at a "rising junior" exam—that is, an exam given at the end of the sophomore year. In fact, the committee's name initially was "The Committee on Testing of College Sophomores." However, it became clear fairly early in our deliberations that no one felt that a "rising junior" exam was the answer for a mandated statewide test. We realized that if we were serious about remediation—and remediation is crucial if we are going to improve skills—then it is important to identify those students who need help as early as possible in their college careers—early in their freshman year.

Here, then, are the unanimous recommendations of our committee.

One, we recommended that beginning in fall 1989, or as soon thereafter as feasible, all freshmen entering a public college or university in Texas be tested in reading, writing, and mathematics skills at levels required to perform effectively in college. The test should be uniform across institutions and should be administered after admission. In no case should such a test bar entry to any student otherwise qualified; assessment should be a tool of the education process, not the selection process.

Two, we recommended that colleges and universities develop strong advising programs so that appropriate course placement occurs early in a student's degree program.

Three, we recommended that each public institution be required to offer or make available nondegree credit remedial opportunities on its own campus to those students identified by the test as needing assistance.

Four, we recommended that remediation be required when a component of the basic skills test is failed. All components of the test must be passed on or before the completion of sixty semester credit hours of degree credit. If not, further course work would be limited to lower-division courses until all components of the test have been passed.

Five, we recommended that each college and university be required to evaluate the results and effectiveness of remediation and to report annually to the Texas Higher Education Coordinating Board.

Six, we recommended that the Coordinating Board be directed to have these tests developed with the active participation at the decision-making level of faculty members from Texas colleges and universities.

Seven, we recommended that the legislature provide the necessary funding to develop and administer the tests and to support remediation. We said we would oppose a statewide basic skills test without the necessary financial support, especially for remediation.

These were rather far-reaching proposals—and frankly, we didn't have any idea how they would be received.

When I presented our report to the Coordinating Board, I told its members that they had loosed a genie that might prove difficult to get back into its bottle. "I sincerely hope," I said, "that the state of Texas is prepared for this report and prepared to act on it, because its findings are going to be difficult to ignore. If we are not prepared to act," I said, "we would have been better off without the report— better off not knowing what a problem we had."

I reminded them that we were now somewhat like the lady Charlie McCarthy used to talk about who didn't know her husband drank until the night he came home sober. Our report was a sobering document, and I need not have worried about the board's reception. The Coordinating Board adopted our recommendations unanimously and forwarded them to the legislature.

Several months later, the Select Committee on Higher Education also adopted our recommendations and incorporated them in its own far-reaching legislative package. And, in winter 1987, under the superb leadership of Representative Wilhelmina Delco in the House and Senator Carl Parker in the Senate, House Bill 2182—The Testing

HARDESTY (CONTINUED):

> Bill—was enacted by both houses of the Texas legislature and subsequently signed into law by Governor Clements.
>
> It is a chapter of my life that I will always recall with pride.

ALLAN:

> Before we move on, Wilhelmina tells me that there is another point that she thinks is important and ought to be made at this point.

DELCO:

> It is important for you to know that part of that bill is that those test results must be reported back to the institutions from which those youngsters came. I was waiting to see if Bob had this in his recommendations, and he did, as usual. We never take something somebody else does and return it pure. We have to kind of embroider it. And the reason that we return results to institutions is that it is all very well and good to say that it is the kid's fault or the student's fault, but any time an institution sees that forty percent of their kids, or twenty percent of their kids, are failing a segment of that test, they need to redirect inward the concern about how they are teaching certain subject areas. And I think the articulation aspect of the law is an important one to emphasize, the responsibility of education and communication in education up and down the line.

ALLAN:

> Bill Sanford, it seems to me that we sort of jump a hurdle from the synergism between legislative intent and research recommendation to what actually is happening. If you could give us a little bit more nuts-and-bolts detail on what this program will look like as it gets implemented, I think that would be in order next.

SANFORD:

> There are a lot of possible things to say. I do not want to take but just a couple of minutes to try to say them. We are about two-fifths, or about forty percent, of the way through the developmental stages of this program. This process involves two agency staffs, a very large number of committees, and representatives from institutions. We have already taken and will continue to take all content components of this exercise out to a very large representation of the higher education and public school community of the state. This happens at designated points in the process. One of the issues I suggested

in my presentation earlier in the conference was that of ownership. How do we get people to feel like it is their test and not something imposed by the legislature or a testing company or agencies? We are doing it by trying to involve in the development process in one way or another somewhere between four and five thousand of the professionals in the system. A piece of that representation is the group of about twenty distinct advisory committees.

Let me sketch very briefly these committees for you.

We do have one major advisory committee called the Texas Academic Skills Council. It is made up of community college and university representatives and state department of education staff.

We have seven committees dealing with developmental aspects and eight committees addressing various major questions regarding implementation. Just to give you some sense of it, we have a tests and measurements committee providing oversight of all test development activities. We have six regional forum panels, each one made up of, I believe, over fifty people from technical institutes and private universities (remember this is going to be given to the private universities as a substitute for the teacher education entrance exam; Pam Tackett will outline those components in a moment).

We have a special committee focusing all its attention on the question of bias, or potential bias, on the test. By the way, just because you would be curious to know this, we have only three Anglo professionals on that committee out of a total of thirty.

We have a mathematics advisory committee, a reading advisory committee, a writing advisory committee, and all those have had the privilege of hearing the specialists that you got a chance to hear this morning. They have all come to Texas and worked with those committees to give them their views on these matters.

We have a standard-setting committee—the two agencies must agree upon the cutscore at some point.

In the implementation component we have an academic skills development committee working to provide information about existing practices in academic support areas and to disseminate information about model programs and practices. We also have an advisement and placement committee working to provide information about existing practices relative to academic advisement and to disseminate information about model programs around the country on that matter.

We have a special committee on English as a Second Language to deal with special issues of bias with regard to those students and with how to implement a test where some of the students in fact have English problems.

We have an evaluation committee, a faculty development committee. If you are from an institution you may already begin to think about how to implement this kind of thing on your campus. If twenty percent of your students are not doing well now, and this test comes along and the cutscore causes thirty or forty percent of your students not to do well, how are you immediately going to manage that change in your curriculum and your assignment of faculty, your assignment of space, those incredibly complex matters? We have a special committee of the academic officers in the state trying to deal with some of those issues and we have some excellent experts from other states come in and talk with these folks.

We have a technical advisory committee, four nationally known specialists who have extensive experience in other states and nationwide programs in testing, giving us a totally independent external perception.

We have ten upper-level campuses in our state. Those are campuses that do not have any freshman- or sophomore-level activities—they only have junior-, senior-, and graduate-level activities. They face some very special problems, because they do not have control over the first two years of their students' curricula. We have those folks grabbed together. In this composite we now have over six hundred faculty members. Again, we are engaging somewhere between four and five thousand people. We do have in the game representatives from every one of the more than one hundred campuses in the state. We have their names and addresses. They are acting as campus liaisons and in various advisory capacities. And, for Ms. Delco's information, about sixty percent of the entire faculty committee groups are Anglo and the other forty percent are Hispanic and Black and other types of ethnic groups. All are professional educators at various segments in the state. I do not think you had the oppor-

tunity to hear that particular item before. For the sake of time and
the fact that you will probably want to ask some questions of us,
I think I will quit there, Richard.

ALLAN:

Thank you, Bill. Bob Hardesty mentioned that the PPST has been
an entrance requirement for those students moving into the teacher
preparation programs in their junior year. This new program, the
TASP Test, will subsume that effort. There will no longer be a need
for the PPST to be administered since all students will be taking this
basic skills test. Pam Tackett will be talking a little bit about the TEA's
perspective on what they were doing and what they will be doing,
and why it seems reasonable.

TACKETT:

I want to start by giving you a little bit of background about how
we got involved with the TASP. I think that Dick has alluded to
that, but I'll provide a little bit more detail. The Texas Education
Agency is responsible for administering public elementary and
secondary education in Texas, and part of that responsibility includes
the approval of teacher education programs and the responsibility
for certifying teachers. As far back as 1981, the legislature passed
a law that required that we test all students who were going into
teacher education programs. We were to determine their competency
in the basic skills of reading, writing, and mathematics. In addition,
that same law called for certification testing of teachers prior to being
certified to teach in Texas public schools.

As we looked at implementing that law, it was not possible to do
it immediately because in 1981 the legislature did not appropriate
funds for us to move immediately into that testing program. The
first thing that was done was to study how we were going to move
into a dual program of this nature. And the wisest thing at that point
in time for a state agency to do was to look at existing tests and to
determine if any of those would be feasible for their purposes. For
that reason, the state in 1983–1984, after we did receive a legislative
appropriation, validated the PPST for the purpose of determining
which students should and could be admitted into teacher education
programs. If you are familiar with that test, you know it is not
criterion referenced.

The state of Texas is involved in several large-scale assessment programs; as a matter of fact, four.

We are continuously reviewing our assessment programs and looking at how we are using information to improve our curriculum and our instruction to students. These programs, except for the program for admission into teacher education, are all criterion-referenced, diagnostic, prescriptive assessment programs. As we began to review the outcomes of the PPST administrations after approximately one year, the state was enjoined by an organization, or was enjoined by a federal court, to prevent use of the PPST as an entry requirement into teacher education. During the period of that injunction, which was approximately a year, our state board of education began to study that test even more closely to see how we could help improve the education of these students who were not meeting requirements and were not adequately prepared in the basic skills to go into a teacher education program. At the point when that injunction was lifted, which was in summer 1986, that dialogue between the state board of education and the commissioner continued and there was a commitment to make a change to an assessment program that would be more useful to educators in Texas both at the college level and at the public school level.

In fall 1987 the state board made a commitment to that change. A request for proposals (RFP) was developed, and we moved to identify a contractor that could work with us in the development of the new test. That route was selected in late summer 1987 and we immediately began to work on the new testing program. Now what I did not mention and I think both Bill Sanford and Bob Hardesty did mention was that during this same period of time the legislation mandating testing of college students was approved. It seemed that it was not appropriate for us to have one test for teacher education students only and another test for entering college students. So the TEA, along with the Texas Higher Education Coordinating Board, issued a joint request for proposals.

This program is one that we are very excited about. We are anticipating that its impact on the public schools will be even more than its obvious impact on higher education. It will be a tool for us to use in looking back to the high schools and saying, "Here are the points in our curriculum that we need to strengthen. Here are the weaknesses." We want to point out skills that students do not have but, through the process that Bill Sanford has talked about, will have to obtain in order to be successful in college.

We are hoping and we feel confident that this test will also have an impact on the success of minority students in Texas. With the teacher education testing program, students were taking the test just prior to their junior year. At the point where they had some indication of their interest in teacher education, they took the test. It was too late for them to remedy their skills and move quickly on into the junior level or the teacher education program. Thus they were held back. They did not have access to the appropriate preparation/ remediation programs, and in many cases they never came back and attempted the test again. They either dropped out of school or they pursued other programs. It was very important to us that we moved minority students into teacher education and moved them into the classrooms of Texas. We see now that this program in which we are able to administer a test in all public institutions immediately upon admission of students is going to enhance minority participation and finally numbers of minority teachers in classrooms in Texas public schools.

Additionally, Ms. Delco is concerned about access to the test. We also were concerned about access, and with our current testing program we are limited to only three test administrations per year. One of the things that the TASP offers us is additional administrations of this test, and, we hope, in many, many sites across the state. We do not want any opportunities to be missed by us to identify students who need to take the test so that they have the opportunity to continue education.

So this program offers us a great deal of flexibility that we never had before. This program is owned by the state of Texas. It is jointly administered by the Texas Higher Education Coordinating Board and TEA, and we feel it offers us the flexibility to do the kinds of things that we need to do to meet the students' needs.

I have already mentioned the relationship to the public schools. One of the things that we are doing immediately is to appoint a public schools advisory committee. As Ms. Delco said in the legislation, there is a call for test results to be reported back to the high schools from which students graduated. Without some understanding of this testing program and what the reporting back and the information

TACKETT (CONTINUED):

mean, without taking the time and the effort to explain that to the public schools, we are concerned that there will be some fear of what this means in each local community, what hazards will be brought to the public schools that they previously have not had to endure. In order to enhance the high school curriculum we immediately want to begin work with high school educators and counselors.

So that work is under way and we will be involving a great number of people in that activity. The commissioner of education in Texas is very committed to this program. He is excited about the change and he is excited about the potential for change in the high schools. The tests will give a new direction to the high school curriculum that perhaps we have not had before. As one of our speakers mentioned, we are talking about changing expectations, and I think that we are going to find that instruction will be driven by expectations. These will be higher expectations than we have previously had. The public schools will be affected, and we look forward to these changing expectations for public schools.

ALLAN:

Thank you, Pam. This concludes the formal presentations of the panel. Any questions that the audience has for the panel? I'm going to open this up to the floor.

AUDIENCE:

What happens to a student who continues to fail the test, who continues to demonstrate a lack of proficiency? Is that student condemned to fail and not continue in school?

DELCO:

What we are saying is that a student who comes into an institution is automatically offered freshman and sophomore courses. Then, the student would take the test and would need to pass all three segments. If the student failed, for example, the reading component of the test, he or she would be offered remediation. He or she would then have to take the test again before proceeding past the sixtieth semester credit hour, which in most institutions is the point at which upper-division classes begin. So the point is that a student would be identified early if he or she had problems. The institution would have the responsibility to offer that student remediation. If the institution even wanted to mandate remediation, it could, because then a student would not be permitted to ignore the fact that he or she had a deficiency. He or she would have to deal with the deficiency.

Now there was a persuasive argument made that there are some students who simply do not take tests well. The law reads that they would be up for review by a committee. I'm not sure what the committee is, but I'm sure the Coordinating Board and the TEA will have infinite committees. I'm already looking at a request for increased appropriations. I'm sure they will have a committee that will make the determination as to whether or not other factors show that this student has mastered the skills that were shown deficient in the test. So it is not impossible for a student to proceed, but we are encouraging students, once they have failed a portion of the test, to retake the test at that point where they feel they can pass it as a result of having had remediation.

HARDESTY:

Wilhelmina, may I add to that?

DELCO:

Sure.

HARDESTY:

It is impossible to overemphasize the responsibility that this legislation places on the institution for remediation. And as an institutional president I take the attitude that if a student comes there and fails the test in his or her freshman year and can go on and pass courses and get to the end of his or her sophomore year—if that student still fails after remediation, that's not the student's problem, that's mine.

DELCO:

That's exactly right.

HARDESTY:

I believe that, and I hope and believe that the rest of the institutions are going to take the same attitude.

AUDIENCE:

Is the program at this point fully funded by the legislature, and what are the plans for getting funding for this in institutions?

DELCO:

Nothing is ever fully funded by the legislature. What we are saying is that the costs to the institutions, to the state in preparing the test, are being absorbed somewhere. The cost of the test is one that is borne by the student, as are all costs. The one appropriation that the legislature did make in this regard was to say that for students who found this additional cost an impediment, there would be some resources available to pay for the test. But normally costs are borne by a combination of the company administering the test, NES in this case, and the student who is taking the test.

ALLAN:

And please note the two aspects to that answer. One, the cost for developing and administering the test will be paid for ultimately by the student taking the test. The other is the institutional cost, and that is still up in the air.

Bill, did you want to elaborate on that?

SANFORD:

Let me try to address that institutional cost issue, because I think some of the question had to do not with the cost of the test but the cost of remediation programs. We have a form of assistance in the state of Texas so that public universities do get reimbursed based on credit hours generated. As I mentioned earlier this afternoon, in the last decade the Coordinating Board has approved three credit hours of reading and writing and three credit hours of mathematics for reimbursement if those credit hours are precollegiate, or, if you wish, noncollegiate. In two weeks we will be taking to our board recommendations that came out of the various advisory committees. We are recommending that we double that at least temporarily for the next few years, so there would potentially be funding for six hours of precollegiate mathematics, for lack of a better term, and three hours specifically in reading and three hours specifically in writing. We also believe that there is going to have to be some start-up money because of the transitions—because of the potential sudden increase in the fraction of students at a given campus who will be thrust into a program. We will have to be taking to our board in July an initial appropriations request to deal with that kind of issue, and we are trying to figure out those calculations right now.

ALLAN:

Okay. I saw many more hands. Yes?

AUDIENCE:

What do you mean by start-up costs? The question of funding is very important. Once we identify students with needs, how are we going to support them in a remediation program? The legislature is going to have to give us higher funding for developmental costs. Will the institutions receive additional funding?

SANFORD:

That's exactly what I meant by start-up costs. We are planning to go for an additional pot of money, not reimbursable but front-end money that would be available to each campus or maybe in some kind of a statewide pot for distribution. We are still working on those kinds of problems for fall 1989, not to be reimbursed in 1991.

ALLAN:

The synergism of this program continues as we have a college president, a legislator, a member of the Coordinating Board, and a member of TEA all up here, with notes going back and forth, questions about funding, and so on.

SANFORD:

We are solving policy questions right here this afternoon—we are doing all kinds of good work.

DELCO:

That's the good news. The bad news is the legislature does not meet again until January 1989, and everything I say requires seventy-five additional votes.

Let me add this. What we wanted to do was to set in place a concept, and we have charged both agencies and the institutions in a very real sense with taking the concept and coming back with specific recommendations. It was very deliberate on the part of the legislature not to appropriate a lot of money on the assumption that this is what it would take, because we thought that would automatically trigger a process that it would not be enough, and therefore in some way we would limit the commitment to the program. We clearly stated that we knew that there were going to be start-up costs, but no one at that point had any realistic idea of the ultimate cost until the test

DELCO *(CONTINUED)*:

was developed, until all the specifics were determined and we could get a sense of what that first wave of students would be like. We are committed to additional funding. I am not going to sit up here and tell you we are going to give the institutions all they ask, but I do not think there is any question that there will be additional revenues available from the legislature.

ALLAN:

Question over there.

AUDIENCE:

I have a comment, really. If what we heard today from Dr. Pine is accurate, it appears that remediation of math skills, in particular, involves a lot more than a bandaid on a flesh wound. What we are dealing with here is a bloody corpse, and if we are going to revive that corpse it is going to take a lot of work beyond remediation— into instruction.

ALLAN:

The comment is that if Dr. Pine knows what he is talking about we have a lot of work to do. He does know what he is talking about, by the way. Yes, right there.

AUDIENCE:

How are you defining basic skills and for whom are you defining them? I am going back to what we heard first thing this morning. How should tests be constructed and for whom?

SANFORD:

I would suggest that Joan Matthews might be able to discuss a little bit of the debate—a rather extensive debate—that has been going on in the various faculty committee meetings on what level of skills needs to be tested.

ALLAN:

The question involves how we are defining basic skills, how we are going beyond the traditional layperson's definition. Is something being done to expand the notion of basic skills? The suggestion is that Joan Matthews is probably the best person to answer this. Joan, would you like to come up?

DELCO:

> Could I just answer that from a public policy perspective while Joan is coming up? Let's look at it this way. Does it make a difference that a person went to college? Does it make a difference in the job place that they have invested all this money in advanced education? Whether you define basic skills as a better ability to read, write, and compute, or whether you define it as I think Dr. Pine did earlier, and I like that definition, as not just subject areas but also essential elements of learning—the question still remains. Does education make a difference in what you know and how you are able to access the knowledge you will need to be functional in society? However you place that in educational structure and terminology is fine, but that is the bottom line as far as the average taxpayer is concerned.

MATTHEWS:

> Let me provide some details. We have worked with the testing company and advisory committees. We have had two meetings on several issues and are ready to go into our third. In our second meeting we debated for a very, very long time about the definition of the basic skills and how it would be appropriate to measure them. We developed a list of skills. It was sent out to over six thousand educators and students in Texas and it is now in the process of being analyzed. I cannot give you a very specific answer because the validation surveys are at this moment coming in. But in the next meetings, which will be held at the beginning of June, we will have an opportunity to look at those validation surveys and see if our colleagues and students across the state agree with us. Shortly after that, I think that those skills will be made public.

AUDIENCE:

> Are you trying to define those skills for the University of Texas at Austin as well as for any other schools?

DELCO:

> Yes, yes.

ALLAN:

> For all of the institutions.

EDWARD WHITE (MORNING SPEAKER):

Let me go to a question that I think is very profound. I was sensing a real difference between the definition the three academic people used this morning of basic skills and the definition I felt the panel this afternoon was using. Let me just try to say what I saw as the difference. The morning speakers were defining these basic skills in a quite sophisticated and substantial way and were suggesting that there is no very easy way simply to say, "This is what should be done in high school" or "This is what should be done in college." I thought the panel this afternoon was suggesting that it is a relatively easy thing to identify the difference between precollegiate- and collegiate-level basic skills, and that the test will take care of that in a relatively easy way. And then we can provide remediation and bring students up to this ascertainable point and then go on with college work. The question about who is going to define basic skills is very, very important and obviously there is no answer to it at this point. But I think it is important to notice that there is a real difference in the kinds of definitions that were used this morning and the kinds I have heard so far this afternoon.

SANFORD:

Let me make two quick responses to that, Ed. One is that you are coming to Texas and working with these committees in their first meeting and others to which you are invited. You should be instrumental in bringing the theory and the practice together to some extent. Secondly, although it may sound defensive, those of us who are charged by the leadership of the state to put this test into practice are going to have to do that and cannot begin with any kind of presumption that this whole thing is too complex for us to achieve. We may not end up succeeding, but we must assume that we can.

MATTHEWS:

When our committee came up with the language, we agreed that we would not try to define basic skills. We did not have the expertise to do it, and we probably could not have come to closure on what the definition would be if we tried. We would have just tied ourselves up in knots. So we agreed just to call it "the levels necessary to function effectively in college."

TACKETT:

> Yes, I would like to add just a bit. We have ninety people who have met together twice now and will be convened again in May. They have struggled with defining what it is that a person entering college needs in order to be successful. Because, as was pointed out here, persons who are in community colleges, persons who are in technical institutes across the state, persons who are entering four-year institutions, must all pass the same test in order to move on after sixty hours. So the debate rages on, and we feel that it will until early summer, at which time there has to be consensus among these ninety people. We are going to be very dependent upon what these additional thousands of people across the state are telling us in the surveys that are out right now. But initially, the discussions have been labored and difficult and the approaches have been several. Finally there was some general consensus about what skills we should have on this survey, which is the document from which the final skills will be selected. Some of the aspects of item development that were discussed earlier this morning by you and others will indeed be approaches that we use to develop items for this test. I think that we should continue to look for any new, any different approaches to focusing more holistically on how people obtain skills in reading, writing, and mathematics, and then how we measure these skills. So I think we have every intention of doing that. We'll have to look to people like you to keep us going in that direction, however.

ALLAN:

> The answer to that is not simple. It is obviously complex. Experts such as the content people who spoke this morning are involved. College faculty are involved from all across the state from the junior colleges, the senior colleges, the UTs, the Laredos, Texas Southern, and so forth—all are being involved in this. Six thousand will be surveyed to validate the results, and so on. Next question?

AUDIENCE:

> What about listening and speaking skills and some other areas that might or might not be included in the basic skills test? Why were they excluded?

TACKETT:

Listening and speaking skills, specifically, will not be included on this test because we have to develop a test that we can administer in a cost-efficient manner. However, those things were noted by committee members as being important. They were all wistful and wishful about having them on the test. In terms of critical thinking skills, definitely, we hope and we foresee that the committee will choose skills and measure those at a level that is beyond the application level. We anticipate that several of the skills that are on the test will definitely focus on only higher-order thinking skills. Some of the test skills will perhaps be somewhat easier than others, but I think all of those we look to measure beyond an application level only.

AUDIENCE:

Do you plan to have an assessment program to ensure that upper-division students are picking up upper-division skills and knowledge?

SANFORD:

We debated whether to add to this a rising junior exam as well and decided that it might be something the state may wish to add at a later time. We decided that two tests would be a bit much to ask the legislature and universities to take on at one time. But you are absolutely right; if you were going to have a rising junior exam, that would be at a higher level and then you would see what value you were really adding to your education. And we are going to keep our rising junior exams at Southwest Texas to do just that, to see how well we are doing in adding upper-division skills to what the students already had.

MATTHEWS:

Let me comment on that also. The Texas Academic Skills Program is just an assessment of the entry-level student in the first two years of college. The Select Committee on Higher Education saw beyond that and did call for other assessment programs that are currently under development. However, these will be institutionally based, so each institution will be drawing together a variety of assessment instruments. Those will possibly include assessing the graduates, but there will not be a big state mandate that the same instruments be used across each institution. There will be separate ones for each institution.

ALLAN:

Let's have one last question, and then we will call it an afternoon. Yes?

AUDIENCE:

Two questions. What happens to the students who have not passed the PPST when TASP becomes implemented? And will teacher education students and other students be scored differently?

TACKETT:

Students who have not passed the PPST will be required to pass the TASP. The TASP is the test to be used in lieu of the PPST. We are hoping and anticipating that our state board of education will allow students who have passed any part of the PPST to have that count toward the requirement and then the other parts would be accomplished by the TASP test. In terms of differential scores between teacher education students and other students, we have no indication whatsoever that there will be different scores, and our commissioners of higher education and education in the public schools seem intent on there being one passing score for all students. So, I think our state board of education and the higher education boards will be supportive of that; at least that is what we are hoping.

ALLAN:

I will say thank you to the panel members, and thank you to the audience. We hope you enjoyed the day as much as we did.

Part Two

Components of the Texas Approach

A Generation of Failure:
The Case for Testing
and Remediation
in Texas Higher Education

Recommendations of the Committee
on Testing to the Coordinating Board
of the Texas College and University System

Executive Summary

Every year more than 110,000 freshmen enter Texas public colleges and universities. Of these, at least 30,000 cannot read, communicate, or compute at levels needed to perform effectively in higher education. Some become college drop-outs—not because they lack the ability, but because they lack the skills. Others receive degrees without ever mastering basic skills. The tragedy is that we often do not know they are deficient until it is too late to help them. We do not know who they are or where they are. But we do know they represent a generation of failure in our educational system.

When our colleges and universities graduate thousands of students each year who cannot write a clear sentence or compute a simple mathematical problem, we have cast a shadow on the quality of our degrees and the integrity of our diplomas.

For ten months the Committee on Testing of the Coordinating Board, Texas College and University System, studied the need for identifying and assisting students who are qualified to enter college but who lack the basic skills needed to perform effectively in all their courses.

The Coordinating Board of the Texas College and University System (later named the Texas Higher Education Coordinating Board) published *A Generation of Failure* in July 1986.

The committee held nine meetings, visited two states that have implemented testing programs, listened to experts on testing, interviewed representatives of the business community to hear the views of employers, and conducted five hearings around the state to obtain the views of educators, students, concerned citizens, and policymakers. We learned that the basic skills problem is one of enormous magnitude. We learned also that it can be corrected—that students deficient in basic skills, when identified early, can benefit greatly from remedial instruction. In fact, with sufficient remediation they are three times more likely to be successful in college than those who need such instruction but do not receive it.

First, however, they must be identified—and that requires a statewide assessment program.

Based on the findings of our study, the Committee on Testing unanimously makes the following recommendations:

1. We recommend that beginning in the fall of 1989, or as soon thereafter as feasible, all freshmen entering a public college or university in Texas be tested in reading, writing, and mathematics skills at levels required to perform effectively in college. The test should be uniform across institutions and should be administered after admission. In no case should such a test bar entry to any student otherwise qualified; this assessment should be a tool of the education process, not the selection process.

2. We recommend that colleges and universities develop strong advising programs so that appropriate course placement occurs early in the student's degree program.

3. We recommend that each public institution be required to offer or make available nondegree credit remedial opportunities on its own campus to those students identified by the test as needing assistance.

4. We recommend that remediation be required when a component of the basic skills test is failed. All components of the test must be passed on or before the completion of 60 semester credit hours of degree credit. If not, further course work would be limited to lower division courses until all components of the test have been passed.

5. We recommend that each college and university be required to evaluate the results and effectiveness of remediation and report annually to the Coordinating Board.

6. We recommend that the Coordinating Board be directed to have these tests developed with the active participation at the decision-making level of faculty members from Texas colleges and universities.

7. We recommend that the legislature provide the necessary funding to develop and administer the tests and to support remediation. We would oppose a statewide basic skills test without the necessary financial support, especially for remediation.

We believe that the implementation of these recommendations is absolutely imperative if we are to prevent another generation of failure. Higher education can no longer afford to ignore the needs of thousands of bright, young students simply because the public schools have failed to demand of them the basic skills mastery they need to become more productive citizens.

Further, we believe that an assessment and remediation program is the best way to improve the quality of education for *all* students. By developing fundamental skills in remedial courses and through other assistance, the level of instruction in regular college classes improves because the quality of the class itself is better and can rise to a greater challenge.

The Case for Testing and Remediation

Every year thousands of young Texans fall between the academic cracks. They are high school graduates; most of them are bright. They are qualified to attend college but many of them won't succeed—not because they lack the ability, but because they lack the skills.

They are not alone. Across the nation, the three Rs are making headlines. Despite having one of the best and most extensive education systems in the world, America is producing high school graduates who have failed to master the basic skills of reading, writing, or mathematics. Even worse, the nation's colleges and universities are perpetuating the problem.

In recent months, some disturbing statistics have come to light.

- Nationwide, forty percent of entering college students appear to need remedial education. Many of them complete college without much improvement. The Southern Regional Education Board reports, "Increasing numbers of employers complain that the communication and computation skills of college graduates are deficient." The knowledge that many of the students who lack basic skills have received passing grades and in many cases baccalaureate degrees is, notes SREB, "disquieting."

- In Texas, of the approximately 30,000 students who took the Pre-Professional Skills Test (PPST) from 1984 to 1986 to qualify for admission to teacher education programs, 30 percent failed to pass the test; and of those who took the test more than once, approximately half continued to fail.

- Math skills are the worst. Remedial math courses offered by America's public four-year colleges increased by 72 percent between 1975 and 1980, and some estimates indicate that as many as 65 percent of our nation's freshmen are math deficient.

Virtually every educator can back these statistics with horror stories about bright students who are woefully ignorant when it comes to writing a clear sentence, communicating a thought or idea, or computing a simple math problem. The exact dimension of the problem in Texas is not known, but the indicators are clear: too many Texas students do not read, communicate, or compute at the college-level. We do not know who they are or where they are, but we do know that they represent a generation of failure in our educational system—a failure we can no longer afford to ignore.

The Committee and Its Mandate

Texas took an important step toward addressing this problem when Coordinating Board Chairman Larry Temple appointed the Committee on Testing in August 1985. He asked the committee to consider the merits of a state testing program that would measure the basic skills of college students and provide a basis for improving the quality of higher education in Texas.

He also raised a number of questions for the committee to investigate:

1. What purpose should the tests serve?
2. What tests would be appropriate?
3. How would a statewide test affect institutions and students?
4. In what ways can institutions best assist students both before and after testing?
5. How should a test be selected or developed?
6. What are the costs of a testing program and who should bear these costs?
7. What uses should be made of the test data by institutions and the Coordinating Board?

He emphasized that the purpose of any testing program should not be to weed out or reduce the number of students in Texas colleges, but rather to provide a measurement of both the quality of the teaching and the quality of learning. He asked, "How can we improve the quality of the higher education product unless we know what product is actually being delivered and received?"

To carry out this mandate, committee members studied the status of basic skills among college students and the use of postsecondary testing and remediation programs in several states. The review included various types of tests and their merits, the impact of testing on minority students, the implications of requiring a test at the sophomore level, the effectiveness of remedial and developmental education programs, and the basic skills levels of college graduates from the point of view of employers in different industries.

Committee members held nine meetings, attended a national conference on testing in South Carolina, visited testing programs in Florida and New Jersey, and conducted five public hearings throughout Texas to obtain testimony from more than 50 educators, students, concerned citizens, and policymakers on the proposed testing program.

Identifying the Problem

The committee's first task was to identify the problem. We learned that Texas is not alone in experiencing a crisis in higher education. Across the nation there has been a serious decline in the ability of students to read, write, use mathematics, and think critically at the college-level. In New Jersey, for example, where reading, writing, computation, and elementary algebra skills of some 400,000 entering freshmen have been tested since 1978, test results consistently show that entering students' deficiencies range from 31 percent in verbal skills to 60 percent in algebra.

The ultimate burden of this failure is not borne by the schools but by America's businesses and industries. Thirty-seven percent of businesses participating in a recent national survey said they are forced to teach skills to their employees that the secondary schools should have taught. And three out of four major corporations are training new workers in basic reading, writing, and mathematics. Some economists are saying that, next year, businesses will hire more than a million people who lack the basic skills for the job. In fact, private corporations spend nearly as much on education and training for their employees each year as the nation's colleges and universities spend on their students. In 1982, corporate education cost more than $60 billion. A significant portion of this expenditure each year is used for remedial courses in reading, writing, and mathematics. Many corporate managers are dissatisfied with the basic skills of their new employees. This dissatisfaction and other concerns about education were echoed by Texas employers who addressed the committee.

A bank vice president told the committee that while job applicants are well-trained in finance, they often fail to pass a screening for oral and written communication skills. He told of countless letters and resumés that are discarded on the basis of spelling, grammatical errors, or poor sentence structure.

A major aerospace corporation hires only top engineers from a carefully-screened list of colleges and universities across the nation, including two Texas institutions. Even so, this corporation is compelled to provide additional training in advanced problem solving. And, when it is time for some engineers to move into management, poor writing and verbal communication skills prevent many of them from being promoted to administrative positions.

Other employers reported similar problems:

- One of the nation's largest insurance companies employs a full-time instructor to teach basic language and writing skills to employees, many of whom are college graduates.

- A metropolitan police department reported that the basic skills of recruits are so poor that they have to teach new cadets how to write clear and understandable sentences just to be able to fill out accident reports. Police recruits also must be taught how to work relatively simple mathematics problems so that they can perform routine duties.

- At another corporation, college graduates take five to six years on the job to learn appropriate problem-solving and critical-thinking skills.

- A journalist reported on a survey of newspaper editors conducted by the Associated Press. What the survey showed was depressing. Apparently, journalism graduates don't have a broad enough education; their basic skills are insufficient, they lack a real world perspective, they have low reporting and writing skills, and they don't even have the newspaper-reading habit.

And employers all agreed on the need for improved grammar, punctuation, vocabulary, style, sentence structure, and spelling.

We hasten to point out that the committee sought comments about Texas college graduates in order to learn the extent of the basic skills problem. Our report deals with just one aspect of higher education and is not an indictment of the whole system. We learned in our studies that the academic programming in Texas and the overall ability of our students compare favorably with other states. There is much to praise, including an increasing awareness on the part of faculty and administrators across the state that reforms are needed. Indeed, improvements are already being made in many institutions, particularly in curriculum reform. Nonetheless, the basic skills problem is pervasive and, if left unattended, can have a detrimental impact on overall quality.

There is no simple explanation for the lack of basic skills among such a large number of college students. Clearly, part of the problem has been the rapid growth of our schools to accommodate the increasing population. Colleges and universities inherited the results of this growth: an erosion of quality. The National Commission on Excellence in Education reports that while the average United States citizen is "better educated today than a generation ago, the average graduate of American high schools and colleges is less well educated."

During almost two decades of steady decline in college admissions test scores, the Educational Testing Service noted a pervasive trend which reflected fewer basic courses and more electives in high school, less thoughtful and critical reading, less careful writing, and a decline in the study of foreign languages. These factors are paralleled by reduced homework requirements, greater absenteeism, and automatic promotion from grade to grade.

Examining Potential Solutions

There is a growing recognition of the problem across the country. Many states, among them New Jersey, Florida, Georgia, Maryland, Ohio, South Dakota, Tennessee, Missouri, and California, are attempting to overcome basic skills deficiencies through assessment programs. We visited two of these states: New Jersey and Florida. The experience of both states makes it clear that testing and remediation must go hand in hand. There is no point in identifying problems unless there is a willingness to do something about them.

In New Jersey, all college and university students take the Basic Skills Assessment Test, which measures reading comprehension, sentence sense, computation, and elementary algebra. The test is given after admission to place entering students in appropriate courses. Results do not affect admission in any way. The state requests institutions to retest students at the end of the sophomore year on a voluntary basis. Enough institutions comply to make pre- and post-test evaluations possible.

The testing program provides New Jersey with enough information to define the problem and to identify the students in need of help. State colleges and universities follow up with remediation.

The program is working. Studies show that students who need and complete remedial programs have better retention rates and nearly comparable grades to students who did not need remediation in the first place. Furthermore, these students have a three-times greater chance for success in college than students who need remediation but do not complete it. Students who complete remediation show significant test score gains and pass their sophomore level courses at rates comparable to nonremedial students.

In Florida, students take the College Level Academic Skills Test (CLAST). This is a "rising junior" test commonly given during the second semester of the sophomore year to measure reading, writing, and math skills. Florida students in general have improved their test scores over the past two years. The most dramatic improvement is among minorities. Florida A&M University, an historically black institution, reported an increase in students passing the CLAST from 39 percent in 1983 to 61 percent in 1985.

The CLAST examination, which measures skills at approximately the tenth-grade level, has a graduated set of standards to be instituted between 1984 and 1989. This process was designed to enable Florida to accommodate the changes in graduation standards that the state has mandated for the secondary schools. The 1989 CLAST pass-fail standards will be tougher than the present ones.

Our committee learned from these visits that testing programs benefit all students, not just those who lack basic skills. These programs drive curriculum reform, they stimulate innovative teaching, and they motivate students. For those who need help, a testing and remediation program provides a tangible hope, a way to overcome deficiencies which students know they have.

Committee Recommendations

After ten months of study, the committee estimates that at least 30 percent of Texas students entering their freshman year in college are deficient in the basic skills of reading, writing, or mathematics that are needed in college. Too often these students are not identified; in turn, too few of them are helped. The need for testing and remediation is obvious. We must put an end to basic skills deficiencies for the sake of our young people, our universities, and our nation.

The Committee on Testing unanimously makes the following seven recommendations.

1. Basic Skills Test

We recommend that beginning in the fall of 1989, or as soon thereafter as feasible, all freshmen entering a public college or university in Texas be tested in reading, writing, and mathematics skills at levels required to perform effectively in college. The test should be uniform across institutions and should be administered after admission. In no case should such a test bar entry to any student otherwise qualified; this assessment should be a tool of the education process, not the selection process.

It is obvious that the first step in solving the basic skills problem is to identify those students who need help. The only way to do this is to test them. And it is clear to the committee that the test ought to be given at the beginning of the college experience. We seriously considered the Florida "rising junior" exam, but we rejected it because it would mean losing two valuable years before identifying the students who really need help.

We recommend a college-level basic skills test to be administered by the college or university to new students after they have been accepted, to avoid influencing admission decisions, but with the condition that students must pass all parts of the test by the time they have earned 60 credit hours. Students who have not passed the test would be limited to enrollment in lower division courses until they pass it. This proposal combines the diagnostic and placement strengths of the New Jersey test with the effective exit measures of Florida's rising junior exam.

Diagnostic or placement testing is already employed in many Texas colleges and universities. More than half of the community and junior colleges test students' basic skills for placement in remedial programs, and many of the other community colleges are setting up similar programs. Of the senior universities, 44 percent require students to take placement tests in mathematics, 33 percent require placement tests in English, and 19 percent require students to pass advancement tests in writing at the end of the sophomore year.

What Are College-Level Skills?

There are different levels of basic skills and different measures to identify them. The difference between high school and college basic skills generally involves the mastery of specific content areas and the ability to reason at increasingly complex levels.

The College Board identifies six broad areas in which students should be competent to perform effectively in college: reading, writing, speaking and listening, mathematics, reasoning, and studying. Examples of these college-level basic skills include:

- the ability to recognize different purposes and methods of writing, to identify a writer's point of view and tone, and to interpret a writer's meaning inferentially as well as literally;
- the ability to vary one's writing style, including vocabulary and sentence structure, for different readers and purposes;
- the ability to use effectively the mathematics of integers, fractions, and decimals; ratios, proportions, and percentages; roots and powers; algebra and geometry.

Why Test Everyone?

We recommend that all students be tested, even those who post good high school grades and score well on college entry exams. Testing experts tell us that neither high school grades nor entrance examination test scores are appropriate criteria for measuring basic skills. The committee is concerned about the legal implications that will arise if some students are required to take a basic skills test while others are exempted on the basis of such inappropriate criteria. Furthermore, there is no way to realize fully the magnitude of the problem or to provide adequate basic skills remediation until a single, valid test to assess college skills is administered statewide to all entering students.

Why Not Just Raise Entrance Requirements at Four-Year Institutions?

The students we are trying to help already meet the entrance requirements of our colleges and universities but they are handicapped by their weaknesses in basic skills. Raising entrance requirements will not eliminate the problem; it will only eliminate some of the qualified students. Most state colleges and universities use entrance test scores or test scores and high school grades in some combination as the basis for admission. These selection methods reveal information about a student's innate ability and motivation but they do not, nor were they designed to, reveal deficiencies in basic skills. While raising entrance requirements might weed out those whose basic skills are weakest, it would also deprive thousands of able people of the chance to earn a baccalaureate degree. This would be a tragic mistake, especially for the growing number of minority students entering colleges and universities.

Why Not Use the ACT, SAT, or PSAT for Testing Basic Skills?

This is an attractive alternative, and the committee considered it seriously. However, every testing expert we talked with told us that scores on college entrance examinations are not accurate indicators of basic skills deficiencies. The test we propose would be diagnostic in nature—which the ACT Assessment (ACT) and the Scholastic Aptitude Test (SAT) are not—and would detect such a weakness, making remediation and course placement possible.

Tests such as the Texas Education Assessment of Minimum Skills (TEAMS) and Florida's CLAST are designed to assess high school level skills rather than skills needed to perform effectively in college. At the other extreme, the SAT and the ACT are designed to measure achievement or aptitude beyond the college basic skills level. These tests are accepted measures for admission purposes since their strength is in their ability to predict a student's first-year performance. Such tests do not provide information on a well-defined set of skills that are either mastered or not mastered. Other tests—such as the PPST—are not constructed for diagnostic purposes either.

What Will It Take to Pass the Test?

The committee supports a state-wide minimum passing score to be established with the assistance of an advisory committee. All students would be required to achieve a minimum level of competency before graduation from a college or university, thus adding much-needed credibility to all baccalaureate degrees conferred by state institutions. Individual institutions should have the option of setting their own passing scores which could be higher than the state minimum; in no case, however, should an institution accept a score lower than the state requirement.

2. Advising Programs

We recommend that colleges and universities develop strong advising programs so that appropriate course placement occurs early in the student's degree program.

A college advising program is an essential link between testing, identification, and remediation. The probability of success in college is increased by early identification of problem areas, followed by guidance toward appropriate support systems and remediation. The proposed testing program, with its strong advising component, makes early remediation and success much more probable.

Every freshman class contains some students who have charted their life's course—young men and women who have specific goals and definite plans for achieving them. But such students are rare. Most college freshmen need advice to help them decide what specific courses to take or what general direction to follow.

For all students, advising is essential for course selection. Beyond that, it offers contact and support from a knowledgeable faculty or staff member, someone to turn to for advice and encouragement. It can make the difference between a negative college experience and a positive one, and many studies show that it is the key to retention.

It is evident that strong advising has suffered in these years of rapid enrollment expansion. As a consequence, students also have suffered. Colleges and universities must redouble their efforts to strengthen their advising programs and place more emphasis on individual student direction and support.

It also is evident that a testing program cannot stand alone. To be effective, it must be followed by advising that directs students toward the best course of skill development and learning available. In turn, this advising program must be followed by solid opportunities for remediation.

3. *Remedial Opportunities*

We recommend that each public institution be required to offer or make available nondegree credit remedial opportunities on its own campus to those students identified by the test as needing assistance.

If it is clear that strong advising must follow testing, it is just as clear that remediation must follow advising.

In this matter of basic skills, we have only three choices:

1. Continue our present system and fail to provide a full education to thousands of students who have the native ability but not the skills for college;

2. Weed out those who can't pass the entry-level basic skills test on the first attempt and, therefore, deny many bright students the chance for a college education; or

3. Test all entering students, identify those who need help, and provide them the necessary remediation.

Why Should Colleges Be Doing the Work of the Public Schools?

Ideally, basic skills should be developed throughout the school years. The state of Texas recently implemented far-reaching educational reforms in grades K through 12 which should insure the development of basic skills. These reforms include: tutorials, summer programs, pre-school programs, smaller classes, attendance standards, limits on extracurricular activities, and remedial instruction. However, their effectiveness reforms cannot be measured until an entire school generation has experienced them. The first generation of students to be affected by public school reforms has not yet completed high school; it will be 12 years at best before students who receive the full benefit of these reforms complete high school and enter college.

All of these education reforms will have an impact on traditional college students who enter as freshmen at age 18, but this is a group decreasing in number and percentage. Reforms will not have any effect on older students, who are attending college in increasing numbers each year. Many of these students will have bypassed the reforms.

It is not enough to wait for public school reforms to improve the quality of our high school graduates. Higher education must institute its own reforms if we are to prevent another generation of young people from being caught in a cycle of failure, if we are to remove the shadow that skill-deficient graduates cast on our diplomas.

Yet, there are those who say that it is not practical to provide basic skills instruction in colleges and universities. There are those who say that if our public schools cannot teach their students basic skills, there is nothing higher education can or should do about it. And there are still others who say that if we must offer remedial instruction at the college level, it should be done by community and junior colleges even when the students needing remediation meet the entrance requirements of four-year institutions.

The committee finds these statements to be nothing more than excuses to maintain the status quo. We must intervene at every level. It is bad enough that our high schools are graduating students who are seriously deficient in reading or writing or computation, but it is inexcusable that our universities are graduating them with virtually the same deficiencies. The people of Texas have a right to expect a college education to have some meaning.

Why Not Let the Community Colleges Handle the Remediation?
The committee feels strongly that remediation needs to take place on the primary campus where the student is enrolled and under the supervision of that institution. An institution might wish to contract with a community college to deliver remediation, but students should not have to leave campus to receive it.

In the first place, many students will find it inconvenient to attend community colleges while they are enrolled at other institutions. Still others do not live close enough to a community college to make it feasible for them to receive remedial instruction this way.

But the primary reason for having remedial instruction offered on campus is to hold the institution accountable. We learned, particularly from the experience in New Jersey, that if the institution doesn't have the *responsibility* for providing the remediation, it doesn't have the incentive to be sure that it is done properly. We can't continue to let the universities wash their hands of the responsibility to see that deficiencies in basic skills among their students are corrected.

Does Remediation Really Work for College Students?

Studies show that underprepared college students who participate in basic skills courses show measurable gains in skill development— and greater gains than similar students who do not participate in such courses. More progress has been measured in reading, study skills, and composition than in mathematics. Such courses seem to reduce the differences between underprepared and better-prepared students, as measured by standardized tests. Further, students who participate in developmental programs often perform better academically than their admissions credentials would suggest. Students with low grade point averages, for example, tend to improve their grades beyond those predicted on the basis of high school grades and achievement test scores. Underprepared students who participate in developmental programs are more likely to remain in college than those who do not, and they often outperform better-prepared students who have superior admissions credentials. Remediation also contributes to persistence: the positive effects of developmental programs are greatest when the programs begin early in the students' college experience. They are least effective when started later than the freshman year.

How Much Remediation Do Our Colleges and Universities Provide at Present?

Texas community colleges are expected to offer remediation to students. Senior colleges can also offer six semester credit hours of remedial instruction. The state supports this instruction through formula funding, although the courses do not count toward the hours required for a degree.

Most junior and senior colleges also provide nonformula-funded remedial opportunities such as learning assistance centers or writing or mathematics laboratories. The combination of credit and noncredit remedial opportunities makes it difficult to determine exactly how much remediation is currently offered. National data suggest that the majority of all universities have learning assistance courses or laboratories and that the number of remedial mathematics courses offered in four-year universities increased by 72 percent between 1975 and 1980.

A Coordinating Board study shows that Texas spent $37 million for remedial courses in the 1984 and 1985 biennium. The committee believes that the funds already devoted to remediation for college students can be more effectively spent with a statewide testing program. At present we have no true picture of the scope of the problem. Our current remediation, especially in senior colleges, suffers from a lack of direction. We have applied a bandage without knowing the extent of the wound.

4. Required Remediation

We recommend that remediation be required when a component of the basic skills test is failed. All components of the test must be passed on or before the completion of 60 semester credit hours of degree credit. If not, further course work would be limited to lower division courses until all components of the test have been passed.

Even if remedial opportunities are available on all campuses, most students will not take advantage of them unless they are required to do so.

Each institution should be able to offer programs designed to meet the needs of its students. One of the most cost-effective forms of remediation, and one already in place in many Texas institutions, is the traditional college course which can serve a number of students simultaneously. Many students, however, because of individual learning styles, familiarity with the course content, or the pace of the course, need other forms of remediation in addition to or in place of these courses.

Learning and study skills laboratories frequently supplement classroom instruction by offering tutorial services, computer-assisted instruction, and programmed or modular materials. Learning labs, counseling centers, and student development offices frequently offer noncredit minicourses that focus on study skills, testing skills, reading improvement, and test-anxiety reduction. Tutorials can be offered in residence halls and special study halls. Many institutions with a high percentage of commuter students make portable remediation programs available for students to work on at home.

What Happens If Teachers "Teach to the Test"?

All remediation programs, regardless of how they are delivered, should provide students with feedback on their skill development progress. Because skill mastery rather than content knowledge is tested, "teaching to the test" is appropriate for a basic skills program. Students need numerous opportunities to practice and to be evaluated on the skills they are learning.

Why Should Failing This Test Prevent Students from Advancing to Upper-Level Work?

Research and experience indicate that with adequate supporting resources, a large percentage of the students identified by the test as skill-deficient can effectively overcome the deficit *if they are motivated* to learn the skills they lack. The requirement to pass all sections of the test on or before the completion of 60 hours of degree-credit work or before advancing to upper-level work should be a sufficient motivator. It will insure that a degree from a Texas institution of higher education stands for college-level skill proficiencies in reading, writing, and mathematics in addition to the content knowledge acquired in specific fields of study.

Most importantly, if all students have mastered the basic skills, the entire instructional experience is strengthened and the quality of higher education for all students is improved. The students who testified before the committee offered strong support for a testing and remediation program which would place students on a more equal footing in the classroom. They complained that fellow students who lack skills tend to require too much instruction time in class, thus reducing the effectiveness of instruction for others. The only way to overcome this criticism is to require students who need remedial work to take it promptly and to demonstrate skill mastery early in their college work.

5. *Evaluation*

We recommend that each college and university be required to evaluate the results and effectiveness of remediation and report annually to the Coordinating Board.

Annual evaluation is used to determine a program's overall effectiveness—its success in meeting established goals. If we are going to place the responsibility of remediation with the individual institution, we need a way to determine the effectiveness of these remediation programs. Evaluation eliminates guesswork and anecdotal reporting and replaces assumptions with accepted forms of measurements. Several states, for example, have found that a testing and remediation program not only improves the basic skills of students, but it also increases their retention in college.

Evaluation verified the success of the New Jersey program. In its January 1985 report on the "Effectiveness of Remedial Programs," the New Jersey Basic Skills Council reported that retention rates were higher for students completing remediation than for students who did not need remediation. Seventy-five percent of state college students and 55 percent of community college students who completed their remedial sequences were enrolled in the fourth semester, compared with 70 percent and 51 percent of nonremedial students in the respective college sectors. The report emphasizes that skills-deficient students who complete the appropriate remedial course sequence have a far greater chance of college success than students who do not complete remediation.

The committee predicts that the Texas program also will show improved retention. The number of students helped, the extent of their skills development, and the cost effectiveness of the program must be quantified. We believe an annual evaluation and report of the testing program is essential to substantiate the gains made and to use as a basis for future plans.

6. *Test Development*

We recommend that the Coordinating Board be directed to have these tests developed with the active participation at the decision-making level of faculty members from Texas colleges and universities.

For the proposed program, standardized tests must be selected or developed to assess students' basic skills of mathematics, reading comprehension, and writing needed to perform effectively at the college level. An advisory committee that includes faculty representatives should be established to guide the development and approve the content of the tests.

Advisory committee tasks should include specifying the skills to be measured and the levels of proficiency to be required, as well as reviewing tests and test items for recommendation to the Coordinating Board. It should be their responsibility to recommend whether test components be norm-referenced or criterion-referenced, to assist institutions in planning for computer-adaptive versions of the test, to assure that the test has no cultural bias, and to establish a statewide minimum cut-off score.

Faculty involvement in the basic skills testing program is crucial. In visits to New Jersey and Florida and in consultations with personnel in other states, we learned that faculty participation is essential for program excellence, for widespread acceptance of a basic skills testing program, and for acceptance of the whole concept of testing and remediation.

Of all the tests reviewed, the New Jersey College Basic Skills Placement Test is most similar to the type envisioned by this committee. Since the Texas test also would be used to diagnose basic skills deficiencies and to place students in appropriate remediation programs, it might even be economically prudent to study the feasibility of using the New Jersey test in its existing or in a modified form to meet the specifications outlined by Texas faculty members before steps are taken to create a new test.

We feel strongly that all institutions, community colleges as well as senior universities, employ the same basic skills test. This will enable educators to compare data across institutions and to answer questions concerning such topics as entry standards and institutional accountability on a state as well as an institutional level.

How Will the Test Impact Minority Students?

A crucial question for the state of Texas is the effect of testing on different ethnic groups. Any test adopted by the state must be free of bias.

The committee spent considerable time addressing this issue. In meetings with experts from across the nation, we asked repeatedly if tests could be devised that are devoid of ethnic bias. We were told that they can and they are. This issue is important today, and it will be more so in the future.

Texas demographics are changing rapidly. By the year 2000, Hispanics and blacks will form a majority of the population. Yet, both black and Hispanic students are underrepresented at all levels of postsecondary education. All programs designed to improve higher education must offer appropriate curriculum reform and provide support to minority students to assure both their preparation for and their access to a college education of high quality.

The academic performance of minority students has been improving steadily. On the SAT, the scores of the nation's black students continue to increase. This year, Hispanic students had the strongest gain in average SAT scores in more than two decades. The gap in scores between black, Hispanic, and white students is still large, but it is shrinking.

A common explanation for this reversal is that educational reforms put in place in public schools a school generation ago are finally showing their effects. This appears to be true in Texas. At Lincoln High School in Port Arthur, the valedictorian of this year's graduating class and many other top students were graduates of the Head Start program 12 years ago.

The committee was told repeatedly that the greatest benefits from testing and remediation were reaped by minority students. In Florida, where increases in basic skills were shown for all groups, the university with the greatest gains was Florida A&M, a traditionally black college. Students with poor elementary and secondary education, when identified early in their college years, often prove willing and able to increase their skills and their knowledge.

We expect that Texas colleges and universities will respond to basic skills test results as they have to PPST results. In institutions with appropriate advising, counseling, learning assistance, and course placement programs, the pass rates and scores of minority students rose the second year of the PPST. Texas results of special programming seem to parallel national results: when we improve services and curricula, performance improves.

7. *Program Funding*

We recommend that the legislature provide the necessary funding to develop and administer the tests and to support remediation. We would oppose a statewide basic skills test without the necessary financial support, especially for remediation.

Public education is based on the premise that educated and enlightened citizens are vital to the nation's well-being. The cost of public education in Texas is shared by all Texans. Since a basic skills testing and remediation program would be an integral part of public higher education, the cost should logically be borne by the state. We are firm in recommending state support. Unless the legislature is willing to appropriate funds for this program, particularly for the remediation part of the program, none of these recommendations should be initiated. To ask institutions to bear the increased cost is to take scarce resources away from the students who do not need remediation.

Moreover, the number of students who would be tested each year— more than 110,000 new students—is so large that colleges and universities cannot carry the burden with present funding. The major obstacle in accomplishing the objectives of the Florida testing and remediation program has been the lack of state support.

How Much Are We Spending Now?

Only part of the cost to provide remediation to currently enrolled students is funded through the state formula system for higher education—through semester credit hours generated at senior colleges and universities and contact hours at two-year institutions. Almost every state university conducts six semester credit hours of remedial courses in writing, related language skills, and mathematics. In FY 1985, $14 million was distributed to two-year institutions, and more than $4 million to 23 state universities for remedial courses. In the fall semester 1984, 54,000 students in two-year schools and 21,000 others in four-year institutions were enrolled in remedial courses.

At present only one remedial course in English and one in mathematics can be covered under formula funding for the state universities. It should be noted, however, that some additional flexibility will be required if these universities are to make the best use of their remedial course work.

Without knowing how many students may be required to take remedial work and precisely which methods they might need, the committee is unable to offer more than estimates of the additional funds required to support the program we recommend. We assume that the total formula support to institutions will not change. Students who take remedial courses will forego taking some other formula-funded course; their average semester credit-hour load will not increase.

Academic advisement to 110,400 entering freshmen probably could cost the state $4 million a year in salaries and benefits if professional counselors are employed statewide. Costs are greater if faculty members provide advisement. Since most colleges and universities are already providing advising—some better than others—some of the cost for advisement to support the basic skills testing program would not be new for the state.

Assuming the present state formula is adequate for classroom remedial instruction, we would still fall short of funds to cover the costs of other forms of remediation. Testing centers, learning assistance centers, tutorial programs, and writing and math laboratories—all important academic support services—are not directly funded. In institutions where these kinds of operations exist, they exist at the expense of other programs. In too many instances, they do not exist at all because of the scarcity of funds. Yet these programs can reach thousands of students who may not require classroom instruction or may need more than a large classroom can offer.

Because of the way such programs operate on individual campuses and since they are not considered a separate cost item in formula funding, we do not know how many students across the state are served by them, nor do we know their cost. Almost ten percent of the undergraduate student enrollment at one large state university take advantage of the testing center, learning assistance center, writing and math labs, or special tutorial services. If services were available to meet student demand, that percentage would double. The university estimates that for every student participating in these services, $250 is spent each year, but these services are underfunded already and cannot meet student demand, let alone absorb additional responsibilities.

How Much Support Is Needed?

The testing and remediation program will require additional state support for two purposes: supplemental noncredit academic services and test development and implementation. We recommend the development of an additional formula to cover the cost of

TABLE 1

ESTIMATED COSTS[1]

	FY 88	FY 89	FY 90	FY 91
TEST DEVELOPMENT/ADMINISTRATION				
Test Development	$300,000	$100,000	$ 100,000	$ 100,000
Administration: scoring, reporting at $15 per student[2]	0	0	1,656,000	1,656,000
Test retake cost	0	0	1,200,000	1,200,000
Advisory Committee expenses	40,000	40,000	10,000	10,000
SUBTOTAL	$340,000	$140,000	$2,966,000	$2,966,000
SUPPLEMENTAL ACADEMIC SERVICES	0	0	$2,000,000	$2,000,000
COORDINATING BOARD EXPENSES				
Program Staff	$115,000	$115,000	$ 160,000	$ 160,000
Office operations	110,000	110,000	115,000	115,000
SUBTOTAL	$225,000	$225,000	$ 275,000	$ 275,000
GRAND TOTAL	$565,000	$365,000	$5,241,000	$5,241,000
BIENNIUM TOTALS		$930,000		$10,482,000

[1] These costs do not reflect additional costs for advising.
[2] Based on estimated 110,400 entering students, 5 percent of whom have fees waived.

supplemental support services. Such a formula could be based on a minimum number of contact hours and should be structured to provide at least $200 a year for each student who meets the minimum contact hour requirement. These funds would support testing centers, learning labs, and other academic support services. It should be noted that this does not include the cost of additional advising, which is very difficult to estimate.

Without good information on the number of students who might require remedial support services, we can only estimate specific cost figures. Of the 30,000 entering students who are expected to enroll in formal classroom remediation, about one-third of them will need additional remedial assistance. In that case, about 10,000 students statewide at a cost of $200 a year would require $2 million in additional state support.

State support also is needed for developing and implementing the basic skills test for an estimated 110,400 students entering state colleges and universities each year. Some of these students will be required to retake the test in order to fulfill the state requirements. The committee is informed that it will cost almost $500,000 to develop the basic skills test over the FY 88–89 biennium and almost $6 million in the following biennium to implement the test. In addition, operating costs for program and staff support will cost approximately $500,000 each biennium. Cost estimates are presented in Table 1.

Our strong preference is that the state pay all costs associated with the basic skills test. In our judgment this diagnostic tool is so fundamental that it cannot be separated from the instructional program.

A much less desirable alternative to full state support would be to pass the costs of testing on to students, either through a fee levied by the institution or as a direct payment to a testing service. We estimate the cost of testing to be $15 per student. About five percent of students taking the test would have the cost waived because of financial hardship. Under this arrangement, students would pay $2.7 million in FY 90, reducing state costs for testing in that year to $2.5 million, as noted in Table 2.

Without accounting for increases in enrollment in formula-funded remedial courses, which are likely to occur, but which should not increase total funds for higher education, total costs for testing,

TABLE 2

ESTIMATED COSTS WITH STUDENT PAYMENTS

	FY 88	FY 89	FY 90	FY 91
PROJECTED COSTS				
Test Development/Administration[1]	$340,000	$140,000	$2,966,000	$2,966,000
Coordinating Board Expenses	225,000	225,000	275,000	275,000
Supplemental Academic Services	0	0	2,000,000	2,000,000
SUBTOTAL	$565,000	$365,000	$5,241,000	$5,241,000
LESS STUDENT PAYMENTS				
Initial Testing	0	0	<1,573,200>	<1,573,200>
Retakes	0	0	<1,140,000>	<1,140,000>
SUBTOTAL	0	0	<2,713,200>	<2,713,200>
STATE SUPPORT REQUIRED	$565,000	$365,000	$2,527,800	$2,527,800
BIENNIUM TOTALS	$930,000		$5,055,600	

[1]Based on 110,400 entering students @ $15.00 each, less 5% for whom fees are waived.

supplemental academic services, and operating expenses could cost the state an additional $5.2 million a year for higher education beginning in FY 1990. The committee acknowledges the burden this places on limited state resources, particularly at a time when revenues are declining. But we urge the state not to be tempted to fund one aspect of the program without the other. The two—testing and remediation—are inseparable. To discover inadequacies in basic skills and ignore the need to correct them is self-defeating. Similarly, to provide remedial work haphazardly is inefficient and probably ineffective.

What Happens If We Don't Provide This Program?

We ask the state to examine the cost of not supporting basic skills in higher education as carefully as it will examine the cost of implementing these recommendations. As Texas moves from an economy based on oil, gas, and agriculture to one in which diversification, including technology, is the cornerstone, a well-educated workforce is fundamental. Admiral Bobby Ray Inman, president of Microelectronics and Computer Technology Corporation (MCC), told a San Antonio audience recently, "We are going to have to make the investments now to produce the human resources and infrastructure that will be necessary to carry the technology push in the 1990s."

Texas must improve education across the board to meet the requirements of tomorrow's economy. We have taken the first step in the education reforms of 1984. Now we must take the next step; we must provide for those students who simply have not mastered the skills needed to perform effectively in higher education. Diagnostic testing and remediation for those who need it are basic to that process. We have learned from other states that remediation works, and in Texas one estimate suggests that it could mean an additional 13,000 college graduates available in our workforce each year and many thousands more with stronger skills.

The state benefits also from the increase in personal income which accrues to those with college degrees. Personal income rises significantly with educational attainment, particularly for minority groups. In 1973, each additional year of schooling raised the average annual earnings of black and Hispanic workers by about three percent. In 1980 the incremental benefit of education was about four percent for blacks, while Hispanics and whites earned a premium of six to seven percent. Historically, studies have shown that among all males (at age 42), college graduates earn 50 percent more than high school graduates.

Conclusion

More than 30,000 Texas high school graduates enter higher education each year without having mastered the skills needed to perform effectively at the college level. These are students who meet the admission requirements of our colleges and universities; many of them have posted good scores on college entrance examinations. Some of them graduate with good marks in their majors but they are woefully deficient in reading, writing, or mathematics.

Required examinations, especially in writing and English language usage, are not uncommon in higher education in the state. Many Texas colleges and universities already ask students to demonstrate proficiencies in some skill areas before graduation from college. Still, such arrangements are scattered and have no commonality. A passing grade at one institution may not be adequate at another. This sporadic approach to basic skills testing is both inefficient and inadequate. Worse, without knowing who is deficient in basic skills, we are turning out college graduates who cannot write a clear sentence, cannot comprehend complex written materials, and cannot use mathematics effectively. Employers are criticizing colleges and universities for the poor quality of some graduates, and in some cases, the integrity of the degree is questioned.

Early identification of and appropriate instruction for these students are essential to the health of the state's educational system and are absolutely necessary for the intellectual development of our students. The high school exit examination (TEAMS) will identify those students who are the most deficient before they graduate, but this test will not screen for skills needed in college because it tests for lower level basic skills.

Are We Testing Too Much?

There is some concern that we are testing students too much. The committee believes that ultimately the benefits of a standardized statewide testing program will override these concerns. For one thing, it would replace existing institutional testing and placement programs, thus eliminating some local testing. For another, the benefits to the individual student are expected to compensate for the disadvantage of taking another test. This was the case in New Jersey and Florida, and we can expect our students to react similarly. In any event, frequent testing is an accepted and integral part of our educational system.

We believe that the program outlined in these recommendations is the most effective way of dealing with basic skills deficiencies among college students. Though we recognize the rights of institutions and governing boards to develop curricula and instructional policies, the critical need to identify and instruct these students is so great that it demands a statewide solution. We cannot afford another generation of failure.

References

Academic preparation for college: What students need to know and be able to do. (1983) New York: The College Board.

Blankmeyer, E. (1986) *Remedial courses in higher education in Texas: An outline of benefits and costs.* Unpublished manuscript, Southwest Texas State University, Department of Finance and Economics, San Marcos.

Boylan, H. R. *Is developmental education really working—An analysis of the research.* (1983) Chicago: National Association for Developmental Education.

Kulik, C. C., Kulik, J. H. and Shwalb, B. J. (1983) College programs for high-risk and disadvantaged students: A meta analysis of findings. *Review of Educational Research.*

The National Commission on Excellence in Education. (1983) *A nation at risk: The imperative for educational reform.* Washington, D.C.: Department of Education.

New Jersey Basic Skills Council. *Effectiveness of remedial programs in New Jersey public colleges and universities: Fall 1982–spring 1984.* Newark: Department of Education.

On further examination: Report of the advisory panel on the Scholastic Aptitude Test score decline. (1977) New York: The College Entrance Examination Board.

Southern Regional Education Board. (1985) *Access to quality undergraduate education.* Atlanta, GA: Southern Regional Education Board.

Committee on Testing

Coordinating Board, Texas College and Univeristy System

Robert L. Hardesty, President of Southwest Texas State University, Committee Chair

Larry Johnson, Regent, Texas Tech University

Dr. H. Paul Kelley, Director of the Measurement and Evaluation Center, The University of Texas at Austin

Dr. George Magner, Professor of Social Work, University of Houston-University Park

Dr. Miguel A. Nevarez, President, Pan American University

Laurie Plessala, Student, Angelo State University

Dr. Ruth Shaw, President, El Centro College

Dr. Leonard H. O. Spearman, President, Texas Southern University

Sister Elizabeth Anne Sueltenfuss, President, Our Lady of the Lake University, San Antonio

James R. Vasquez, Superintendent, Edgewood Independent School District, San Antonio

Dr. Marvin Veselka, Assistant Commissioner for Assessment, Texas Education Agency

Dr. Jim M. Williams, President, Grayson County College

Staff

Dr. Joan Matthews, Program Director, Coordinating Board, Texas College and University System

Carol Dochen, Acting Director, Student Learning Assistance Center, Southwest Texas State University

Louise Iscoe, Director of University Relations, Southwest Texas State University

Dr. Leatha Miloy, Vice President for Student and Institutional Relations, Southwest Texas State University

Committee Itinerary

August 27, 1985—Coordinating Board, Austin, Texas. First committee meeting. Speakers: Mr. Robert L. Hardesty on the nature and importance of the committee's work; Mr. Larry Temple on the charge of the committee; Dr. Joan Matthews on postsecondary testing programs across the nation.

September 19, 1985—Coordinating Board, Austin, Texas. Second committee meeting. Speakers: Mr. John Fainter on the Texas Desegregation Plan; Dr. Paul Kelley on major concepts and issues related to testing.

October 13–15, 1985—Columbia, South Carolina. National Conference on Assessment in Higher Education attended by Drs. Kelley, Matthews, Raffeld, Williams, Mr. Hardesty, and Ms. Plessala.

October 18, 1985—Coordinating Board, Austin, Texas. Third committee meeting. Speakers: Dr. Marvin Veselka on the Texas Educational Assessment of Minimum Skills (TEAMS) test and the Pre-Professional Skills Test (PPST); Mr. Hardesty on the National Conference on Assessment in Higher Education.

November 11, 1985—Coordinating Board, Austin, Texas. Fourth committee meeting. Speakers: Dr. Paul Raffeld on the Regents' test of Georgia; Dr. Myron Blee on the College Level Academic Skills Test (CLAST) in Florida; Dr. Joan Matthews on the Northeast Missouri State University value-added testing program; Dr. Anthony Lutkus on the New Jersey Basic Skills Project.

December 12, 1985—Coordinating Board, Austin, Texas. Fifth committee meeting. Speakers: Ms. Laurie Plessala on students' views on testing; Dr. James Popham on test bias and the impact of testing on minority students; Dr. Anita McDonald on the efficacy of developmental preparation programs and the impact of testing on minority students.

January 10, 1986—Coordinating Board, Austin, Texas. Sixth committee meeting. Speakers: Mr. Jeff Bruce from the Austin-American Statesman; Mr. Charles Simpson from MBank Austin; Ms. Beth Pyndus from USAA; Mr. William Flick from Lockheed; Captain Robert Shirley from the Austin Police Department.

January 27–29, 1986—Trip to Florida made by Drs. Kelley, Matthews, Nevarez, Williams, Ms. Dochen, Mr. Hardesty, Sr. Sueltenfuss, and Mr. Vasquez. Met with the following people about the CLAST:

The Honorable Robert Graham, Governor, State of Florida

Ms. Shelley Boone, Deputy Commissioner for Special Programs, State of Florida

Dr. Myron Blee, CLAST Manager

Dr. Bruce Mitchell, Director of Academic Programs, Division of Universities, State of Florida
Dr. William Proctor, Executive Director—Division of Community Colleges, State of Florida

We visited the following institutions (only our host is listed by name):

Florida Agricultural and Mechanical Univ.—Dr. Eva Wanton, Dean of General Studies

Tallahassee Community College—Dr. Perry Adams, Dean

Florida State University—Dr. Augustus Turnbull, Vice President for Academic Affairs

St. Petersburg Junior College—Dr. Ernest Ross, Dean of Academic Services

University of South Florida—Dr. William Schuerele, Dean of Undergraduate Studies/Academic Affairs

Miami-Dade Community College—Dr. Piedad Robertson, Vice President for Education

Florida International University—Mr. William Beesting, Assistant to the Dean of Undergraduate Studies

February 10–11, 1986—Trip to New Jersey made by Drs. Clarkson (for Spearman), Magner, Matthews, Raffeld, Shaw, Ms. Dochen and Ms. Plessala. We met with Dr. T. Edward Hollander, Chancellor of Higher Education and Dr. Anthony Lutkus, Director of Basic Skills Testing Program.

We visited the following institutions (only our host is listed by name):

New Jersey Institute of Technology—Dr. Edward Morante, Director of the Counseling Center

Rutgers, Newark campus—Dr. David Hosford, Dean of Arts and Sciences

Essex County College—Dr. Rupert Jemott, Dean of Academic Affairs

Trenton State College—Dr. Anthony Evangelisto, Director of Academic Development Instructional Program

February 23, 1986—Corpus Christi, Texas. Seventh committee meeting. Committee members travelling to Florida and New Jersey reported on their trips.

February 24, 1986—Corpus Christi, Texas. First public hearing, hosted by Corpus Christi State University.

March 14, 1986—Arlington, Texas. Second public hearing, hosted by The University of Texas at Arlington.

March 31, 1986—Lubbock, Texas. Third public hearing, hosted by Texas Tech University.

April 22, 1986—Austin, Texas. Fourth public hearing, hosted by the Coordinating Board.

May 5, 1986—Houston, Texas. Fifth public hearing, hosted by Texas Southern University.

May 5, 1986—Texas Southern University, Houston, Texas. Eighth committee meeting. Draft preliminary recommendation.

May 19, 1986—Southwest Texas State University, San Marcos, Texas. Final committee meeting. Final recommendations were written and unanimously adopted.

Acknowledgements

Assistance

Dr. Eric Blankmeyer, Associate Professor, Finance and Economics, Southwest Texas State University

Dr. Llayron Clarkson, Professor, Texas Southern University and former Vice President for Academic Affairs

Mr. James English, Superintendent, Kennard Independent School District

Dr. Mary Griffith, Program Director, Coordinating Board

Ms. Susan Griffith, Planning Analyst, Southwest Texas State University

Dr. Paul Gowens, Dean, School of Business, Southwest Texas State University

Ms. Colleen Klein, Coordinating Board Secretary

Ms. Jane Koepp, Coordinating Board Secretary

Dr. Paul Raffeld, Director, Southwest Texas State University Testing Center

Ms. Denise Watts, Director of Planning and Analysis, Southwest Texas State University

Consultants

Dr. Myron Blee, Director, College Level Academic Skills Test (Florida)

Mr. Jeff Bruce, Managing Editor, Austin American-Statesman

Mr. John Fainter, Attorney, Austin

Mr. William Flick, Vice President for Operations, Lockheed Corporation, Austin Division

Dr. Anthony Lutkus, Director, New Jersey College Basic Skills Placement Testing Program

Dr. Anita McDonald, Associate Dean, University of Missouri-St. Louis and Past President, National Association of Developmental Educators

Dr. James Popham, Professor of Education, University of California at Los Angeles

Ms. Beth Pyndus, Instructor, United Services Automobile Association, San Antonio

Captain Robert Shirley, Austin Police Department

Mr. Charles Simpson, Senior Vice President for Loans, MBank, Austin

Testimony—Corpus Christi 2-25-86

Dr. Wallace Davis, Dean, College of Education, Corpus Christi State University

Dr. William Davis, Instructor, Texas Southmost College and Past President, Faculty Association

Mr. Al Kauffman, Attorney, Mexican American Legal Defense and Educational Fund

Mr. Jim Maloney, Vice President for Finance, Lantana Corporation

Dr. Kevin Morse, Professor of Education, Pan American University

Mr. Michael R. Putegnot, Vice Chair, Texas Southmost College Board of Trustees (statement read by Dr. William Davis)

Mr. Mike Stewart, Vice President for Administration, Lantana Corporation

Dr. O. Rex Whiteside, Academic Dean, Victoria College

Dr. Carlton Williams, Vice President of Instruction, Del Mar College

Dr. Roger Worsley, President, Laredo Junior College

Testimony—UT-Arlington 3-14-86

Dr. Wilkes Berry, Provost of the University, Texas Woman's University

Dr. Joe E. Cude, Chair, Department of Mathematics and Physics, Tarleton State University

Dr. Norbert Elliott, Professor of Literature and Languages, East Texas State University

Dr. Tom Hinkson, Assistant Vice President for Academic Affairs, Tarleton State University

Dr. R. Jan LeCroy, Chancellor, Dallas County Community College District

Dr. Dennis Michaelis, President, Paris Junior College

Dr. Charlotte Phillips, Coordinator of Developmental Studies, Henderson County College, and President, Texas Association of Developmental Educators

Dr. Maximo Plata, Coordinator, Professor of Special Education, East Texas State University

Mr. Walter Price, President, Student Congress, The University of Texas at Arlington

Mr. Jimmie C. Styles, Vice Chancellor, Tarrant County Junior College District

Dr. Paul Zelhart, Associate Vice President for Academic Programs and Services, East Texas State University

Testimony—Texas Tech University 3-31-86

Ms. Cindy Barela, student, Texas Tech University

Mr. Gracey Cates, Southwestern Public Service, Lubbock

Dr. Bill Dean, Director, Texas Tech Ex-Students Association

Dr. Ken Van Doren, Graduate Dean, West Texas State University

Mr. David Fishner, Vice President, Student Association, Texas Tech University

Mr. Duane Hood, Dean of Student Services, Western Texas College

Dr. Teddy Lanford, Dean of School of Nursing, Texas Tech University Health Sciences Center School of Nursing

Mr. Joe Minkley, Senior Vice President/Personnel Director, First National Bank, Lubbock

Ms. Gail Platt, South Plains College, Levelland

Dr. Philip T. Speegle, President, Odessa College

Dr. Nolen Swain, Division Personnel Manager, Southwestern Public Service, Amarillo

Mr. Darrell L. Vines, Associate Dean of Undergraduate Programs in Engineering, Texas Tech University

Testimony—Austin 4-22-86

Dr. T. Dary Erwin, Associate Director of Measurement and Research Services, Texas A&M University

Dr. John R. Grable, Vice President, Brazosport College and President, Texas Association of Junior and Community College Instructional Administrators

Mr. Mark Heatherington, Vice President-elect, United Students' Association, East Texas State University

Dr. Clay G. Johnson, Vice President for Instruction, Texas State Technical Institute

Dr. De Johnson, Acting Dean, College of General Studies, Southwest Texas State University

Mr. Neal Kocurek, Vice President, Technical Staff, Radian Corporation

Mr. Rob Patterson, President Associated Student Government, Southwest Texas State University

Dr. Roberto Reyes, Dean of College and Community Educational Development, El Paso Community College

Mr. Michael Smith, Vice President of United Students Association, East Texas State University and Vice President of Texas State Students Association

Dr. Belle Wheelan, Director of Developmental Education, San Antonio College

Testimony—Texas Southern University 5-5-86

Dr. L. L. Clarkson, Chair, Texas Southern University Committee on Testing

Dr. Elbert Hutchins, President, Wharton County Junior College

Dr. John Kerrigan, Vice Chancellor for Academic Affairs, University of Houston Downtown

Mr. Aubrey Lewis, Director of Assessment Services, Southwest Region, American College Testing Programs, Inc.

Dr. William Moore, Vice President for Academic Affairs, Texas Southern University

Mr. Charles W. Nix, Assistant Superintendent for Instruction, McAllen Independent School District

Dr. Gerald E. Osborne, Director of Counseling and Testing, University of Houston University Park

Ms. Teresa Phillips, President, Texas Association of Collegiate Registrars and Admissions Officers

Dr. Edward Powell, Professor, Department of Sociology, Texas Southern University

Ms. Carol Ritter, parent

Dr. R. Hugh Walker, Vice President for Academic Affairs, University of Houston System

Legislation

The following is the section of the Texas Education Code that implements the mandates of House Bill 2182, passed by the 70th Legislature in May 1987.

§ 51.306. Testing and Remedial Coursework

(a) In this section, "board" and "institution of higher education" have the meanings assigned by Section 61.003 of this code.

(b) All students in the following categories who enter public institutions of higher education in the fall of 1989 and thereafter must be tested for reading, writing, and mathematics skills:

(1) all full-time and part-time freshmen enrolled in a certificate or degree program;

(2) any other student, prior to the accumulation of nine or more semester credit hours or the equivalent; and

(3) any transfer student with fewer than 60 semester credit hours or the equivalent who has not previously taken the tests.

For that purpose, the institution shall use a test instrument prescribed by the board. The same instrument shall be used at all public institutions of higher education.

(c) The test instrument adopted by the board must be of a diagnostic nature and be designed to provide a comparison of the skill level of the individual student with the skill level necessary for a student to perform effectively in an undergraduate degree program. In developing the test, the board shall consider the recommendations of faculty from various institutions of higher education.

(d) An institution may not use performance on the test as a condition of admission into the institution.

(e) The board shall prescribe minimum performance standards for the test instrument. A student whose performance is below the standard for tested skill must participate in a remediation program. An institution may require higher performance standards.

(f) If the test results indicate that remedial education is necessary in any area tested, the institution shall refer the student to remedial courses or other remedial programs made available by the institution. Each institution shall make available those courses and programs on the same campus at which the student would otherwise attend classes. The courses or programs may not be considered as credit toward completion of degree requirements.

(g) A student may not enroll in any upper division course completion of which would give the student 60 or more semester credit hours or the equivalent until the student's test results meet or exceed the minimum standards in all test scores. The board shall establish other assessment procedures to be used by institutions in exceptional cases to allow a student to enroll in upper division courses in cases where student test results do not meet minimum standards.

(h) The state shall continue to fund approved nondegree credit remedial courses. Additionally, the board shall develop formulas to augment institutional funding of other remedial academic programs. The additional funding required under such formulas shall be met by state appropriation for fiscal years 1990–1991 and thereafter.

(i) Each institution shall establish an advising program to advise students at every level of courses and degree options that are appropriate for the individual student.

(j) The unit costs of each test shall be borne by the student. Costs of administering the tests to students shown to be financially needy under criteria established by the board shall be borne by the state through appropriation to the board for that purpose or other sources of funds. Additionally, appropriation shall be made to the board to cover overall administrative costs of the testing program.

(k) Each institution shall report annually to the board, on or before a day set by rule of the board, concerning the results of the students being tested and the effectiveness of the institution's remedial program and advising program. The report shall identify by name the high school from which each tested student graduated and a statement as to whether or not the student's performance was above or below the standard. For the purposes of this report, students shall not be identified by name.

Added by Acts 1987, 70th Leg., ch. 807, § 1, eff. Aug. 31, 1987.

1987 Legislation

Section 2 of the 1987 Act provides: "The test required by this Act shall be administered to students beginning with those students entering institutions of higher education for the first time no later than the fall semester 1989."

The following is the section of the Texas Education Code that implements the mandates of a bill passed by the 65th Legislature in 1977.

§ 51.403. Reports of Student Enrollment and Academic Performance

(a) All higher education institutions of this state shall offer only such courses and teach such classes as are economically justified in the considered judgment of the appropriate governing board.

(b) After the end of each spring semester the chief executive officer of each institution shall provide its governing board a report for the preceding fall and spring semesters indicating for each instructor the number of students enrolled in each class, the number of semester-credit hours accrued to each course, the course number and title, the department in which the course is offered, and the identity and academic rank of the instructor.

(c) A report prepared under Subsection (b) of this section must compare student enrollments in each class on the last day of each semester with enrollments at the beginning of that semester.

(d) Each institution shall file with its governing board and the coordinating board a small class report, excluding individual instruction courses, indicating department, course number, title of course, and the name of the instructor. "Small classes," for the purpose of this report, are undergraduate-level courses with less than 10 registrations, and graduate-level courses with less than 5 registrations. No small classes shall be offered in any institution except as authorized by the appropriate governing board, within the guidelines established by the Coordinating Board.

(e) Under guidelines established by the Coordinating Board, Texas College and University System, and the State Board of Education, postsecondary institutions shall report student performance during the first year enrolled after graduation from high school to the high school or junior college last attended. This report shall include, but not be limited to, appropriate student test scores, a description of developmental courses required, and the student's grade point average. Appropriate safeguards for student privacy shall be included in the rules for implementation of this subsection.

Amended by Acts 1987, 70th Leg., ch. 665, § 2, eff. Aug. 31, 1987.

1987 Legislation

The 1987 amendment, in the heading, added "and Academic Performance"; and added subsec. (e).

Texas Higher Education Coordinating Board Rules and Regulations

In July 1988 the Texas Higher Education Coordinating Board adopted under emergency rules the following Texas Academic Skills Program testing and remediation rules and regulations, known as Subchapter P.

§ 5.311. Purpose

In accordance with Texas Education Code 51.306, this subchapter is intended to delineate policies relating to the Texas Academic Skills Program and the treatment of students in public institutions of higher education who do not pass one or more sections of the examination.

§ 5.312. Definitions

(a) For purposes of this subchapter, "freshman" is defined as a matriculated student who has accumulated fewer than thirty college-level semester credit hours or the equivalent.

(b) The "Certification Form" of the TASP examination is a version that shall be uniformly administered statewide on days prescribed by the board and shall be scored by National Evaluation Systems, Inc.

(c) The "Campus Form" of the TASP examination is a version that may be administered and scored by qualified campus personnel on a schedule determined by the institution. The Campus Form may not be used to satisfy the requirements of 5.313(e) or (g).

(d) A certificate program subject to the requirements of TASP is one which contains nine or more semester credit hours or the equivalent of basic core general education courses as defined by the Southern Association of Colleges and Schools.

(e) For the purposes of this section, an upper division course shall be defined as any degree credit course beyond the sophomore level as defined by a four year senior university, and any degree credit course offered by an upper level institution.

§ 5.313. Eligibility

(a) Any student with at least three college-level credit hours accumulated prior to the fall of 1989 shall not be required to take the examination. If the student is transferring to an institution affected by the TASP, any previous college-level hours must be acceptable to the receiving institution as counting toward a certificate or degree program not exempted under paragraph (f) below.

(b) All students in the following categories who enter public institutions of higher education in the fall of 1989 or thereafter must be tested for reading, writing, and mathematics skills:

(1) all full-time and part-time freshmen enrolled in a certificate program or degree program;

(2) any other student, including transfers from private or out-of-state institutions, prior to the accumulation of nine or more college-level semester credit hours or the equivalent in a Texas public institution of higher education;

(c) High school students may take the examination prior to graduation only if they have previously passed all sections of the exit level TEAMS test, and have been admitted to, or are currently enrolled in, an institution of higher education.

(d) Pre-collegiate or non-credit courses may not be counted toward the accumulation of the semester credit hours referred to in paragraph (b) above.

(e) No student may graduate from a certificate program defined in paragraph 5.312(d) above, an associate degree program, or a baccalaureate degree program without having passed all sections of the "Certification Form" of the examination, unless the student is exempted under paragraph 5.313(a).

(f) Students in certificate programs other than those defined in paragraph 5.312(d) are exempted from the requirement of taking the examination unless and until they become eligible under the provisions of paragraph 5.313(b).

(g) A student may not enroll in any upper division course completion of which would give the student sixty or more college-level semester credit hours or the equivalent until the student's examination results meet or exceed the minimum standards in all test sections (reading, writing, and math).

(h) An institution which by law may not offer lower division courses may use performance on the "Certification Form" of the examination as a condition of admission.

(i) A health science center may use performance on the "Certification Form" of the examination as a condition of admission only to upper level programs.

(j) To assist with placement decisions only, institutions may elect to administer to freshmen entering a Texas Public Institution of Higher Education for the first time the "Campus Form" of the TASP or any appropriate diagnostic instrument designated by the institution. Such students must then take the "Certification Form" of the TASP prior to the end of the semester in which they accumulate fifteen or more college-level semester credit hours.

(k) All students not included in paragraph (j) above, who enter a Texas public institution of higher education for the first time in fall 1989 or thereafter, other than those exempted by this subchapter, must take the "Certification Form" of the examination prior to the end of the semester in which they accumulate nine or more college-level semester credit hours.

(l) If any student tested under either paragraph (j) or (k) above fails to take the "Certification Form" of the TASP during the designated semester, the student may not be permitted to re-enroll or to enroll in any other Texas public higher education institution in any courses other than non-credit remedial, developmental, or pre-collegiate courses until he or she has taken the examination.

§ 5.314. Administration

(a) All institutions shall use TASP test instruments and testing procedures prescribed by the Board. The same instruments shall be used at all public institutions of higher education.

(b) The test instruments shall be diagnostic in nature and be designed to provide a comparison of the skill level of the individual student with the skill level necessary for a student to perform effectively in an undergraduate degree or certificate program.

For the purposes of this provision it is the intent of the Board that the diagnostic feature of the TASP assures that for each of the three examination sections—Reading, Writing, and Mathematics—the student score report will provide an indication of student performance on both the examination and on the specific skills assessed by the examination. This information will help to identify areas of student academic strength and weakness, and thereby will facilitate student remediation and preparation for retaking any section not passed.

Also, even in cases where a student has demonstrated minimum skill proficiency, the diagnostic score report may help the student to identify skills where further improvement may be needed in order to increase the likelihood of benefiting from collegiate instruction.

(c) Once a student has passed any section of the "Certification Form" of the examination, his or her score shall remain active.

(d) A public institution of higher education serving as a testing site may not charge students for site costs.

(e) An institution may not charge a student more than $3 for the administration and scoring of the "Campus Form" of the examination.

§ 5.315. Alternative Assessment
[Rules to be added at a later date.]

§ 5.316. Standards
(a) The Board shall set statewide standards for the "Certification Form" of the examination, but an institution may require higher performance standards than those set by the Board.

§ 5.317. Remediation and Advisement
(a) For initial placement of a student, an institution may use any appropriate assessment procedures.

(b) A student whose performance is below the standard set by the Board for a tested skill area on the "Certification Form" of the examination must participate in a remediation program.

(c) If the examination results indicate that remedial education is necessary in any area tested, the institution shall refer the student to remedial courses or other types of remedial programs made available by the institution.

(d) Each institution shall make available those courses and programs on the same campus or center at which the student would otherwise attend classes. Where there are multiple centers or sites for classes, an institution may designate a principal site or sites where remediation will be held.

(e) An institution may elect to provide remedial programs or courses on its campus by contracting with a second institution to deliver the instruction. If such an arrangement is made, the host institution will be responsible for the quality and effectiveness of remediation.

(f) An upper level institution or health science center that admits a student who has not passed the "Certification Form" of the examination is responsible for providing remedial instruction on campus either through the provision of non-credit remedial programs or by contracting with another institution, as provided in paragraph (e) above.

(g) Remedial courses and programs may not be considered as credit toward completion of degree or certificate requirements.

(h) Each institution shall establish an advising program to advise students at every level of courses and degree options that are appropriate for the individual student.

(i) Each institution shall formulate policies to require and monitor students' continuous participation in appropriate remedial courses and/or other types of programs until such students have passed all sections of the "Certification Form" of the TASP examination.

(j) The faculty of each institution should review its degree credit and certificate courses, and may identify those courses for which students must demonstrate prior successful performance on one or more parts of the TASP examination. Each institution adopting such a placement plan shall file it with the Texas Higher Education Coordinating Board.

(k) When students are concurrently enrolled in multiple public institutions of higher education, the institution where the student pays the tuition base fee takes precedence for the provision of remediation in accordance with (d) and (e) above.

§ 5.318. Institutional Reporting

(a) Each institution shall report annually to the board, on or before a day set by rule of the board and in a manner prescribed by the board, concerning the results of the students being tested and the effectiveness of the institution's remedial program and advising program. The report shall identify by name the high school from which each tested student graduated and a statement as to whether or not the student's performance was above or below the standard. For the purposes of this report, students shall not be identified by name.

(b) Annual reports on the effectiveness of advising shall contain information about the institution's total advisement program.

The TASP Program Summary

Introduction

Throughout Texas and the rest of the nation there is growing evidence that large numbers of college students and college graduates lack academic skills in reading, writing, and mathematics. Increased student attrition, inadequately prepared college graduates, and impaired social and economic opportunities for many individuals are among the significant negative effects of these weaknesses in academic skills.

The Texas Academic Skills Program (TASP) is an instructional program designed to ensure that students attending public institutions in Texas have the academic skills to perform effectively in college-level course work. The TASP will provide advisory programs and support for those students who demonstrate a need to develop the academic skills to perform effectively in undergraduate degree programs. Further, the TASP includes a testing component. The purpose of the test is to identify and provide diagnostic information about the academic skills of each student.

The major impetus for the development of the TASP has been *A Generation of Failure: The Case for Testing and Remediation in Texas Higher Education,* a report published by the Texas Higher Education Coordinating Board (THECB) in July 1986. It contained specific recommendations about strategies for improving the academic skills of students in public institutions in Texas, including the commitment of resources at higher education institutions to help those students identified as needing advisory and academic skills development assistance. The report also recommended the creation of a test (developed with the ongoing guidance and participation of Texas educators) to ensure a common level of preparedness for Texas students. The TASP seeks to implement those recommendations.

The TASP Program Summary is a working document first distributed in December 1988 and again in August 1988. Its purpose is to provide an overview of legislative requirements and information about how the program addresses those requirements. In the form of a four-page flier, it is sent to TASP committee members, college and university campus liaisons, district superintendents, college presidents and vice-presidents, and high school guidance counselors across Texas.

Legislation

The legislature's response to *A Generation of Failure* accepted nearly all the recommendations from the report. House Bill 2182, passed in spring 1987, requires testing for all entering students and mandates developmental education for students who do not meet established criteria. Advisory programs must be established on each campus to assist students early in their careers, and developmental education must be provided for students not passing the test. Students must take the academic skills test before completing their first nine semester credit hours of college course work and must pass it before completing 60 semester credit hours, or be limited to lower-division course work until they pass.

The Texas Higher Education Coordinating Board and the Texas Education Agency (TEA) agreed to develop jointly a single test that would serve both as one of the criteria for admission to public and private teacher education programs and as the test mandated by House Bill 2182 for students entering public colleges and universities. In June 1987, a Request for Proposals was issued for this testing program. National Evaluation Systems, Inc. (NES) of Amherst, Massachusetts, was selected to develop and administer the testing component of the new academic skills program. Development of the TASP began in September 1987 and the first administration of the TASP Test will be in March 1989.

Program Design

The Texas Academic Skills Program focuses on instruction. Its primary purpose is to support and improve the academic skills of students entering Texas colleges and universities. The program encompasses student advisement and academic skills development, faculty development, and program evaluation.

The TASP also includes a testing component. The design for the test and its administration will reflect the following purposes of the TASP:

- to assess the academic skills students should have if they are to perform effectively in an undergraduate degree program; and
- to identify which individual students need to participate in academic skills development programs.

Test Development

The development of the TASP Test will follow professional practice for assessment instruments. The development will therefore meet the following criteria.

- The content of the test will be valid in relation to the skills important for effective performance in college-level courses. Test materials will be reviewed at several stages from this perspective. The development process includes the participation of professional educators in Texas through regional forums, content advisory committees, a bias review panel, a skills survey of Texas educators, a field test, standard-setting panels, and involvement with the staffs of the Texas Higher Education Coordinating Board and the Texas Education Agency.

- Reliability statistics, among a number of other indicators of psychometric quality, will be calculated.

- Minority groups will be involved in test development to review the test for potential bias.

- A passing score that represents a standard of knowledge and skills required for effective performance in college courses will be established.

The resulting test will reflect the participation of thousands of educators in Texas, particularly higher education faculty and administrators who best know the academic skills students should have for effective performance in Texas colleges and universities.

Test Administration

For the test administration to be fair to examinees, it will include the following features:

- convenient registration procedures;

- administration under secure and consistent conditions across all sites;

- standard and accurate procedures for scoring all three parts of the test, including the writing sample;

- test results reported for specific subareas of the test; and

- new test forms comparable to previous test forms.

The following factors will contribute to achieving these goals for test administration.

- Large-scale test administrations will be regularly scheduled each year to enhance the reporting of results to students and their institutions.

TEST DEVELOPMENT PROCESS

Participation of Texas Educators   **Activities conducted by Texas*/NES**

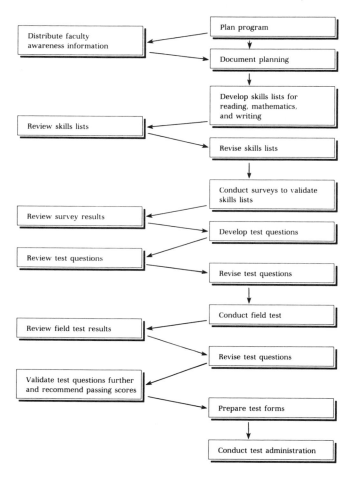

*The Texas Higher Education Coordinating Board and the Texas Education Agency.

NOTE: Each review by Texas educators will involve regional review panels, bias review, and content advisory committees.

- A Pre-TASP Test will be available for use on college and university campuses. It will be comparable in content to the regular academic skills test and will be semi-secure. The Pre-TASP Test will allow a college to assess the academic skills of entering students and to generate scores on a schedule set by the institution for those individuals. While the Pre-TASP Test will not count toward the requirement of passing the academic skills test, it will offer students an opportunity to assess their performance status and to begin needed developmental education.

- In the first year of the TASP Test, there will be several test administrations at over one hundred test centers across the state of Texas.

Program Support

The major purpose of the various program support activities for students and their institutions is to address the needs of students who may be "at risk." These needs will be addressed in the following ways.

- Early notification about this program will be provided to examinees and affected Texas institutions of higher education by the Texas Higher Education Coordinating Board and the Texas Education Agency.

- Substantial and timely information about the test will be available to examinees and institutions of higher education both before and after test administration. This information will include listings of the test skills, sample test questions, a preliminary test, diagnostic score reports, a study guide, and other resources. These materials are intended to support individuals as they prepare to take or retake the test.

- Developmental education will be made available by institutions to students who demonstrate weaknesses in one or more skill areas. While developmental education will take different forms on different campuses, instruction will focus on bringing students up to the standards set by the state.

- The test administration schedule will include convenient opportunities to retake the examination.

Summary

The ability of students to benefit from the talent and wisdom of our college faculty rests, in no small part, on the level of academic skills students possess. Without an adequate foundation in reading, writing, and mathematics, students are handicapped in their ability to benefit from higher education.

Most college students possess the academic skills to perform effectively in college course work; however, a significant group of students must be provided with additional developmental education to obtain these necessary skills.

Through recent legislation and educational reforms, Texas has made the commitment to deal directly and aggressively with this problem. Under the Texas Academic Skills Program, institutions will identify students with difficulties in reading, writing, or mathematics and will provide them with activities to improve their levels of skills.

The benefits of this important undertaking will be far reaching. Ultimately, the economic and social well-being of Texas will be improved by graduates who are better qualified and better able to participate in a rapidly changing society.

TASP Skills

Introduction

The Texas Academic Skills Program (TASP) is an instructional program designed to ensure that students attending public institutions of higher education in Texas have the academic skills to perform effectively in college-level course work. The TASP includes a testing component designed to provide information about the reading, mathematics, and writing skills of students entering Texas public colleges and universities.

The purpose of this document is to provide general information about the academic skills that may be assessed by the test.

Test

The TASP Test consists of three sections: reading, mathematics, and writing. Each section of the test is defined by a list of five to ten broadly stated academic skills. The academic skills defining each section of the test have been reviewed and judged by thousands of Texas college faculty, the Texas Higher Education Coordinating Board, and the State Board of Education. The skills represent the knowledge students entering college in Texas should have if they are to perform effectively in their courses.

The academic skills that are eligible to be assessed by the TASP Test are listed on the pages that follow. Each skill is accompanied by a description of aspects of the skill that may be assessed by this test.

Each section of the test will consist of approximately forty to fifty four-option, multiple-choice questions. Only one of the options will be the correct or best answer. The writing section will also include a writing sample.

Registration Bulletin

The TASP Test Registration Bulletin will help students register for the test. The bulletin will include general information about the TASP and its testing component, instructions for registering for the test

---

TASP Skills is distributed to Texas state colleges and universities in the form of a four-page flier. It was first produced and distributed in fall 1988.

and receiving test scores, and background information about the development of the test. The bulletin can be ordered, starting in November 1988, from the address listed below.

Study Guide

The Official TASP Test Study Guide will help students prepare for the TASP Test. The guide will include a description of the TASP and its testing component, strategies for preparing for the test, a description of the skills eligible for the test, a chapter of study materials and exercises for each skill, and a practice test. The guide can be ordered, starting in January 1989, from the address listed below.

To obtain copies of *The TASP Test Registration Bulletin* and *The Official TASP Test Study Guide,* contact:

TASP Project
P.O. Box 140347
Austin, Texas   78714-0347

TASP Reading Section

General Description

The reading section of the TASP Test consists of approximately ten to twelve reading selections of 300 to 750 words each. The selections were chosen from a variety of subject areas; they are similar to reading materials (e.g., textbooks, manuals) that students are likely to encounter during their first year of college. Students will be asked to answer several multiple-choice questions about each reading selection.

Skill Descriptions

The reading section of the TASP Test is based on the skills listed below. Each skill is accompanied by a description of the content that may be included on the test.

Skill: Determine the meaning of words and phrases.

Includes using the context of a passage to determine the meaning of words with multiple meanings, unfamiliar and uncommon words and phrases, and figurative expressions.

Skill: Understand the main idea and supporting details in written material.

Includes identifying explicit and implicit main ideas and recognizing ideas that support, illustrate, or elaborate the main idea of a passage.

Skill: Identify a writer's purpose, point of view, and intended meaning.

Includes recognizing a writer's expressed or implied purpose for writing; evaluating the appropriateness of written material for various purposes or audiences; recognizing the likely effect on an audience of a writer's choice of words; and using the content, word choice, and phrasing of a passage to determine a writer's opinion or point of view.

Skill: Analyze the relationship among ideas in written material.

Includes identifying the sequence of events or steps, identifying cause–effect relationships, analyzing relationships between ideas in opposition, identifying solutions to problems, and drawing conclusions inductively and deductively from information stated or implied in a passage.

Skill: Use critical reasoning skills to evaluate written material.

Includes evaluating the stated or implied assumptions on which the validity of a writer's argument depends; judging the relevance or importance of facts, examples, or graphic data to a writer's argument; evaluating the logic of a writer's argument; evaluating the validity of analogies; distinguishing between fact and opinion; and assessing the credibility or objectivity of the writer or source of written material.

Skill: Apply study skills to reading assignments.

Includes organizing and summarizing information for study purposes; following written instructions or directions; and interpreting information presented in charts, graphs, or tables.

TASP Mathematics Section

General Description

The mathematics section of the TASP Test consists of multiple-choice questions covering three general areas: fundamental mathematics, algebra, and geometry. The test questions focus on a student's ability to perform mathematical operations and solve problems. Appropriate formulas will be provided to help students perform some of the calculations required by the test questions.

Skill Descriptions

The mathematics section of the TASP Test is based on the skills listed below. Each skill is accompanied by a description of the content that may be included on the test.

FUNDAMENTAL MATHEMATICS

Skill: Use number concepts and computation skills.

Includes adding, subtracting, multiplying, and dividing fractions, decimals, and integers; using the order of operations to solve problems; solving problems involving percents; performing calculations using exponents and scientific notation; estimating solutions to problems; and using the concepts of "less than" and "greater than."

Skill: Solve word problems involving integers, fractions, or decimals (including percents, ratios, and proportions).

Includes determining the appropriate operations to solve word problems and solving word problems involving integers, fractions, decimals, percents, ratios, and proportions.

Skill: Interpret information from a graph, table, or chart.

Includes interpreting information in line graphs, bar graphs, pie graphs, pictographs, tables, charts, or graphs of functions.

ALGEBRA

Skill: Graph numbers or number relationships.

Includes identifying points from their coordinates, the coordinates of points, or graphs of sets of ordered pairs; identifying the graphs of equations or inequalities; finding the slopes and intercepts of lines; and recognizing direct and inverse variation presented graphically.

Skill: Solve one- and two-variable equations.

Includes finding the value of the unknown in one-variable equations, expressing one variable in terms of a second variable in two-variable equations, and solving a system of two linear equations in two variables.

Skill: Solve word problems involving one and two variables.

Includes solving word problems that can be translated into one-variable linear equations or systems of two-variable linear equations and identifying the equation or equations that correctly represent the mathematical relationship(s) in word problems.

Skill: Understand operations with algebraic expressions.

Includes factoring quadratics and polynomials; adding, subtracting, and multiplying polynomial expressions; and performing basic operations on and simplifying rational expressions.

Skill: Solve problems involving quadratic equations.

Includes graphing quadratic equations, solving word problems involving quadratics, identifying the algebraic equivalent of stated relationships, and solving quadratic equations.

Geometry

Skill: Solve problems involving geometric figures.

Includes identifying the appropriate formula for solving geometric problems, solving problems involving two- and three-dimensional geometric figures, and solving problems involving right triangles using the Pythagorean theorem.

Skill: Apply reasoning skills.

Includes drawing conclusions using the principles of similarity, congruence, parallelism, and perpendicularity; and using inductive and deductive reasoning.

TASP Writing Section

General Description

The writing section of the TASP Test consists of two parts: a multiple-choice part and a writing sample part. The multiple-choice part will include questions assessing a student's ability to recognize various elements of effective writing. The writing sample part will require students to demonstrate their ability to communicate effectively in writing on a given topic.

Skill Descriptions: Multiple-Choice Part

The multiple-choice part of the writing section of the test is based on the skills listed below. Each skill is accompanied by a description of the content that may be included on the test.

Please note that the term "standard" as it appears below refers to language use that conforms to the conventions of edited American English.

ELEMENTS OF COMPOSITION

Skill: Recognize purpose and audience.

Includes recognizing the appropriate purpose, audience, or occasion for a piece of writing; and recognizing writing that is appropriate for various purposes, audiences, or occasions.

Skill: Recognize unity, focus, and development in writing.

Includes recognizing unnecessary shifts in point of view or distracting details that impair the development of the main idea in a piece of writing and recognizing revisions that improve the unity and focus of a piece of writing.

Skill: Recognize effective organization in writing.

Includes recognizing methods of paragraph organization and the appropriate use of transitional words or phrases to convey text structure, and reorganizing sentences to improve cohesion and the effective sequence of ideas.

SENTENCE STRUCTURE, USAGE, AND MECHANICS

Skill: Recognize effective sentences.

Includes recognizing ineffective repetition and inefficiency in sentence construction; identifying sentence fragments and run-on sentences; identifying standard subject-verb agreement; identifying standard placement of modifiers, parallel structure, and use of negatives in sentence formation; and recognizing imprecise and inappropriate word choice.

Skill: Recognize edited American English usage.

Includes recognizing the standard use of verb forms and pronouns; recognizing the standard formation and use of adverbs, adjectives, comparatives, superlatives, and plural and possessive forms of nouns; and recognizing standard punctuation.

Description: Writing Sample Part

The writing sample part of the TASP Test consists of one writing assignment. Students are asked to prepare a writing sample of about 300 to 600 words on an assigned topic. Students' writing samples are scored on the basis of how effectively they communicate a whole message to a specified audience for a stated purpose. The following characteristics may be considered in scoring the writing sample.

- APPROPRIATENESS—the extent to which the student addresses the topic and uses language and style appropriate to the given audience, purpose, and occasion.

- UNITY AND FOCUS—the clarity with which the student states and maintains a main idea or point of view.

- DEVELOPMENT—the amount, depth, and specificity of supporting detail the student provides.

- ORGANIZATION—the clarity of the student's writing and the logical sequence of the student's ideas.

- SENTENCE STRUCTURE—the effectiveness of the student's sentence structure and the extent to which the student's writing is free of errors in sentence structure.

- USAGE—the extent to which the student's writing is free of errors in usage and shows care and precision in word choice.

- MECHANICAL CONVENTIONS—the student's ability to spell common words and use the conventions of capitalization and punctuation.

Bias Concerns in Test Development

The test development process should be designed to create test materials that are fair to groups against whom there historically has been discrimination (e.g., racial and/or ethnic minorities, women, older persons, persons with disabilities). It is important, therefore, to address issues of bias at the beginning stages of test development as well as to provide reviews of test materials to address bias concerns at the end of the development process. All who are involved in test development—including writers, editors, content reviewers, bias reviewers, psychometricians, policy makers, sponsoring agency personnel, program managers, and technical experts—should be guided by an awareness of and sensitivity to bias concerns. These concerns should be a part of the way in which those involved in test development approach their work.

This document has been designed to alert those involved in the test development process to several major areas in which bias in tests may be found. It provides concrete examples of bias and suggests alternatives. In general, it attempts to assist test developers in constructing materials that are free from discriminatory bias by focusing on several major areas in which bias in tests may occur. These include language usage, stereotypes, representational fairness, and content inclusiveness.

This document focuses primarily on bias issues related to minority groups (mainly Blacks, Hispanics, Native Americans, and Asians), women, and people with disabilities. Other forms of bias can occur, such as bias related to age, socioeconomic status, geography, and religion. These are briefly discussed, especially in Chapter V. The

Bias Concerns in Test Development is distributed in booklet form to agencies, panels, committees, writers, and editors involved in the development of test questions for the Texas Academic Skills Program. This manual draws heavily on the paper "Preventing Bias in Tests: Guidelines for Writing and Reviewing Test Materials," written for National Evaluation Systems, Inc., by Rose Caporrimo and Carol Kehr Tittle of the City University of New York, and on *Guidelines for Bias-Free Publishing*, produced by the McGraw-Hill Book Company.

guidelines and suggestions in this document should provide analogies and methods for avoiding these forms of bias as well as those more extensively discussed herein.

In order to provide a concrete discussion of bias issues, this document contains hypothetical test objectives and test items that include biased language and concepts. These are presented for illustrative purposes only.

I. Categories of Test Bias

Language Usage

There is no doubt that bias exists in any culture. Language, as a reflection of that culture, often reinforces and perpetuates bias. Language, moreover, can play a powerful role in shaping reality and reinforcing commonly accepted cultural standards. It is important for these biases to be dealt with directly in the educational setting, and specifically in testing materials that are presented to both educational personnel and students.

Test developers should exercise care to use language that has the same basic semantic and affective content for all persons who encounter it, regardless of their gender, race, ethnicity, age, or physical or mental condition. Choice of vocabulary and of diction should be guided by the need to communicate just what is intended, neither more nor less. Words and expressions can carry both a literal meaning (their denotation) and an extended meaning (their connotation). Both denotation and connotation must be matters of concern in test development.

Stereotyping

A stereotype is an image formed by ascribing certain characteristics (e.g., physical, cultural, personal, occupational, historical) to all members of a group. It is based on a custom or practice that it isolates and exaggerates. Because it is a standardized image, a stereotype describes the individual wholly in group terms, making recognition of individuality difficult; it may be inaccurate because it over-simplifies. It may reinforce preconceptions of people, whether positive or negative, and insulate the reader or viewer from the real person or group.

The following are unacceptable underlying assumptions that often form the basis for stereotypes:

- that a population group is deserving of a particular fate
- that a population group is by nature dependent on help from the majority culture (paternalism)
- that a population group lacks some positive quality fairly common to humans
- that a population group has an excess of a quality fairly common to humans
- that a population group has a genetic deficit or surplus in some area of intellect, talent, or ability
- that what may be a norm only in Western culture is "truth" or that European civilization is "better than" (as opposed to "different from") other civilizations
- that a causal link exists between membership in a particular population group and poverty, crime, intelligence, physical stamina, mental alertness, etc.

Representational Fairness

Discrimination and bias may occur either through the under-representation of females, minorities, older persons, and persons with disabilities in educational testing materials or through their overrepresentation. The former fails to acknowledge the roles and achievements of such groups in society. The latter tends to create stereotypes that do not reflect the reality of life for many members of these groups.

The legitimacy of portraying equal and fair representation has been questioned on the grounds that proportionally equal representation of a group in various activities and occupations may not reflect reality. However, there are individuals who are involved in areas not seen as traditional for their particular group. By not representing them, test developers may undermine and undervalue their important contributions.

Representational fairness includes depicting females and males in nontraditional occupations. It also involves representing women; older persons; religious, ethnic, and racial minorities; and persons with disabilities in many different environments and occupations and in roles of diverse status and power. This section provides guidelines and examples to assess whether test materials reflect representational fairness for these groups.

Categories for Analyzing Text

The set of guidelines listed below outlines the three main categories of analyzing text for representational fairness.

1. **Main and secondary characters:** Care should be taken not to depict White individuals, particularly young males, consistently as main characters or in positions of power. Females, racial and ethnic minorities, older people, and people with disabilities should not be consistently depicted as secondary characters or those devoid of power and status.

2. **Type of environment:** Females, racial and ethnic minorities, older persons, and individuals with disabilities should be depicted, mentioned, or discussed in a variety of settings and environments: home, outdoors, place of business, schools, etc.

3. **Behavior exhibited:** Females, minorities, older persons, and persons with disabilities should be depicted in ways that reflect a wide variety of behavior and not those associated with stereotypes. For example, Hispanic women should not always be depicted as homemakers and nurturers; older persons should not always be presented as "retirees."

Examples of Statements of Power and Status

Below are some examples of how written materials can wrongly depict relations of status and power, important components of equal and fair representation. Also presented are more accurate statements of power and status relationships.

Misleading	Accurate
Congress finally granted Blacks broad enforcement and protection of their right to vote in 1964.	Blacks finally won broad enforcement and protection of their right to vote in 1964.
In many Native American societies, men allowed women to control the family and the home.	In many Native American societies, women controlled the family and the home.
Blacks faced many obstacles before Whites allowed them equal access to jobs and education.	Blacks fought hard to gain equal access to jobs and education.

Misleading	Accurate
Ms. Teodoro's husband disapproves of her job, although he allows her to pursue her own interests.	Ms. Teodoro is pursuing her interest in computers and has accepted a job in a major corporation.
Many universities are now permitting retirees to take courses for enjoyment and even to enroll in degree programs.	Older persons are enrolling in university courses and degree programs in ever-increasing numbers.
Through recent legislation and regulations, the federal government has been opening doors for economic opportunity for handicapped persons.	By working successfully for federal legislation and regulations, persons with disabilities have been achieving increased access to economic opportunities.

Categories for Analysis of Gender Balance

Below are examples of traditional and nontraditional occupations, activities, roles, and emotions ascribed to males and females.

Occupations

Female traditional:	nurse, teacher, librarian, secretary
Male traditional:	laborer, professional, boss, principal
Female nontraditional:	laborer, professional, boss, principal
Male nontraditional:	nurse, elementary school teacher, secretary

Activities

Female traditional:	school, playing with dolls, onlooker, domestic chores
Male traditional:	school sports, games, other physical activities, adventurer

Activities *(continued)*

Female nontraditional: sports, games, physical
                                activity

Male nontraditional: domestic chores,
                                child-rearing

Roles

Active: main character, problem
                                solver, giver of help or gift

Passive: secondary character, needing
                                help, recipient of help or gift

Emotions

Female traditional: fear, nurturance, tenderness,
                                dependency

Male traditional: aggression, courage,
                                emotional strength, "strong,
                                silent type"

Female/Male nontraditional: attribution of "traditional"
                                male emotions to females and
                                vice versa

Representational Fairness and Older Persons

The recommendation to represent older persons fairly does not mean
that test developers are required to stretch test content unnaturally
in order to include references to characters' ages in an effort to
demonstrate that a proportion of them are older. Rather, the test
developer should accept the responsibility of depicting older persons
in a variety of roles and activities whenever they naturally appear
in test content. It is too easy to present older persons as grandparents,
bookworms, sedate hobbyists, and wise but frail bit players with
nothing but past experiences to revisit and leisure time to struggle
to occupy. Needless to say, these depictions are stereotypes that tend
to rob older persons of their vitality. When older persons appear in
test items or reading passages, they should be depicted as active,
intelligent, and even fallible—the same as persons of any other age.

Representational Fairness and People With Disabilities

Due to the dedication and persistence of people with disabilities, the public is now aware, particularly through media exposure, of an increasing number of individuals with disabilities who are functioning in many situations. Unfortunately, not all of the images presented are positive. Story lines often revolve around the person with the disability, perhaps with the disability (or acceptance or denial of it) being the main focus. This is not fair representation. Like all other productive members of society, these individuals should be depicted in daily activities that reflect the versatility of their lives. Their participation should be presented as commonplace, matter-of-fact; it should not have special attention drawn to it. Specifically identifying a computer programmer as a paraplegic or an artist as learning-disabled, for example, is probably gratuitous and irrelevant to the programmer's or the artist's work. On the other hand, it may be acceptable to present a reading passage that describes how one person successfully manages a particular disability. Remember that these individuals do not want to be noticed or remembered for their disability but for the lives they lead and the work they accomplish.

Context of Questions and Test Performance

Students may perform differently depending on the context of testing material. Since familiarity and recognition appear to influence test scores, context becomes a consideration in developing test materials. For example, Black high school students may score higher on items on a reading test when the questions pertain to language usage and literary material that reflect the cultural experience of Blacks. Similarly, women's scores on mathematics problem-solving items may increase when the context changes from one that is traditionally more familiar to men to one that is either general or traditionally more familiar to women. This is particularly the case with items that measure basic skills (e.g., reading, mathematics), but it is also true of questions testing problem-solving or reasoning skills. Even questions in science or other technical areas should be reviewed for their applicability or level of interest to a mixed audience.

Content Inclusiveness

The question of fairness in test materials also involves the issue of content inclusiveness (i.e., the contributions, issues, and concerns of racial and ethnic minorities, females, older persons, and persons with disabilities in the domain definition of a subject area). Bias can result from omitting certain areas of information from the knowledge base in any subject area.

The issue of content inclusiveness is relevant to any subject area when cultural and/or historical topics are included in the domain definition. History is an area in which the contributions of minorities, for example, often have been overlooked. Black Americans such as W. E. B. DuBois and Hispanics such as Joaquin Murieta and Juan Cortina are important leaders and scholars. Women such as Margaret Sanger, Harriet Tubman, Sojourner Truth, and Dorothea Dix made significant and lasting contributions to social change. Literature and art are other areas in which the inclusion of references to minorities and women can be both natural and beneficial. The works of Cervantes, de la Vega, Garcia Lorca, and other Hispanic authors have influenced the literature of many cultures; the same is true of writers such as Sappho, de Beauvoir, George Eliot, and the Brontës. American literature has been enriched by the writings of Black authors such as Langston Hughes, Richard Wright, Alice Walker, Toni Morrison, and James Baldwin. Artists such as Goya, Orozco, Diego Rivera, Mary Cassatt, and Grandma Moses have valid places in educational materials and tests. Issues of content inclusiveness may apply to foreign language tests as well, particularly when cultural objectives and topics have been included in the selection of subject matter. In all fields of endeavor, significant contributions have been made by individuals of all ages; the work of persons in their older years should be included on the same footing as that of younger persons (or the same persons in their younger years). Generally, materials should include participation in all fields by women, minorities, older persons, and persons with disabilities, with particular attention to areas in which members of these groups may be underrepresented (e.g., science, mathematics). The contributions of groups and cultures should also be considered as part of the issue of content inclusiveness. For example, when the domain of content includes world civilizations, the achievements of African, Asian, Native American, and Pacific cultures should be addressed as well as the European and Near Eastern cultures that have traditionally been included. Even scientific subjects can legitimately address the accomplishments of world cultures: Mayan astronomy, for example, or Aztec mathematics.

II. Guidelines for Fair Representation of Minority Groups

Content of Test Materials

Wherever appropriate, in materials showing people in everyday situations, groups should be depicted as fully integrated, reflecting the multicultural composition of American society and conveying clearly that equal status and nonsegregated relationships are the ideal toward which society is striving.

In presenting the background of individuals, there should be no suggestion that any racial, ethnic, or religious group is more or less worthy than any other. Materials should provide reasonable representation of various minority groups in all areas of life and culture. Whenever appropriate, it should be made clear that every group has its share of achievers, thinkers, writers, artists, scientists, builders, and leaders. Test material taken as a whole should not convey the impression that any pattern of success or failure is correlated with a particular group or that any single group is more or less talented than any other group.

While people of different backgrounds participating in group activities should be depicted as equals in a social and political sense, this should not be done by neutralizing the distinguishing characteristics of diverse minority groups. Rather, the presentation should convey the idea that such differences are valuable.

Materials should not suggest that a particular minority group can be characterized by any isolated custom or lifestyle to the exclusion of others. The portrayal of people from minority groups in roles to which they have been traditionally restricted by society (e.g., Blacks as sports figures or entertainers) must be balanced by material showing individuals from the same groups in nonstereotypical activities and roles. In analyzing materials for balance, however, resist the temptation to apply strictly quantitative criteria.

In materials dealing with history, accuracy should be the goal, and assumptions about present-day society and politics should not be imposed upon the past. Situations involving members of minority groups should be accurately portrayed. It is true, for example, that the United States has provided a haven for many succeeding waves of immigrants and that these immigrants have made unique contributions to American society and culture. It is also true that many groups, particularly those discriminated against because of their background, have had to struggle against prejudice and discrimination, the extent of which should not be hidden or played down.

While it is important to include substantive material about minorities in test materials, it is not necessary to restrict the inclusion of minority references and examples to such fields as history, English, and art. It is also possible to include such material in other fields. For example, in testing a person's computational skill, topics or references relevant to bias issues might be included instead of references to material having no relationship to bias concerns at all. Instead of calculating the number of cars in a parking lot or the number of soup cans produced in a factory, examinees might be asked to interpret a graph showing the increase in the number of Black persons holding political office in the country.

Examples of Bias Toward Minority Groups in Test Objectives and Items

There are several ways in which a test item can be offensive. The following are hypothetical objectives and test items that are offensive and discussions of why they are so as an aid to avoiding these characteristics in actual test materials.

Objective for a History Test

Analyze the causes for the preeminence of Western civilization since the Middle Ages.

Discussion. This objective displays a cultural and ethnic bias toward Western civilization (by which is normally meant European civilization and its derivatives) and ignores the simultaneous existence of other civilizations in Asia, Africa, and elsewhere. If only Western civilization is the focus of this objective (with other civilizations to be covered in other objectives), it may be reworded: "Analyze causes and effects of the development of Western European civilization since the Middle Ages." If all civilizations are to be covered, this may be reworded: "Analyze the development of world civilizations since the fourteenth century."

Objective for a Health Test

Analyze the effects of poor diet on Black women.

Discussion. This objective reflects a racial and gender bias. It makes a direct connection between poor diet and the female members of a particular ethnic group. Why single out one sex and one ethnic group as a focus for poor diet? The objective should be more inclusive and relate poor diet to people in general (e.g., "Analyze the effects of diet on health") or put the issue of poor diet into some broader context having to do with the particular effects of low income, poor health, or bad eating habits on different groups in the society (e.g., "Analyze the relationships among income, eating habits, and health").

Item for a Special Education Test

Which of the following is a characteristic of persons with Down's syndrome?

    ★A. larger than normal head

    B. obesity

    C. oriental-like skin folds over the eyes

    D. above-average height

Discussion. In alternative C, there is no need to associate a physical characteristic seen in Down's syndrome with a physical characteristic associated with Asians. Further, the term *oriental* is offensive to some. Why not simply say "a downward-sloping skin fold over the eyes"?

Item for a History Test

Which of the following countries during the 1970s turned away from Western values and returned to a more primitive style of living?

    ★A. Iran

    B. Iraq

    C. Turkey

    D. Afghanistan

Discussion. The stem assumes a hierarchy with Western values superior to non-Western ones and also suggests that non-Western values are less modern and advanced and, therefore, less

*indicates correct response

worthwhile than Western lifestyles and beliefs. Perhaps reword the item stem as follows: "Which of the following countries returned in the 1970s to its former religious and cultural values?"

Item for a Social Science Test

Which of the following non-White groups has had the most rapid population increase in the last ten years?

    A. Blacks
    *B. Mexican Americans
    C. Indians
    D. Orientals

Discussion. The problem here is with both the stem and the responses. The term *non-White* should not be used unless it is necessary for accuracy as, for example, in a census table that groups data according to White and non-White populations. In other uses, to describe people of color as non-White is to use Whiteness as the standard or the norm against which all others are defined. In addition, the list of minority groups is problematic. The four entries are not parallel: the term *Mexican Americans* is more specific than the other terms, since it refers to Americans from one particular national heritage. The list also uses the words *Indians* and *Orientals,* neither of which is the preferred term. To remedy, delete *non-White* from the stem and use as alternatives such groups as Asians, Blacks, Hispanics, and Whites.

Other Dimensions of Bias in Test Items

Test items that deal with minority groups have both a cognitive and an affective dimension. One should seek to develop items that are cognitively accurate and convey a neutral or positive image and set of associations about minority groups or individuals. Both aspects of test items—the cognitive and the affective—must be taken into account along with those related to the particular kinds of offensiveness discussed in the previous section. The following item contains an example of an affective bias.

*indicates correct response

Item for a Social Science Test

Which of the following groups has the highest birth rate?

    A. Black Americans

    B. Asian Americans

   ⋆C. Hispanics

    D. Polish Americans

Discussion. This item is probably offensive to various minority groups. Although it may be cognitively accurate, it is affectively negative. Such an item, therefore, is best excluded from test materials.

Guidelines for Choosing Ethnic Names

When it is necessary to use ethnic names in test items, consider the following guidelines.

- Do not invent ethnic names. Use the telephone book if you wish, but take care not to use any full name exactly as it appears there. Consult with individuals familiar with the cultural group being presented to determine the accuracy and appropriateness of the name(s) to be used.

- Names should be relatively common (e.g., common Hispanic names in Texas include Aguilar, Benavides, Cantu, Castillo, Flores, Garcia, Garza, Gonzalez, Hernandez, Jimenez, Lopez, Martinez, Ramirez, Rodriguez, Sanchez, and Villarreal).

- Avoid overrepresenting particular groups. Ethnic names can come from a wide variety of groups, such as Spanish, African, eastern European, Chinese, Japanese, etc.

- Avoid names that might inadvertently convey a negative image, e.g., *von Klutz*.

- In text discussing Native Americans, consider presenting the name as it is pronounced in its own language either instead of or in addition to the English-language version, e.g., *Tashunka Witko* for *Crazy Horse,* or *Tashunka Witko (Crazy Horse).* Consult with individuals familiar with the cultural group being presented to determine the accuracy and appropriateness of the name(s) to be used.

Terms Referring to Minorities

Terms describing a nationality, race, or ethnic group may be controversial, but some terms are more acceptable than others. Terms acceptable to people involved, however, may vary over time, and careful test developers should become sensitive to what the groups

⋆indicates correct response

being described prefer. As a general rule, be as accurate and specific as possible about the group being discussed: *Iroquois* (the name of a specific people) is preferable to the term *Native American,* and *Chinese* and *Dominican* (adjectives derived from the names of specific countries) are preferable to general terms such as *Asian* and *South American.* Slang, colloquialisms, or awkward phrasings should be avoided since they may not be familiar to the reader and are most likely to change. For some commonly encountered terms referring to minorities, see Appendix A.

III. Guidelines for Equitable Treatment of the Sexes

Educational and Career Opportunities

Girls and boys and women and men should be shown obtaining education and training in all fields and at all levels. Implications that either sex has a greater or lesser need for education of any kind should be avoided. Stereotypes derived from ideas of inherent aptitudes should not be presented.

In objectives and test items, women and girls should be portrayed participating in the same activities with the same frequency as men and boys.

Job Stereotypes

Every attempt should be made to eliminate job stereotypes for both women and men. No job should be sex-typed, and it should never be implied that holding a particular job is incompatible with being a woman or being a man. All work should be treated as honorable and worthy of respect. No job or job choice should be downgraded or considered intrinsically inferior to another job choice. All job choices should be shown to be open to all people.

Women's full participation in the work force should be assumed, and women should be shown at all professional levels, including top levels, in both public and private sectors. Both men and women should be shown in management and nonmanagement positions. Implications that work relationships are necessarily affected by the gender of the people involved should not be presented.

Job and career stereotypes pertaining to men also should be avoided. No set of interests or attitudes, or choice of careers, should be considered as incompatible with any concept of masculinity. It should not be implied that a man's worth is predicated solely upon his income level or job status. Notions that men should earn more than women or that women are not competent supervisors should not be suggested. It should not be implied that men are necessarily the only sources of economic support for their families. Rather, men should be shown in a broad spectrum of pursuits and roles.

It should be made clear that men and women have the same motivation for working: to earn a living, to contribute to society, and to satisfy intellectual and psychosocial needs.

Lifestyles

Stereotyping in regard to an individual's lifestyle should be avoided. It should not be implied that some interests and activities are intrinsically masculine or feminine. Women and men should be shown as participants and spectators at sports and games, as producers and consumers of art and literature, as political and community leaders and contributors, and so forth. It should not be suggested that boys and girls necessarily have separate interests, but rather that they pursue interests based on their individuality, not their gender. Women, like men, have many choices: to remain single, to marry early or late in life, to have children or not to have them, and— whether married or unmarried, a parent or childless—to have a career outside the home. It should not be implied that a family suffers or is deprived simply because a woman works.

On the other hand, the value of housework should be recognized, as long as such work is not glorified as the exclusive domain of women. Both men and women should be shown engaging in home maintenance activities ranging from cooking and housecleaning to washing the car and making household repairs; this should be the case in the depiction of children's activities as well. The stereotype that only girls should help with traditionally female household chores (while boys do not) should be avoided.

Historical and Cultural Materials

When the activities and experiences of men are discussed, attempts should be made to include the achievements of women. This is true even in historical and cultural settings in which women were or are accorded inferior status or when historical works have overlooked the role of women. The fact that women's rights, opportunities, and accomplishments have been limited by the economic, political, and social customs of a particular historical period should be openly discussed when relevant.

The implementation of this policy is accomplished partly through the choice of nonbiased language and the avoidance of stereotypes. This does not mean, however, that the actual language, events, or case studies of a historical period should be altered in any way.

Item developers should diversify their choices of case histories and examples so as to represent a broad spectrum of historical and cultural reality.

Gender Traits

There are, of course, indisputable physical differences between males and females. When these are germane, they should be mentioned without apology or irony. When they are not germane, they should not be mentioned. The real effects of physical differences between the sexes should not be exaggerated, nor should they be assumed to exist when they do not: it should not be implied, for instance, that women in general lack strength or stamina or that men lack gracefulness or dexterity. Test developers should bear in mind that there is a large area of overlap between males and females in regard to size, strength, endurance, and many other physical attributes.

Since individual men and women differ, it should not be assumed that specific traits, whether positive or negative, are necessarily associated with men or with women. For example, it should not be implied that all women have, or should have, a "maternal instinct" or that all men are, or should be, naturally aggressive. It should not be assumed that people have, or lack, certain aptitudes simply by virtue of being men or women, that men have a "knack for machinery," for instance, or that women are "good with people." It should not be assumed or implied that certain aspects of personality, ways of reacting to experiences, or modes of thought are characteristic of men or women; for example, that men are competitive or that women are sentimental, that women are intuitive or that men are logical.

It should not be assumed that because of physical or psychological differences men and women are confined to certain roles, or that some roles are natural or unnatural for men or for women. Rather, women's and men's shared capacities as human beings should be stressed.

Techniques for Writing Tests Free of Gender Bias

Consider the following guidelines in developing tests that are free of bias.

Using Parallel Language

Parallel language should be used for women and men. Avoid the subtle stereotyping of women by terminology and role assignment. Use parallel adjectives to describe parallel situations.

Women should be referred to as *ladies* only when men are being referred to as *gentlemen*. Similarly, women should be called *wives* and *mothers* only when men are referred to as *husbands* and *fathers*.

Potentially Biased	Alternatives
men and ladies	men and women or ladies and gentlemen
The man and wife are both economists.	The husband and wife are both economists.
The girls' locker room is on the right; the men's locker room is on the left.	The women's locker room is on the right; the men's locker room is on the left. or The girls' locker room is on the right; the boys' locker room is on the left.

Names

Women should not be identified in terms of their roles as wife, mother, sister, or daughter unless these roles are specifically at issue, nor should their marital status be indicated unless the form is paired with similar references to men.

Men's and women's names should be treated comparably.

Potentially Biased	Alternatives
Albert Einstein and Mrs. Mead	Dr. Einstein and Dr. Mead or Albert Einstein and Margaret Mead
Einstein and Mrs. Mead	Einstein and Mead

Unnecessary reference to or emphasis on a woman's marital status should be avoided. A woman should be referred to by the name she prefers, whether that name is her birth name or her name by marriage.

Titles

The same nomenclature should be used for the same job or position whether it is held by a woman or a man.

Whenever possible, terms should be used that include both sexes.

Potentially Biased	Alternatives
Francis MacIntyre, chairman of the policy committee, and Alison Copely, chairwoman of the executive committee	Francis MacIntyre, chair of the policy committee, and Alison Copely, chair of the executive committee
	or
	Francis MacIntyre, chairperson of the policy committee, and Alison Copely, chairperson of the executive committee

Gender-specific terms should be replaced by terms that can include members of either sex.

Potentially Biased	Alternatives
Today, businessmen are doing billions of dollars of business.	Today, companies are doing. . . .
	or
	Today, businesspeople are doing. . . .
John Taylor is a salesman for a construction business, and his wife is a saleswoman for a word-processing firm.	The Taylors are both sales agents. John sells lumber for a building supply company, and Gloria is a sales representative for a word-processing firm.

Gender-specific pronouns should not be used to refer to workers in particular occupations, or to individuals engaged in particular activities, on the assumption that such individuals are always (or usually) female or male. Instead, use a plural form, or use *he or she* or *she or he*.

Potentially Biased	Alternatives
the consumer or shopper . . . she	consumers or shoppers . . . they
the assistant . . . she	the assistants . . . they
the breadwinner . . . his earnings	the breadwinner . . . his or her earnings or breadwinners . . . their earnings

See the vocabulary list in Appendix B for other suitable suggestions.

Women as Participants

Women should be spoken of as participants in the world in their own right, not as appendages of men.

Terms like *pioneer, farmer,* and *settler* should clearly include females as well as males.

Potentially Biased	Alternative
Pioneers moved west, taking their wives and children with them.	Pioneer families moved west.

Women should not be portrayed as needing permission from men in order to function in the world or to exercise their rights (except, of course, for historical or factual accuracy).

Potentially Biased	Alternative
George Weiss allows his wife, Ruth, to work part time.	Ruth Weiss works part time.

Women should be recognized for their own achievements.

Potentially Biased	Alternative
Mrs. Paul Sager, whose husband is president of Software Enterprises and was instrumental in the Parks campaign, was granted tenure today by the English Department of City University.	Helen Sager was granted tenure today by the English Department of City University.

Intelligent, daring, and innovative women should be included in both historical and fictional contexts and should be treated with respect.

Describing Women and Men

Women and men should be treated with the same respect, dignity, and seriousness. Neither sex should be trivialized or stereotyped.

Women should not be described in terms of physical attributes when men are being described in terms of mental attributes or professional status. Instead, both sexes should be dealt with in the same terms. References to a man's or a woman's appearance, charm, or intuition should be avoided when irrelevant.

Potentially Biased	Alternatives
Mike Rivera is a respected officer, and his wife, Annette, is a striking blonde.	The Riveras are highly respected in their fields. Annette is a noted musician, and Mike is a successful law officer.
	or
	The Riveras are an attractive couple.

Language that assumes that the subject being written about is always either male or female should be avoided.

Potentially Biased	Alternatives
Doctors often neglect their wives and children.	Doctors often neglect their families.
The staff and their wives were invited.	The staff and their spouses were invited.
Give your wife a copy of this diet so that she can prepare your meals accordingly.	You and your spouse should go over this diet together so that you can plan meals at home that will be satisfying and still enable you to follow the diet.
Make sure that your cap, dress, hose, and shoes are clean and neat, because an unkempt uniform can be offensive to patients.	Make sure that your clothing is clean and neat, because an unkempt uniform can be offensive to patients.

Writers should avoid showing a "gee-whiz" attitude toward women who perform competently.

Potentially Biased	Alternative
Although a woman, she ran the business efficiently.	She ran the business efficiently.

In the overall context, women should not be represented merely as sex objects nor portrayed as weak, helpless, or hysterical; they should not be depicted as absurd or ridiculous, nor should their concerns be represented as trivial, humorous, or unimportant. A patronizing tone should be avoided.

Similarly, descriptions of men, especially in the context of home and personal life, should not caricature nor stereotype them. Men should not be shown as dependent upon women for advice on what to wear, what to eat, and so on. Nor should they be characterized as inept in household maintenance or child care. Such expressions as *henpecked husband* and *boys' night out* should be avoided.

Terminology

Terms that have in the past been applied to women in American society can be offensive; they often reflect a social situation and sensibility that no longer obtain.

Although many of the inappropriate terms listed below are being used less often, they still appear occasionally and should be avoided.

Potentially Biased	Alternatives
the fair sex, the weaker sex	women or females
the girls, the ladies (in reference to adult females)	the women
I'll ask my girl to check that.	I'll ask my assistant (or use name) to check that.
lady lawyer (i.e., lady as a modifier)	lawyer
male nurse	nurse
authoress, poetess, Jewess, and other female-gender word forms	author, poet, Jew
actor/actress	These terms and others like them, such as *waiter/waitress,* are widely accepted, but some people prefer the term *actor* for either sex.
suffragette, usherette, aviatrix, and other diminutive word forms	suffragist, usher, aviator
libber	feminist
coed (as a noun)	student
housewife	homemaker
career girl or career woman	Name the person's profession.
cleaning lady, cleaning woman	housekeeper, house cleaner, or office cleaner

"Man" Words and the Word "Man"

In references to humanity at large, gender-specific terms should be avoided whenever possible.

"Man," long used to denote all of humanity, may in certain contexts and word combinations perpetuate bias.

Potentially Biased	Alternatives
mankind, man	humanity, human beings, human race, people, men and women
man's achievements	human achievements, society's achievements
manpower	human power, human energy, workers, workforce, personnel
manhood	adulthood, manhood or womanhood
man-made	artificial, synthetic, manufactured, constructed, of human origin
the average man	the average person
This phenomenon has been observed in men and other mammals.	This phenomenon has been observed in humans and other mammals.
There are only six crews available to man the trucks.	There are only six crews available to operate the trucks.
There are only six people to man the campaign headquarters.	There are only six people to staff the campaign headquarters.

For a more comprehensive list of bias-free alternatives, including occupational titles, see Appendix B.

Choosing Figures of Speech

Figures of speech that are, or seem to be, sexist should be avoided.

Expressions such as *man in the street* are best reworded entirely.

Potentially Biased	Alternatives
man in the street	average citizen, average person, average American
old wives' tales	superstitions, folk wisdom
sob sister	exploitive journalist, do-gooder, sentimentalist
right-hand man	closest associate
straw man	unreal issue, misrepresentation

Occasionally, a historical context makes such an expression appropriate: *no-man's land,* for example, in the context of World War I. As a rule, however, rewording avoids possible bias and improves clarity.

Note that descriptive terms deriving from historical or fictional personages should be applied to persons of either sex: for example, *a Pollyanna, a Cassandra, a quisling.*

Some expressions, *tomboy* or *sissy,* for example, may embody potentially biased ideas. In such expressions, the concept itself—not just the choice of words—should be reconsidered.

Using Pronouns

The English language lacks a nongender-specific singular personal pronoun. Although masculine pronouns have generally been used for reference to a hypothetical person or to humanity in general (in such constructions as "anyone . . . he" and "each child opened his book"), the alternatives outlined below are recommended as preferable.

Potentially Biased

When a mechanic is checking the brakes, he must observe several precautions.

Alternatives

Recast to eliminate unnecessary gender-specific pronouns:

When checking the brakes, a mechanic must observe several precautions.

Use a plural form of the pronoun—a very simple solution and often the best:

When mechanics check the brakes, they must observe several precautions.

Recast in the passive voice, making sure there is no ambiguity:

When a mechanic is checking the brakes, several precautions must be observed.

Use *one* or *we*:

When checking the brakes, we must observe several precautions.

Use a relative clause:

A mechanic who is checking the brakes must observe several precautions.

Potentially Biased

The committee must consider the character of the applicant and his financial responsibilities.

Alternatives

Recast to substitute the antecedent for the pronoun:

The committee must consider the character and the financial responsibilities of the applicant.

Use *he or she, him or her,* or *his or her* (these constructions have passed easily into wide use):

The committee must consider the character of the applicant and his or her financial responsibilities.

Potentially Biased

I've often heard supervisors say, "He's not the right man for the job," or "He lacks the qualifications for success."

Alternative

Alternate male and female expressions and examples:

I've often heard supervisors say, "She's not the right person for the job," or "He lacks the qualifications for success."

IV. Guidelines for Fair Representation of Persons with Disabilities

Legislation such as Section 504 of the Vocational Rehabilitation Act of 1973 (PL 93-112) and the Education for All Handicapped Children Act of 1975 (PL 94-142) has focused attention on the need for fair and adequate representation of people with disabilities. Such legislation has resulted in increasing participation of students with disabilities in all public schools.

Discrimination against people with disabilities receives less attention than sexism, racism, or ethnocentrism, yet it appears in both written and illustrated materials and in the media. Individuals with disabilities have been portrayed as villains or comic figures. In other cases, they are presented solely because of their disability. Such treatment amounts to the subordination of people because of a physical or mental disability. In the context of education, it is important that students be aware that people with disabilities have an equal right to employment, decent pay, transportation, education, and a full social life.

Avoid stereotyping, belittling, or depersonalizing people with disabilities. Do not imply that people who are blind bump into things or that people who are mentally retarded are unkempt. Avoid expressions of condescension, such as *poor little cripple*. Be careful not to use terms that tend to depersonalize. For instance, *the blind* and *the deaf* should be replaced with *blind people* and *deaf people,* or *persons with a visual* (or *hearing*) *impairment.*

Language that discriminates against people with disabilities should be recognized and corrected. It dehumanizes individuals and separates them from the rest of society. Below are examples of terminology that may be considered biased. Preferred alternatives are listed to the right.

Preferred Terms in Referring to Persons with Disabilities

Potentially Biased	Alternatives
handicap, handicapped person	disability, person with a disability
deaf and dumb, deaf-mute, the deaf	deaf, person with a hearing disability or a hearing impairment, deaf person
Mongoloid	person with Down's syndrome
cripple, crippled	orthopedic disability, person with a disability, mobility impairment
the blind	blind person, sight disability, visually impaired
retard, retardate, idiot, imbecile, feebleminded	retarded, person with a mental impairment, mentally disabled
crazy, maniac, insane, mentally ill	person with an emotional disability or an emotional impairment, developmentally disabled

Guidelines for Fair Representation

Test developers should consider the following five guidelines in representing persons with disabilities.

1. **Amount of representation:** There should be adequate representation of people with disabilities in text and illustration.
2. **Disabilities represented:** Do not limit the portrayal of people with disabilities to those who are deaf, blind, or physically handicapped in an obvious way (e.g., in a wheelchair, on crutches). Whenever possible, represent those with other types of impairment as well. The full range of conditions includes behavioral problems, hearing impairments, learning disabilities, mental retardation, multiple handicaps, neurological problems, physical handicaps, and serious emotional problems.

3. **Avoidance of stereotypes:** In both text and illustrations, avoid representing people with disabilities as objects of curiosity.

4. **Integration and interaction:** Show people with disabilities as integrated with other members of society. Nothing should be said nor shown that fosters a "one of them as opposed to one of us" attitude or in any way separates persons with disabilities from the mainstream of society. Do not always depict people with disabilities as being helped by others; the roles should be reversed whenever possible. Show people with disabilities interacting positively in a variety of interpersonal relationships and communicating naturally in a variety of situations.

5. **Portrayal of achievement:** Materials should provide a broad range of appropriate role models. A variety of occupational situations should be described or illustrated. Whenever possible, show people with disabilities who are community leaders, business executives, or parents.

V. Further Areas of Potential Bias

Examples of hypothetical objectives and test items that might reflect one or more kinds of bias are presented below. These examples focus, in part, on some areas of bias not covered in detail in other chapters of this document. They include age, socioeconomic status, geography, culture, and religion.

Age bias can be subtle and yet real and damaging in educational materials and tests. Attention to age bias is especially important now that large numbers of older people are entering college programs. Just as college administrative and instructional personnel have a responsibility to make such "nontraditional students" feel welcome and equally regarded with their fellow students, so do the developers of educational materials and tests have a responsibility to present written and graphic materials that are free of age bias and fair for students of all ages. Furthermore, it is not only the older persons who benefit from age-neutral educational materials. All students profit from their interactions with materials that portray older persons fairly and realistically instead of as only partial participants in this country's life and culture.

Stereotypes about age, even seemingly favorable ones, should be avoided. Older persons are not always (or only) fonts of wisdom and experience, nor are they universally gentle, patient, kind, and child-loving. Older persons are as varied in their attitudes and feelings as younger persons, and they should be depicted in the same ways.

In presenting older persons in educational materials, it is important to be careful in the selection of language. Descriptive terms intended to be endearing may be perceived as patronizing and condescending. Older persons should not be described as cute, funny, absent-minded, fussy, or charming any more than younger persons are. They should not be depicted as having twinkles in their eyes, needing afternoon naps, losing their hearing or sight, suffering aches and pains, or constantly engaged in such pursuits as fishing, baking cookies, or knitting.

When older persons are referred to in educational materials (including tests), they should be presented as having the full range of options and opportunities enjoyed by other age groups. They should not be presented as being limited by physical or mental capacities to a restricted range of activities or occupations. It should not be assumed that older persons have retired, are at the end of their careers, have lived the most fruitful years of their lives, or are engaged in a life of leisure activities. Older persons should be depicted as vital parts of American society.

Test questions and reading passages about older persons should portray these persons in the same range of actions and reactions as other persons. Test developers should include, where it is natural and appropriate to do so, references to the achievements and contributions of older persons. In all fields of study, from the arts to the sciences, the fruitful careers of many individuals have spanned the full human lifetime; the achievements of artists, scientists, philosophers, and writers of all ages should be included in ways that are natural and unobtrusive.

Religious bias is also to be avoided. No religious belief or practice should be portrayed as a universal norm, or as inferior or superior to any other. Portrayals of contemporary society should, where religion is discussed or depicted, reflect the religious diversity of the United States. Similarly, the country's diversity of socioeconomic status, geography, and culture should be considered as educational materials and tests are being developed. Materials should not assume that students or examinees are all from the same demographic setting, the same region, the same type of background. Materials that are heavily reflective of one circumscribed kind of experience (e.g., the urban middle class experience) should be avoided unless reasons of content accuracy or coverage require such a focus.

The following examples were created to illustrate the concept of bias in test objectives and items and to aid in developing tests free of bias. Some of the examples illustrate the use of potentially biased language; others illustrate the point that test developers' background experiences and assumptions may—even unwittingly—result in objectives and items that might penalize examinees who do not have similar experiences and assumptions. If other, more general topics are available for testing the same areas of the content domain, test developers should address them instead.

Objective for a Home Economics Test

Understand advantages and disadvantages of preferred stock ownership.

Discussion. Even for the consumer economics portion of the test, this objective addresses content geared toward those who are affluent enough to purchase preferred stock and those who are culturally conditioned to consider the purchase of stock.

Objective for a Business Test

Identify principles of salesmanship.

Discussion. In using the word *salesmanship*, this objective uses language that may be considered offensive. The suffix "-man" generally should be avoided; the objective can be changed to "Identify principles of selling."

Objective for a Physical Education Test

Identify sports appropriate for boys and activities appropriate for girls in the elementary grades.

Discussion. This objective seems to assume that sports are appropriate only for boys, while girls should be steered toward other activities.

Objective for a History Test

Analyze factors in the origin and development of civilization in North America since the arrival of Columbus.

Discussion. This objective ignores the fact that vigorous Native American civilizations preexisted the arrival of Columbus. Civilization in North America did not originate in 1492.

Objective for a Social Science Test

Identify cultural advantages of urban living.

Discussion. This objective displays a cultural bias toward urban life. It would be more appropriate to compare the features of urban and rural life or to refer to cultural characteristics, instead of cultural advantages, of urban life.

Objective for a History Test

Analyze the contributions of the music of Bob Dylan and the Beatles to the popular culture of the sixties.

Discussion. Even if this objective's focus were appropriate, the popular culture of the sixties was influenced by other musical strains than those represented by Bob Dylan and the Beatles. For example, Motown music may be considered equally important.

Objective for a Spanish Test

Differentiate proper Castilian pronunciation from dialectical variants in Hispanic America.

Discussion. The value judgment implied by this objective constitutes cultural bias. The Castilian pronunciation of Spanish is no more "proper" than the Puerto Rican or Mexican (for example), nor are these two latter pronunciations considered dialects.

Objective for a Physical Education Test

Identify techniques of exercise appropriate for maintaining a youthful appearance and attitude.

Discussion. This objective betrays a stereotypical outlook on aging by stressing the desirability of youth. It might be improved by addressing exercise appropriate for maintaining health and vitality, for example.

Objective for a Physical Education Test

Understand regulations and techniques applicable to sailing.

Discussion. This objective seems to be biased toward relatively affluent people and toward those who are geographically located near large bodies of water.

Objective for a Reading Test

Interpret mass transportation schedules.

Discussion. In assuming a familiarity with the format and content of a subway or bus schedule, this objective may be biased against those who do not live in an urban environment.

Objective for a Home Economics Test

Identify traditional food preparation techniques for Thanksgiving, Christmas, and other major holidays.

Discussion. This objective displays a cultural and religious bias and should be modified.

Objective for a Social Science Test

Identify economic and social problems faced by older persons in the United States.

Discussion. This objective seems to imply that older Americans have nothing but problems to look forward to; this is a stereotypically depressing depiction of aging. It might be better to leave room in the objective for both positive and negative aspects of the aging experience. The objective might be reworded: "Identify economic and social characteristics of life in the United States for older persons."

Item for a Health Test

Which of the following is a distinguishing characteristic of first-degree burns?

    *A. pink or red skin
    B. blisters
    C. charred skin
    D. bleeding

Discussion. This item assumes the victim's skin is white.

Item for a Reading Test

The most appropriate way for a reading teacher to divide her class into reading groups is according to students':

    A. grade level.
    B. age.
    *C. reading ability.
    D. interest.

*indicates correct response

Discussion. This item assumes a reading teacher is female, thereby perpetuating a sex-role stereotype.

Item for a Business Test

Carolyn buys on margin 100 shares of stock at 21. If the APR is 8%, what would be the total amount owed after one month?

    A. $1,680
    B. $2,100
    *C. $2,114
    D. $2,268

Discussion. This item is biased both in terminology and content against examinees of lower socioeconomic status. The intention of measuring problem-solving and computational skills is compromised by the content.

Item for an English Test

Which American author is correctly matched with one of his works?

    A. Ernest Hemingway: *Robinson Crusoe*
    B. Nathaniel Hawthorne: *Moby Dick*
    C. James Fenimore Cooper: *The Scarlet Letter*
    *D. F. Scott Fitzgerald: *Tender is the Night*

Discussion. Although this item is not biased per se, it exemplifies a missed opportunity to include either minority or female contributions to a significant area.

Item for a History Test

Which of the following events exemplifies Black revolt and unrest in the 1960s?

    *A. Watts riot
    B. Kent State massacre
    C. Kennedy's assassination
    D. Chicago convention riot

Discussion. By using terms such as *riot* and *revolt* and limiting the causal relationship to the actions of Blacks only, this item reflects a bias against the Civil Rights Movement in general and Blacks in particular.

*indicates correct response

Item for a Home Economics Test

Which of the following is the most appropriate and nutritious supper?

    A. tacos, beans, water
    B. beet soup, blintzes, milk
    C. salami sandwich, potato chips, soda
  *D. steak, potatoes, peas, milk

Discussion. Issues of nutrition aside, there is an obvious bias here against ethnic foods and hence, ethnic cultures.

Item for a Leisure Studies Test

Which of the following leisure activities is most appropriate for an older person living on a fixed income?

    A. scuba diving
    B. sailing
    C. big game hunting
  *D. painting

Discussion. This item may be biased in two ways. First, it contributes to a stereotype of older persons as financially strapped and dependent. Second, it portrays older persons as requiring rather sedentary and passive leisure activities. If item content must address the match between leisure activities and personal characteristics, it is better to describe a particular situation than a falsely generic one. For example, the item might begin: "Which of the following leisure activities is most appropriate for a person of moderate means?" or even more simply: "Which of the following leisure activities is least expensive to pursue?"

*indicates correct response

Appendix A

Commonly Encountered Terms Referring to Minorities

Term	Comment
aborigine/aboriginal	Widely used to refer to the aboriginal peoples of Australia, although some prefer the term *Australian Blacks.* The argument over whether it should be capitalized depends on whether it is regarded as a proper name or as a descriptive term. (See Black/black.)
African American or Afro-American	Widely used term to refer to Black Americans.
alien, resident alien	Acceptable when it refers to non-U.S. citizens.
American	The use of the term *American* to refer to a citizen of the United States is acceptable. *U.S. citizen* or *U.S. resident* may be used when it is necessary to emphasize the distinction between a U.S. citizen and a resident of, for example, South America. Immigrant groups that have settled in the United States are described as *American* (as in *Irish American*).
American of Hispanic background	See Latin American.

Term	Comment
American Indian	Often acceptable. However, the general term should be avoided if a specific tribe or nation is being referred to. Do not use such terms as *Mohawk Indians*, which is redundant. (See also Native American.)
American policy, American economy	The terms *U.S. policy* and *U.S. economy* are preferable. (See also we/our.)
Amerind, Amerindian	Not recommended. The term *American Indian* or *Native American* is preferable.
Anglo-American	Used colloquially for *White non-Hispanic.*
Asian	Acceptable, but be specific if possible (e.g., Chinese, Japanese). (See also oriental.)
Black/black	Opinion is divided on the capitalization of *Black.* Since 1987, the style manual of the American Psychological Association (*APA Publication Manual*) has recommended that both *Black* and *White* in references to ethnicity be capitalized. That is the style used and recommended in this manual.
Boricua	Carib word used in early times to refer to people of Puerto Rico; now enjoying renewed usage. Not recommended as an English-language substitute for *Puerto Rican.*

Term	Comment
Chicano, Chicana	Often used colloquially for a Mexican American born in the United States. Because of a negative connotation for the term among some Hispanic groups, *Mexican American* is highly preferred.
coloured	Used as a color designation by the South African government for people of mixed African and other ancestry. Often considered derogatory.
English	Should be distinguished from *British* and *Briton*. Not everyone in Great Britain is English.
Eskimo	The term *Inuit* is preferred by Arctic and Canadian peoples and is often an acceptable alternative.
ethnic (noun), ethnics	Colloquialism. Usually refers to "new immigrant" nationalities from Southern and Eastern Europe, but often applied to any group.
gringo	A negative Spanish colloquialism used to refer to Whites. Do not use.
Hebrew	A language. Not acceptable when referring to a person or a religion, except in references to ancient Israel.

Term	Comment
Hispanic (adj.)	Widely used and acceptable umbrella term referring to people of Spanish origin. Also used as a demographic category in lists specifying racial or ethnic background (e.g., questionnaires, census forms). (See also Latin American.)
Hispanic American	See Latin American.
Ibero-American	See Latin American.
Indian	Refers to an individual from India. Not to be confused with *American Indian* or *Native American.*
Inuk, Inuit	Preferred over *Eskimo* by Arctic and Canadian peoples.
Irish American	Used in political and sociological writing to refer to people of Irish heritage who live in the United States.
Israeli	Citizen of Israel; not all Israelis are Jews.
Jew	Person whose religion or religious background is Jewish.
Latin American	There is wide confusion over what term to use when referring to Spanish- and Portuguese-speaking people in the Western Hemisphere. *Hispanic* is often used instead of *Latin American* when referring to residents of the United States who speak

Term	Comment
Latin American *(continued)*	Spanish or who are one or two generations removed from Spanish-speaking people from one of the Central American, South American, or Caribbean countries. However, some groups object to the term *Hispanic* on the grounds that it emphasizes a shared European cultural heritage rather than a shared new world cultural heritage. And certainly not all Spanish-speaking people from Central America, South America, or Caribbean countries are of Spanish descent. When possible, be specific. Some resent *Latin American,* saying it is insensitive to national differences; some find it inaccurate, since not all people referred to as *Latin American* speak a Latin-based language. Further, it usually does not include French speakers. Again, when possible, be specific. *Central American* or *South American* can also be used. *Latin American* is preferable to *Hispanic American* (often used of Spanish speakers who have settled in the United States). *Ibero-American* is acceptable, but clumsy; use *Brazilian* instead of *Luso-American.*

Term	Comment
Latino	Preferred by some groups to *Hispanic*.
Mexican American	Acceptable.
minority, minority group	In its strict sense, refers to a statistical minority. However, it is often used to refer to groups within a population who differ in certain respects from the rest of the population and who are treated specially because of their differences.
Mongoloid, Negroid, Caucasoid	Not recommended. The racial classifications from which these terms were derived—*Mongolian, Negro, Caucasian*—are no longer considered valid. Further, "-oid" has a pejorative connotation.
mulatto	Not recommended. The term is from the Spanish *mulo* (mule) and is used to refer to a person of mixed ancestry. Specify ancestry.
Muslim, Moslem, Muhammadan	Used to refer to persons whose religion is Islam. *Muslim* is preferred in the United States. *Muhammadan* is not recommended. Note: The term *Muslim* is not interchangeable with *Arab*.

Term	Comment
Native American	Preferred by some groups to *American Indian*. Note: When it is used with a lowercase "n" it can refer to people born in the United States (sometimes called *native-born Americans*).
native peoples	Acceptable.
Negro	Acceptable when quoting from a historical document in the appropriate historical context.
North American	Acceptable.
oriental	Not recommended. Use *Asian*, or be specific.
primitive	In referring to primitive societies or their cultural manifestations (e.g., dance, music), beware of the danger of stereotyping minority cultures. The term *primitive* can be interpreted pejoratively. Unless it is part of a technical term (e.g., *primitive painting*), consider using *ancient* or *early* instead, or specifying a people and a time period (e.g., the society of the Maya *in the third century A.D.*).
Quebecois, Quebecker, Quebecer	Quebec French speakers prefer *Quebecois*; Quebec English speakers prefer *Quebeckers*; The New York Times prefers *Quebecer* (which might lead to a mispronunciation).

Term	Comment
Scottish, Scots, Scotch	*Scottish* should be the adjective; use *Scot* for the people, *Scotch* for certain products or objects (such as whiskey). *Scottish* is most widely used in Scotland.
Spanish-speaking people	See Latin American.
third world	Not recommended. Often used to refer to developing countries, especially those not aligned with either the Soviet Union or the United States. Also used to refer to "minority groups," taken as a whole, in the United States. If the term is used, care should be taken to make sure that the intended meaning is clear from the context in which it appears.
WASP	Colloquialism of limited application. Stands for "White, Anglo-Saxon Protestant."
we/our (when referring to the United States)	Not recommended.

Appendix B

Using Vocabulary Free of Gender Bias

The following list of alternatives to gender-specific terms is intended as a general guide. Explanatory notes indicate where there is disagreement about the more acceptable alternative.

The recommendations are based on preferences expressed by authors and editors at McGraw-Hill Book Co. and on the 1977 edition of the U.S. Department of Labor *Dictionary of Occupational Titles* (DOT).

Gender-Specific Term	Alternative
Able Seaman	Term refers to holder of U.S. government certificate and often cannot be changed. In some cases a specific designation such as *deckhand* or *stevedore* may be appropriate.
actor/actress	none (Note: These terms and others like them, such as *waiter/waitress*, are widely accepted, but some people prefer the term *actor*.)
airline stewardess	flight attendant
anchorman	anchor, anchorperson
authoress	author
aviatrix	aviator, pilot
boatman	boat operator (Note: All analogous "-man" words, such as *cameraman, brakeman,* and *motorman,* can be changed by substituting with *operator*. If in doubt, check DOT.)
border patrolman	border guard, border patrol agent

Gender-Specific Term	Alternative
busboy	*Dining room attendant* is the general DOT designation, but a more specific term, such as *runner* or *dish carrier,* may also be used.
businessman	*Businessperson* (plural, *businesspeople*) is sometimes acceptable. *Business executive, business manager, retail store owner, entrepreneur, proprietor,* and *merchant* may also be used depending on the context.
cameraman	camera operator, cinematographer
career woman	Name the profession.
chairman	chair, chairperson (also *presiding officer, head, leader, coordinator, moderator*)
cleaning lady or woman, maid	housekeeper, house cleaner, office cleaner
clergyman	member of the clergy (or use specific title, e.g., *minister, rabbi*)
coed (noun)	student
congressman	member of Congress, representative (but *Congressman O'Neill, Congresswoman Schroeder,* because this is the custom in Congress)
councilman	council member

Gender-Specific Term	Alternative
craftsman	artisan, craftsperson (Note: According to DOT, the terms *crafter* and *craft worker* are acceptable only when referring to makers and crafters of jewelry.)
craftsmanship	none
deliveryman	deliveryperson
divorce/divorcee	divorced person, single person (Avoid unless relevant to discussion.)
draftsman	drafter
early man	See alternative for primitive man.
fellow worker	coworker, colleague
fireman	fire fighter (Note: *Firer* is the DOT title for a worker who maintains or stokes fires.)
fisherman	fisher (Note: For sport-fishing enthusiasts, *angler* is acceptable.)
forefathers	ancestors
foreman	Care should be exercised in replacing this term. *Supervisor* or *line supervisor* is sometimes used, although it is often not specific enough. (According to DOT, a supervisor can be a boss, chief, head, leader, manager, etc., and classifi-cations are made according to process involved, craft or workers supervised, product

Gender-Specific Term	Alternative
foreman *(continued)*	manufactured, or industry in which work occurs. Other alternatives are *group leader* and *straw boss*.)
freshman	first-year student
girl	woman, young woman (but *girl* is acceptable when referring specifically to female children)
groundsman	ground worker
handyman	repairer, maintenance worker
hero/heroine	none
horsemanship	riding skill
housewife	homemaker (sometimes *consumer,* if appropriate)
insurance salesman	insurance agent
journeyman	none (Note: The term *journey worker* is a DOT term referring to a worker who has completed an apprenticeship.)
landlord/landlady	owner
layman	layperson, nonspecialist, nonexpert, nonprofessional
lineman	line maintainer
longshoreman	stevedore (Note: DOT differentiates between stevedores who operate loading and unloading equipment [*stevedore I*] and those who load and unload manually or by handtruck [*stevedore II*].)
lumberman	logger

Gender-Specific Term	Alternative
mailman	mail carrier (DOT), letter carrier
manhood	adulthood, manhood or womanhood
man-hour	worker-hour, employee-hour
mankind	humanity, human beings, human race, people, men and women
man-made	artificial, synthetic, manufactured, constructed of human origin
manpower	work force, human resources, personnel, workers
middleman	intermediary, wholesaler, broker (finance)
newsboy	newspaper carrier or newspaper vendor
newsman	newscaster, reporter, journalist
office boy	messenger, officer helper
ombudsman	none (Note: The term ombudsperson may be emerging, but dictionaries have not yet accepted it.)
policeman	police officer
pressman	press operator
primitive man	primitive people or peoples, primitive human beings, early human beings, primitive men and women. (Note: Scholars often use specific terms that one cannot change without altering their meaning. For example, by *early*

Gender-Specific Term	Alternative
primitive man *(continued)*	*man* an author may mean *Homo erectus* but not *Homo sapiens;* it would be incorrect to change *early man* to *early human being* or *primitive men and women* when something more like hominid is meant. See also primitive in Appendix A. Other terms may be preferable.)
public relations man	public relations specialist, publicity writer, publicist
repairman	repairer (Note: The term *mechanic* may be used with a specific designation, such as *automobile mechanic*.)
salesman/saleswoman	salesperson (a person who sells in a retail store), sales representative, sales agent, sales associate (generally used to refer to persons doing wholesale selling), sales worker
seamstress	sewing machine operator, sewer, stitcher, garment worker (if applicable)
sissy	Reword passage (see Choosing Figures of Speech in Chapter III).
spokesman	spokesperson, advocate, representative
sportsmanship	sporting conduct
statesman	leader, public servant

Gender-Specific Term	Alternative
steward/stewardess	none if references to those involved are in water or train transportation (Note: Some people prefer the term *steward* for either gender. See also airline stewardess.)
suffragette	suffragist
tomboy	Reword passage (see Choosing Figures of Speech in Chapter III).
waiter/waitress	none (Note: These terms and others like them, such as *actor/actress,* are widely accepted, but some people prefer the term *waiter.*)
weatherman	weather reporter, meteorologist
widower/widow	widowed or single person (Avoid unless relevant.)
workman	worker, laborer
workmanship	none (or describe quality of work)

References

Anderson, J. D. (1986). Secondary school history textbooks and the treatment of black history. In D. C. Hine (Ed.), *The state of Afro-American history: Past, present and future*. Baton Rouge: Louisiana State University Press.

Bersoff, D. N. (1979). Regarding psychologists testily: Regulation of psychological assessment in the public schools. *Maryland Law Review, 39*, 27–120.

Bogatz, B. E. (Ed.). (1978). *With bias toward none: A national survey of assessment programs and procedures*. Lexington, KY: Coordinating Office for Regional Resource Centers, University of Kentucky.

Breland, H. M., Stocking, M., Pinchak, B. M., & Abrams, N. (1974). *The cross-cultural stability of mental test items: An investigation of response patterns for ten sociocultural groups*. Princeton, NJ: Educational Testing Service.

Cotera, M. P. (1982). *Checklists for counteracting race and sex bias in educational materials*. Austin, TX: WEEA Publishing Center.

Council on Interracial Books for Children. (1977). *Stereotypes, distortions and omissions in U.S. history textbooks*. New York: Author.

Council on Interracial Books for Children. (1980). *Guidelines for selecting bias-free textbooks and storybooks*. New York: Author.

Curriculum Frameworks and Instructional Materials Unit, California State Department of Education. (1982). *Standards for evaluation of instructional materials with respect to social content*. Sacramento, CA: Author.

Darlington, R. B. (1970). Another look at "cultural fairness." *Journal of Educational Measurement, 8*(2), 71–82.

Duffey, J. B., Salvia, J., Tucker, J., & Upseldyke, J. (1981). Non-biased assessment: A need for operationalism. *Exceptional Children, 47*, 427–434.

Educational Testing Service. (1980). *An approach for identifying and minimizing bias in standardized tests: A set of guidelines*. Princeton, NJ: Author.

Glaser, R., & Bond, J. (Eds.). (1981). Testing: Concepts, policy, practice, and research [Special issue]. *American Psychologist, 36*(10).

Goodman, J. (1979). Is tissue the issue? A critique of SOMPA's models and tests. *The School Psychology Digest, 8*, 47–62.

Heaston, P. (1982, August). *Urban school psychology: Current perspectives*. Paper presented at the American Psychological Association Convention, Washington, DC.

Hunter, J. E., & Schmidt, F. L. (1976). A critical analysis of the statistical and ethical implications of various definitions of test bias. *Psychological Bulletin, 83*, 1053–1071.

Hunter, R. V., & Slaughter, C. D. (1980). *ETS test sensitivity review process.* Princeton, NJ: Educational Testing Service.

Jackson, G. D. (1975). On the Report of the Ad Hoc Committee on Educational Uses of Tests with Disadvantaged Students: Another psychological view from the Association of Black Psychologists. *American Psychologist, 30*(1), 88–92.

Jensen, A. R. (1969). How much can we boost I.Q. and scholastic achievement? *Harvard Educational Review, 39,* 1–123.

Jensen, M., & Beck, M. D. (1978, March). Gender balance analysis of the Metropolitan Achievement Tests. Paper presented at the annual meeting of the National Council on Measurement in Education, Toronto, Canada.

Kane, M. B. (1970). *Minorities in textbooks: A study of their treatment in social studies texts.* Chicago: Quadrangle Books.

Klein, S. S. (Ed.). (1985). *Handbook for achieving sex equity through education.* Baltimore: Johns Hopkins Press.

Linn, R. L., Levine, M. V., Hastings, C. N., & Wardrop, J. L. (1981). Item bias in a test of reading comprehension. *Applied Psychological Measurement, 5*(2), 159–173.

Macmillan Publishing Company. (1975). *Guidelines for creating positive sexual and racial images in educational materials.* New York: Author.

McGraw-Hill Book Company. (n.d.). *Guidelines for bias-free publishing.* New York: Author.

Mercer, J. R., & Lewis, J. F. (1978). *System of multicultural pluralistic assessment: Basic kit.* New York: Psychological Corporation.

Meyers, J., Pfeffer, J., & Erlbaum, V. (1982, March). Process assessment: A model for broadening the school psychologist's assessment role. Paper presented at the annual meeting of the National Association of School Psychologists, Toronto, Canada.

Miller, C., & Swift, K. (1980). *The handbook of nonsexist writing.* New York: Harper and Row.

National Council of Teachers of English. (1974). *Guidelines for nonsexist use of language in NCTE publications.* Urbana, IL: Author.

National School Psychology Inservice Training Network. (n.d.). *Non-test-based assessment: A training module.* Minneapolis: The University of Minnesota.

Northwest Regional Educational Laboratory. (1978). *Assessment instrument in bilingual education: A descriptive catalog of 342 oral and written tests.* Los Angeles: National Dissemination and Assessment Center.

Oakland, T. (1977). *Psychological and educational assessment of minority children.* New York: Brunner/Mazel.

Office for Minority Education. (1980). *An approach for identifying and minimizing bias in standardized tests: A set of guidelines.* Princeton, NJ: Educational Testing Service.

Reschly, D. J. (1980). *Nonbiased Assessment.* Des Moines, IA: Iowa State Department of Public Instruction, Iowa State University of Science and Technology.

Saario, T. N., Jacklin, C. N., & Tittle, C. K. (1973). Sex-role stereotyping in the public schools. *Harvard Educational Review, 43,* 386–416.

Sattler, J. (1982). *Assessment of children's intelligence and special abilities.* Newton, MA: Allyn and Bacon.

Scheuneman, J. (1985). *Exploration of causes of bias in test items* (Report No. ETS-RR-85-42; GREB-81-21P). Princeton, NJ: Educational Testing Service.

Sewell, T. (1981). Shaping the future of school psychology: Another perspective. *School Psychology Review, 10,* 232–242.

Sternberg, R. (1981). Nothing fails like success: The search for an intelligent paradigm for studying intelligence. *Journal of Educational Psychology, 73*(2), 142–155.

Tittle, C. K. (1978). *Sex bias in testing: A review with policy recommendations.* Princeton, NJ: ERIC Clearinghouse on Tests, Measurement & Evaluation.

Wigdor, A., & Garner, W. R. (Eds.). (1982). *Ability testing: Uses, consequences, and controversies.* Washington, DC: National Academy Press.

The TASP Test
Registration Bulletin

1989 TASP™ Test
Registration Bulletin

TASP™

TEXAS ACADEMIC
SKILLS PROGRAM™

Texas Higher Education Coordinating Board
Texas Education Agency
National Evaluation Systems, Inc.

This document constitutes a working draft. Neither National Evaluation Systems, Inc., nor the Texas Higher Education Coordinating Board, and/or the Texas Education Agency is committed to any of the statements or positions set forth herein. Content in the final version of the document will fully supersede any inconsistent statements or positions contained in this draft.

IMPORTANT

The purpose of this bulletin is to provide the following:

- general information about TASP,™
- instructions for registering for the TASP Test and for receiving your scores, and
- suggestions on how to prepare for and take the TASP Test.

Please read this entire bulletin carefully before you complete the registration form.

You will find the test registration form and a mailing envelope in the center of this bulletin. The instructions for completing the registration form are found on pages 3 to 6. Please read these instructions carefully before filling out the form; it is very important that the information on the registration form be accurate.

Keep this bulletin after you have registered. It includes important information and forms that you may need later.

Your Social Security Number

Your social security number is used to keep track of your TASP testing records. It is also used in reporting your TASP Test score to the one or more colleges or universities that you want to receive it. As a result, it is very important to make sure your social security number is correctly entered on the registration form. If you do not have a social security number, contact the registrar's office at the college or university to which you have been admitted and/or which you plan to attend.

Further Information

For questions not answered in this bulletin, you should contact the advisory office at the college or university to which you have been admitted and/or which you plan to attend. If you still have questions, contact the following offices:

For questions about TASP **policies** and general administration issues contact:

The Texas Higher Education
Coordinating Board
University and Health Affairs
Division
P.O. Box 12780
Austin, Texas 78711
Telephone: (512) 462-6485

For questions about specific **registration procedures** or your **admission ticket** or **score report,** contact:

TASP Test
National Evaluation
Systems, Inc.
P.O. Box 140406
Austin, Texas 78714-0406
(512) 926-8746

The Texas Academic Skills Program, TASP, and the TASP logo are trademarks of National Evaluation Systems, the Texas Higher Education Coordinating Board, and the Texas Education Agency.

Information About the TASP Test

The TASP Test of Reading, Mathematics, and Writing

The Texas Academic Skills Program (TASP) Test is an examination that provides information about the reading, mathematics, and writing skills of each student entering a Texas public college or university. Mandated by House Bill 2182 (HB 2182), passed by the Texas Legislature in spring 1987, the test was developed in response to growing evidence in Texas and other states that many college students and graduates lack some of these basic academic skills.

To ensure that students in public colleges and universities have the skills necessary to perform effectively in college-level course work, the Legislature also mandated that institutions develop and implement appropriate remedial and advisory support activities. With an improved level of skills, students will benefit more fully from their higher-education course work and be better prepared to succeed after college.

The Texas Higher Education Coordinating Board (THECB) and State Board of Education (SBOE) have passed specific regulations and guidelines under which the TASP activities are conducted. The rules and guidelines governing the administration of the TASP Test are included in this registration bulletin. If you will be taking the test, you are strongly encouraged to read this registration bulletin carefully and completely.

> As used in this bulletin, the terms **college-level courses** and **college-level work** refer to courses or other academic experiences that provide credits toward college or university graduation requirements for the degree or certificate a student is seeking. **College-level work** is different from **precollegiate work** such as developmental courses, which do not provide credit toward college or university graduation requirements.

Each section of the TASP Test is designed to measure a student's academic skills in relation to an established standard of competence. Your score on each section of the test is based on your mastery of the skills being tested. Scores are not related to how well other students have performed on the same section.

The TASP Test scores cannot be used to deny a freshman-level student admission to a Texas public college or university.

The TASP Test consists of the following sections:

Reading. The reading section includes reading passages similar to those found in course materials (e.g., textbooks, lab manuals, essays) that students are likely to encounter during their first year of college. Each passage is approximately 300 to 750 words in length. Students will be asked to answer several multiple-choice questions about each passage.

Mathematics. The mathematics section contains multiple-choice questions covering three general areas: fundamental mathematics, algebra, and geometry. The test questions focus on a student's ability to perform mathematical operations and/or solve problems. Appropriate formulas will be provided for students to use in performing some of the calculations required by the test questions.

Examinees will **not** be permitted to use calculators during the test.

Writing. The writing section consists of two parts: a group of multiple-choice questions and an essay portion. The multiple-choice part of the test assesses student skills in various elements of effective writing. The essay portion requires students to demonstrate their ability to communicate effectively by writing on a given topic. Students will be instructed to write an essay of approximately 300 to 600 words. Generally, topics will allow examinees to draw from personal experiences and general knowledge. Students will **not** be allowed to use dictionaries.

Testing Time Provided

The test is designed so that most students should be able to finish all three sections within **four hours**. However, up to five hours will be provided if needed. You may use the time available to work on any of the three sections of the test.

Who Must Take the Test

The requirements for taking the TASP Test apply to students who are entering or enrolled in a Texas public institution of higher education, and teacher education students at both public and private institutions in Texas. If you are a full-time or part-time student, you must take the TASP Test if any one of the conditions listed below applies to you:

- you are enrolling as a student in a college-level degree program in fall 1989 or afterward;

- you are entering a certificate program that contains nine (9) or more semester credit hours, or the equivalent, of general education courses as defined by the Southern Association of Colleges and Schools;

- you are any other student, including a student transferring from outside Texas or from a private Texas college or university;

- you are a student seeking admission to a Texas upper-level institution or program that requires the TASP Test as a condition of admission.

You are exempt from taking the TASP Test if:

- you are entering or are currently in a certificate program that contains fewer than nine (9) semester credit hours or the equivalent, of general education courses as defined by the Southern Association of Colleges and Schools, and/or

- you have earned at least three (3) semester credit hours of college-level work prior to fall 1989.

Check with the institution you are attending or planning to attend about these policies.

You must take the TASP Test if you are a student seeking to enter a Texas-approved teacher education program, a person renewing a Texas emergency teaching permit, or a person seeking a Texas teacher certificate through an approved alternative certification program (see page 3 for information for teacher education students).

When Students Must Take the Test

You must take the TASP Test before accumulating nine (9) or more college-level semester credit hours, or the equivalent, unless you **have taken a placement test** at the Texas college or university in which you are enrolling as a freshman-level student. If you **have taken a placement test** at the college or university in which you are enrolling, you must take the TASP Test before the end of the semester in which you have accumulated fifteen (15) or more college-level semester credit hours. **Check with your institution about its policies on placement testing.**

If you are a transfer student and have not previously taken the TASP Test, you must take the test prior to accumulating nine college-level semester credit hours at the institution to which you transferred.

If you are seeking admission to a state-approved teacher education program, you should contact the teacher certification officer at your campus for information about when to take the TASP Test. If you are seeking admission to a Texas public upper division university or to an upper-level program at a Texas public health science center, you should contact the admissions office at that institution for information about the TASP Test.

Taking and Passing the TASP Test

To pass the TASP Test, you must pass all three of its sections. You may take one, two, or three sections at a given test administration. Once you pass a section of the test, you do not have to take that section again. If you do not pass one or more sections, you may register again and take only the section(s) of the test that you have not already passed. For further information, see "Preparing for the TASP Test" on page 15.

You must participate continuously in a remedial program for those skill areas of the test that you have not passed. **If you do not pass all sections of the TASP Test, you will not be allowed to enroll in any upper-division courses where completion of such courses would give you 60 or more college-level semester credit hours, or the equivalent.**

Students required to take the TASP Test **may not graduate** from a certificate program that has nine (9) or more semester credit hours of general education courses, an associate degree program, or a baccalaureate degree program until they have passed all three sections of the test.

> For further information about whether you must take the TASP Test, when you must take it, and the results of taking it, contact the advising office at the Texas college or university you currently attend or plan to attend.

2

232

Students Seeking Admission to a Teacher Education Program

In 1981, the Texas legislature enacted a law (TEC 13.032[e]) requiring all students seeking admission to a state-approved teacher education program in Texas to perform satisfactorily on a basic skills examination. This law has applied to teacher education students since its implementation on May 1, 1984.

Beginning on January 1, 1989, students seeking admission to an approved teacher education program must meet the requirements of this law by taking and passing the Texas Academic Skills Program (TASP) Test unless they have previously passed all sections (reading, mathematics, and writing) of the Pre-Professional Skills Test (PPST). In addition, persons seeking a Texas teacher certificate through an approved alternative certification program must pass all three sections of the TASP Test. Persons who want to renew a Texas emergency teaching permit also must pass the TASP Test. Students who have not

passed any section(s) of the PPST must pass the corresponding section(s) of the TASP Test to meet the test requirement for admission to a teacher education program. For example, a student who did not pass the reading section of the PPST but passed the mathematics and writing sections must take and pass only the reading section of the TASP Test.

As of May 1, 1991, scores from the PPST will no longer be valid for determining admission to teacher education programs. The TASP Test will be the only test from which scores for entry into teacher education programs will be recognized.

If you have questions about the requirements for admission to a teacher education program, **contact the teacher certification officer on your campus or the Texas Education Agency** at (512) 463-9525.

Instructions for Completing the TASP Test Registration Form

The registration form is in the envelope stapled to the center of this registration bulletin. Carefully remove the envelope and then the form.

Register carefully. Read all of the instructions before filling out the form. Provide accurate information. Please recheck the information on your form before you mail it.

Remember, your form must be **postmarked** by the Registration Deadline. See the back cover or page 9 for test dates and registration deadlines.

How to Complete Your Computer-Processed Registration Form

Refer to the numbered instructions on the following pages as you fill out the registration form. **Because the form is processed by computer, please do the following.**

- Use only a No. 2 pencil. Do NOT use ink.
- Enter only one letter or number per box. Fill in all the appropriate boxes **before** filling in the matching ovals.
- Fill in the matching oval under each letter or number you enter. Fill in the oval completely.

- Check the accuracy of all the ovals you have filled in and correct any errors.
- Erase all errors completely.

See the example below of a properly completed section of the registration form.

Remember to make sure your social security number is accurately recorded on the registration form.

Problems with your registration form will result either in the form being returned to you or in a delay in the production of your score report. Remember to do the following.

- Sign the registration form on the line provided.

- Enclose the proper fee. (See the back cover or Table 3 on page 8 for fee information.) Be sure to send a money order or check for the correct amount, payable to **NES**. **Write your social security number on the check or money order. Do not send cash. If you do not send the correct payment, or if your check is returned by your bank, your score report will not be produced.** You also will be charged a special check processing fee of $10 by NES in addition to any charges from your bank.

Instructions for Completing Side 1 of the Registration Form

1   NAME

Enter your name in the boxes provided. Enter your last name first, then your first name, and then your middle initial. If your name has more letters than will fit in the spaces provided, enter only as many letters as there are spaces. Enter only one letter per box. Fill in all the appropriate boxes. **After** filling in the boxes, fill in the matching oval under each box. (On your TASP Test score report, your name will appear exactly as you enter it in item 1. Please be sure it is entered correctly.)

2   ADMISSION TICKET MAILING ADDRESS

Enter the complete mailing address **where you wish to receive your admission ticket and score report.** Use the abbreviations in Table 1 on page 4 for street addresses. Enter only one letter per box. Leave a space between your street number and street name. Fill in the matching oval under each box.

Use the two-letter postal code for your state, found in Table 2 on page 4. For example, the two-letter postal code for Texas is TX. Enter the correct zip code and fill in the matching ovals below. If your address is **not** in the United States, enter the code "OC" for other country in the space for the state code and attach a note with your full address to your registration form.

(Your TASP admission ticket and score report will be mailed to the address you enter here. Please be sure it is entered correctly. If your score report address will be **different** from the address for sending your admission ticket, you will have an opportunity to provide that address at the test administration.)

TABLE 1
Street Abbreviations

Apartment	APT	Park	PK
Avenue	AVE	Parkway	PKY
Boulevard	BLVD	Pike	PI
Box	BX	Place	PL
Broadway	BDWY	Point	PT
Circle	CI	Port	PRT
Court	CT	Post Office	PO
Drive	DR	Road	RD
East	E	Route	RT
Fort	FT	South	S
Garden	GDN	Square	SQ
Headquarters	HQ	Street	ST
Heights	HTS	Terrace	TER
Highway	HWY	Trail	TRL
Lake	LK	Trailer	TRLR
Lane	LN	Turnpike	TPKE
Mount	MT	Way	WY
Mountain	MTN	West	W
North	N		

TABLE 2
Two-Letter State Abbreviations

Alabama	AL	Montana	MT
Alaska	AK	Nebraska	NE
American Samoa	AS	Nevada	NV
Arizona	AZ	New Hampshire	NH
Arkansas	AR	New Jersey	NJ
California	CA	New Mexico	NM
Canal Zone	CZ	New York	NY
Colorado	CO	North Carolina	NC
Connecticut	CT	North Dakota	ND
Delaware	DE	Ohio	OH
District of Columbia	DC	Oklahoma	OK
Florida	FL	Oregon	OR
Georgia	GA	Pennsylvania	PA
Guam	GU	Puerto Rico	PR
Hawaii	HI	Rhode Island	RI
Idaho	ID	South Carolina	SC
Illinois	IL	South Dakota	SD
Indiana	IN	Tennessee	TN
Iowa	IA	Texas	TX
Kansas	KS	Utah	UT
Kentucky	KY	Vermont	VT
Louisiana	LA	Virginia	VA
Maine	ME	Virgin Islands	VI
Maryland	MD	Washington	WA
Massachusetts	MA	West Virginia	WV
Michigan	MI	Wisconsin	WI
Minnesota	MN	Wyoming	WY
Mississippi	MS	Other Country	OC
Missouri	MO		

4

3	ETHNICITY

Fill in the one oval that best describes your ethnic background.

4	SEX

Fill in the appropriate oval.

5	SOCIAL SECURITY NUMBER

Enter your social security number. **If you do not have a social security number, contact the registrar's office at the college or university to which you have been admitted and/or which you plan to attend.** Write one number per box. Fill in the matching oval under each number. **The accuracy of your social security number is an essential part of the registration and score reporting process.** It will enable us to keep track of your registration records no matter how many sections of the TASP Test you take or how many times you take one or more sections. Please be sure it is entered correctly.

6	DATE OF BIRTH

Enter the month, day, and year of your birth. Fill in the oval next to the month of your birth. Use two numbers for the day. If the day has only one digit, place a zero in the first box. Enter the last two digits of the year in which you were born. For example, if you were born on September 1, 1971, enter:

6 DATE OF BIRTH		
Month	Day	Year
○ Jan.	0 1	7 1
○ Feb.		
○ Mar.	● ⓪	⓪ ⓪
○ Apr.	① ●	① ●
○ May	② ②	② ②
○ June	③ ③	③ ③
○ July	④	④ ④
○ Aug.	⑤	⑤ ⑤
● Sept.	⑥	⑥ ⑥
○ Oct.	⑦	● ⑦
○ Nov.	⑧	⑧ ⑧
○ Dec.	⑨	⑨ ⑨

Instructions for Completing Side 2 of the Registration Form

7	HIGH SCHOOL DIPLOMA, GED, OR OTHER HIGH SCHOOL COMPLETION EQUIVALENT

Fill in the oval indicating whether you have graduated from high school or have received or will receive a General Equivalency Degree certificate (GED). If you have received or will receive some other form of high school completion equivalent, fill in the oval marked "Other."

If you have not and will not receive any form of high school diploma or equivalent, fill in the oval marked "None."

8	HIGH SCHOOL FROM WHICH YOU GRADUATED OR WILL GRADUATE

If you graduated or will graduate from a Texas public high school, enter the four-digit code for the high school. See Table 6 on pages 31 to 37.

If you graduated or will graduate from a **private** high school in Texas, enter 9000.

If you graduated or will graduate from either a public or private high school **outside** the state of Texas, enter 9050.

If you graduated or will graduate from a Texas public high school not listed on Table 6, enter 9060.

9	SEMESTER AND YEAR OF HIGH SCHOOL GRADUATION

Fill in the oval next to the **semester** (spring, summer, fall) of the year you graduated from high school, received a GED certificate, or other form of high school completion equivalent. Then, in the boxes, enter the last two numbers of the **year** you graduated. Fill in the matching ovals below the last two numbers of the year. If you have not yet graduated from high school or received an equivalent diploma, use the semester and year you **will** graduate.

10	FOR COLLEGE TRANSFER STUDENTS ONLY: MOST RECENT COLLEGE OR UNIVERSITY PREVIOUSLY ATTENDED

Complete this portion of the registration form **only** if you **previously** attended a Texas public college or university **different from** the one you are now attending or are planning to attend. Enter

5

the three-digit code of the institution you attended prior to the school you now attend or plan to attend. If you have previously attended more than one Texas public college or university, enter the code of the institution you **most recently** attended. See Table 7 on page 38 for the three-digit college or university code. Enter the three numbers in the boxes. Fill in the matching oval below each number. **If this section does not apply to you, enter 999 and fill in the matching ovals.**

11   TEST DATE

Select **both** your first-choice and second-choice dates for taking the TASP Test by filling in the ovals next to the dates in the boxes marked "First Choice" and "Second Choice." The test date to which you are assigned will be printed on your admission ticket.

12   TEST CENTER WHERE YOU WANT TO TAKE THE TASP TEST

Refer to Table 8 on page 39 and select your first-, second-, and third-choice test centers. Enter the four-digit code for each test center in the boxes provided, and fill in the matching ovals. For proper registration, you must fill in **all three choices.**

13   INSTITUTION(S) TO BE SENT SCORE REPORT

Enter the code for the Texas college or university you are attending or to which you have been admitted and are also planning to attend. Use the institution codes in Table 7 on page 38. Your fee for the TASP Test includes the cost of sending your score report to the one, two, or three colleges or universities you enter on your registration form.

If, after you have sent in your registration form, you decide that you would like your score report to be sent to additional colleges or universities, complete the Additional Score Report Request Form. The fee is $5 for each additional report.

You may also use this form to request a duplicate score report for yourself. The fee for a duplicate score report is $12.

If you do not want your score report sent to any institution, do not fill in question 13 on the registration form.

14   THE OFFICIAL TASP TEST STUDY GUIDE

The Official TASP Test Study Guide can be ordered when you register for the test. This **study guide** is designed to help you prepare for the TASP Test. If you wish to be sent *The Official TASP Test Study Guide,* fill in the oval next to "Yes." If you do not, fill in the oval next to "No." The fee for the study guide is $12 plus $3 for shipping and handling.

Only use this registration form to order a study guide if you are also registering for the TASP Test. If you are **not** registering for the TASP Test **and** wish to order one or more study guides **or** to order more than one study guide in addition to registering for the test, use the **Official TASP Test Study Guide Request Form** on page 43.

15   FEES AND PAYMENT

To calculate your correct payment, you should: (A) fill in the ovals next to the test fee(s) that apply to you (a table of fees appears on the registration form, on page 8 of this bulletin, and on the back cover); (B) enter the dollar amount for each fee that applies to you in the boxes next to the fee; (C) add the fees to get the total, and write the total in the boxes provided; (D) fill in the ovals matching the numbers in the "Total" boxes; and then (E) make out a money order or check for the correct amount, payable to **NES.**

Make sure that you write your social security number on the money order or check. If your personal check is returned by the bank, your score report will not be produced and you will be charged a check processing fee of $10 by NES in addition to any charges from your bank.

16   SIGNATURE

Carefully review the Rules of Test Participation that follow. After you have read and understood these rules, sign your name on the line provided on the registration form. This states that you agree to the conditions presented in this registration bulletin, including the Rules of Test Participation. Even if your form is received without your signature, submitting your registration form indicates that you agree to the Rules of Test Participation listed on pages 7 to 8.

After you have filled in all the appropriate spaces on the registration form, please check the accuracy of the information you have provided.

6

Rules of Test Participation

The following rules govern your participation in the TASP Test. By registering for the TASP Test, you are agreeing to follow these rules and to any of the penalties for breaking one or more of them.

- I understand that if any or all fees as listed in Table 3 on page 8 are not paid in full for all test dates for which I have registered for the TASP Test, I will not be permitted to register and/or my score report will not be provided.

- I affirm that if I am currently a Texas high school student, I have passed all sections of the exit-level Texas Educational Assessment of Minimum Skills (TEAMS) and either have been admitted to or am currently enrolled in a Texas college or university.

- I understand that if I have previously passed the writing section of the TASP Test and am registering for and complete either the reading or mathematics section of the test or both, I will automatically receive a $8 refund.

- I understand that the Texas Higher Education Coordinating Board, the Texas Education Agency, and National Evaluation Systems, Inc., reserve the right to refuse me admission to the testing room if I do not have the proper identification (valid admission ticket and two pieces of positive identification, one containing a recent photograph) or if the test has already begun when I arrive. If one or both of these occur, I understand that I will receive no refund of any portion of the testing fee. I also understand that no portion of the testing fee can be applied toward the cost of future testing fees.

- I authorize the team of test administrators at my assigned testing room to serve as my agent in maintaining a secure and proper test administration. I acknowledge that the test administrators may relocate me before or during the test session.

- I understand that, if I so choose, my test score(s) will be reported to the Texas institution(s) indicated on my registration form. My score report(s) will be sent even if I leave the testing room before I finish the test (e.g., because of an illness). If I do not want

my score(s) reported, I understand that I must request in writing within one week after the test date that my test score(s) be canceled. In such a case, I will receive no refund of any portion of the testing fee, and there will be no credit against future testing fees.

- I understand that all test booklets and answer documents and all other test materials are the **sole property of the Texas Higher Education Coordinating Board and the Texas Education Agency.** The materials have not been available for me to review before taking the test, and they will not be available for me to review after the test. I am not permitted to take any test materials from the testing room nor to reproduce the test materials as a whole or in part. If I do anything prohibited by this paragraph, my test performance will be canceled and I may be subject to legal action. In such a case, I will receive no refund of any portion of the testing fee, and no portion of that fee can be applied toward future test-taking costs.

- I understand that I will not be permitted to use written notes or make written notes of the contents of the test booklets. Throughout the examination, I will have nothing on my desk but the test, answer documents, pencils, and erasers. The use of scratch paper, calculators, calculator watches, and any unauthorized aids is prohibited. I may use the margins of the test booklet for any written work I need to do to answer specific questions. I will not communicate with other examinees or any unauthorized persons in any way. If I do anything prohibited by this paragraph, I understand that my test score will be canceled and I may be subject to legal action. In such a case, I will receive no refund of any portion of the testing fee, and no portion of that fee can be used to cover future test-taking costs.

- The Texas Higher Education Coordinating Board, the Texas Education Agency, and National Evaluation Systems, Inc., reserve the right to cancel any test score if, in their sole opinion, there is adequate reason to question its validity due either to misconduct or circumstances beyond the candidate's control.

7

If doubts are raised about my score, National Evaluation Systems, Inc., will notify the Texas Higher Education Coordinating Board, the Texas Education Agency, and other parties as deemed appropriate by the agencies. I understand that liability for the accuracy of test materials, the adequacy of test materials, and the adequacy of administration conditions will be limited to score correction or test retake at no additional fee. I waive rights to all further claims against the Texas Higher Education Coordinating Board, the Texas Education Agency, and National Evaluation Systems, Inc.

- I understand that the testing program is subject to change at the sole discretion of the Texas Higher Education Coordinating Board and the Texas Education Agency.
- If, for any reason, I object to the procedures presented above, I will advise National Evaluation Systems, Inc., **in writing**, of the basis of my objection at least four weeks before the test date for which I have registered.

Mailing Procedure

After you complete and check all the requested information on the registration form, sign the form and place it in the envelope provided. Include your money order or check for the correct amount, payable to **NES**. Make sure that you have included your social security number on the money order or check. If you require special testing arrangements or an alternate test date, enclose the appropriate letters mentioned on page 10.

Registration Information

Test Dates, Registration Schedule, and Fees

You will have an opportunity to take the TASP Test in 1989 at any of five administrations. (See Table 4 on page 9 for test dates). The test will be given at selected colleges and universities throughout Texas (see Table 8 on page 39 for a list of test centers) during the 1989 calendar year. You should register for your first- and second-choice test dates. You may take all or any sections of the test on a test date. Any section of the test that you do not pass may be taken at any subsequent test administration.

PLEASE NOTE: *There is no limit to the number of times you may take any section or all of the TASP Test in order to pass. You do not have to pass all three sections of the TASP Test at the same time to satisfy the requirements of the legislation.*

The following sections discuss the procedures for regular registration (including how to make changes in registration) and for registering late for the TASP Test. Table 3 provides information on test registration and other fees.

All registration is on a first-come, first-served basis. Mail in your registration as early as possible before the Registration Deadline. You should indicate three test center choices on your registration form **in order of preference**. You should also list a first- and second-choice test date.

TABLE 3
TASP Test Registration and Other Fees

Fee for regular registration for all or any section of the TASP Test (fee includes sending score report to the institution listed on the registration form)	$24
Other Fees	
Change of Registration (test date, test center)	$15
Late Registration	$20
Additional Score Report to Institution	$ 5
Duplicate Score Report	$12
Score Verification	$10
The Official TASP Test Study Guide	$12
Charge by NES for processing personal check returned by bank	$10

8

238

TABLE 4
Registration Schedule for 1989

Test Date (Saturday morning)	Postmark Deadline for Regular Registration	Late Registration Period (by phone only)
March 4, 1989	February 3, 1989	February 6, 1989–February 22, 1989
June 10, 1989	May 13, 1989	May 15, 1989–May 31, 1989
July 29, 1989	July 1, 1989	July 3, 1989–July 19, 1989
September 30, 1989	September 2, 1989	September 4, 1989–September 20, 1989
November 18, 1989	October 21, 1989	October 23, 1989–November 8, 1989

Regular Registration

A registration form is enclosed in a mailing envelope found in the center of this bulletin. To register:

- fill out the form, carefully following the instructions on pages 3 to 6;

- include a money order or personal check for the correct payment, with your social security number written on the money order or check; and

- mail the registration form and the correct payment in the mailing envelope by the postmark deadline.

Your registration form must be **postmarked** no later than the Registration Deadline for the test date for which you are registering. For example, if you plan to take the test on June 10, 1989, your form must be **postmarked** by May 13, 1989. **Registration forms postmarked after the Registration Deadline will be returned.**

Mail your completed registration form in the envelope provided to:

TASP Test
National Evaluation Systems, Inc.
P.O. Box 140346
Austin, Texas 78714-0346

Changing Your Test Center or Test Date

If you decide to change either the test date or test center for which you had originally registered, you should call National Evaluation Systems at (512) 926-8746 during business hours (8:30 A.M. to 5 P.M., Monday–Friday, not including holidays).

PLEASE NOTE: *Changes in registration will be processed only if there are seats available at the requested test center and on the requested test date.*

An additional $15 processing fee above the registration fee of $24 is charged for all registration changes. You will be given payment information when you phone NES. Problems with payment will result in a delay in sending your admission ticket and/or in producing your score report.

Late Registration

If you missed the regular Registration Deadline, you may seek to register on a space-available basis during the **late registration period.** (See Table 4 on this page for the dates of the late registration period.)

For example, for the July 29, 1989, test date the late registration period begins on July 3, 1989, and ends on July 19, 1989. There is an **additional $20 fee** above the regular registration fee of $24 for registering during this period.

Late registration will be accepted by phone only. For late registration, call National Evaluation Systems at (512) 926-8746 during business hours (8:30 A.M. to 5 P.M., Monday–Friday, not including holidays). If there is space available and you are able to be registered, you will be given a verification number that will allow you to be admitted to the testing room. You will also be given payment information. Problems with payment will result in a delay in producing your score report. **After you phone you must still fill out the registration form included in this bulletin and send it and the proper payment in the enclosed envelope in order to complete your registration.**

9

Withdrawing Your Registration

If you wish to withdraw your registration, fill out the **Withdrawal Request Form** on page 43. You will receive a partial refund of your fee, in the amount of $10, if your request is postmarked by the regular Registration Deadline of the test date for which you originally registered. No refunds will be issued after the regular Registra- tion Deadline (see Table 4 on page 9 for the Registration Schedule).

Send your completed Withdrawal Request Form to:

TASP Test
National Evaluation Systems, Inc.
P.O. Box 140347
Austin, Texas 78714-0347

Special Administration Procedures

Examinees with a Handicapping Condition

Special administration arrangements may be provided for examinees who would not be able to take the test under standard conditions because of a handicapping condition (e.g., hearing impairment, visual impairment). Requests for special arrangements should be made by the **regular Registration Deadline**. These requests must include (a) a completed registration form; (b) a letter from you requesting special test administration arrangements and stating the reasons for these arrangements; and (c) a statement from a professional licensed to diagnose your specific handicapping condition, on the professional's letterhead stationery, with a recommendation for the special testing arrangements required. These three documents **must be submitted together and be received by the close of registration. Make sure that your social security number appears on your letter.**

In some cases, we may contact you directly to make suitable arrangements. Please include in your letter a **phone number** where you can be reached. Before the test date, you will receive confirmation regarding the special procedures that have been arranged.

Examinees Needing an Alternate Test Date for Religious Reasons

Special test dates at a limited number of test centers may be arranged for people whose religious practices do not allow them to take tests on Saturday. These alternate test dates may be arranged only for religious reasons. To request an alternate administration date you must (a) complete the registration form; (b) submit a letter stating your request; and (c) include a letter from your clergy, on the clergy's letterhead stationery, verifying the religious basis for your request. These three documents **must be submitted together and be received by the regular Registration Deadline. Make sure that your social security number appears on your letter.**

After we have received your request, we will correspond with you and may schedule an alternate test date. We may need to contact you directly. Make sure you include in your letter a **phone number** where you can be reached. We will inform you of the test center, day, and time as soon as these have been determined. Alternate test dates will not be available at all test centers.

After You Have Registered

Admission Ticket

After we process your properly completed registration form, we will send you an admission ticket, which will include your name, address, social security number, test center, testing location, test date, and examinee number. Your admission ticket will also indicate any information that you have not provided on your registration form. On the day of testing, you will have an opportunity on the answer document both to correct personal information that is incorrectly listed on your admission ticket (e.g., your social security number) and to provide information that is missing (e.g., high school from which you

10

graduated or will graduate). Make note of any corrections when you receive your admission ticket. Write them on the ticket and bring the correct information with you to the test center. Use the tables provided in this bulletin to look up any missing information that requires a code and note the code on your admission ticket.

Bring your admission ticket to the test center on the day of the test. If you have not received your admission ticket at least one week before the test date or if you lose it, call National Evaluation Systems at (512) 926-8746.

The Day of the Test

There will be one test session on each of the regularly scheduled test dates. You should report to your assigned testing room no later than 8:00 A.M. The test session will end at 1:30 P.M. **Only those students who have officially registered for that test date and test center will be admitted. No others will be allowed into the testing room.**

You should bring the following:

- your admission ticket;

- several No. 2 pencils with erasers (pencils will **not** be supplied at the test center); and

- **two pieces of identification, one with a recent photograph (e.g., driver's license, student identification card, current passport, current alien registration card).**

If you do not have all of these materials, you should report directly to the Chief Test Administrator at your assigned testing room. If you do not have any of the acceptable forms of identification described above, you will be required to sign a declaration of identification statement at the test center. You may **not** use a birth certificate, parent's driver's license, or credit card as a form of identification.

During testing, only pencils, erasers, test booklets, and answer documents will be allowed on your desk. No visitors will be allowed to enter the testing room. Eating, drinking, and smoking will **not** be allowed in the testing room.

> You will **not** be allowed to bring the following into the testing room:
> - calculators,
> - calculator watches,
> - dictionaries,
> - slide rules,
> - briefcases,
> - packages,
> - notebooks,
> - textbooks, or
> - any other written materials.

Taking the Test

The test administration begins at 8:30 A.M. You should plan to arrive at 8:00 A.M. You will have **four hours** to complete one, two, or three sections of the test. One additional hour may be provided if needed.

Before the test begins, the test supervisor will read all the necessary instructions for taking the test. You will be asked to fill out identification information, to provide information missing on your registration form, and to correct any incorrect information. This information will be collected as part of the answer document. The information you provide on your answer document will become part of your registration record; any differences between the information you provide on your answer document and the information you provided on your registration form will be resolved by using the information on your answer document.

During the test, you may take a break to go to the restroom. However, the test supervisor and proctors will use procedures that will maintain test security and minimize any disruption to other examinees.

Leaving the Testing Room

You may leave the testing room whenever you have completed as many sections of the test as you wish to take and are ready to turn in all of your test materials. When you are ready to leave, your test materials will be collected and you will be dismissed. The test session will officially end at approximately 1:30 P.M. At that time, all test materials will be collected and you will be dismissed.

11

After The Test

Canceling Your Score

After the testing session, you may feel that you did not perform to the best of your ability. If this is the case, you may cancel your score on one or more sections of the test by sending a written request to National Evaluation Systems **post-marked within seven days** after the test administration.

The request must include the following information:

- name,
- social security number,
- examinee number,
- date of birth,
- test date, and
- test score(s) to be canceled.

Your request to cancel your test score(s) will cancel your score(s) on the test **taken on that test date**. If you have not received verification of the cancellation of your score(s) within 21 days after the test administration, call National Evaluation Systems at (512) 926-8746. If you choose to cancel your score(s), **you will not receive a refund of any kind.**

After your score(s) is canceled, all records of your test responses for the section(s) you canceled on that test date will be destroyed and you will not be able to have your score(s) for that test date reported.

However, if your score(s) was canceled because you violated one of the Rules of Test Participation (see pages 7 and 8), a report of the incident and of the cancellation of your score will be made to both the Texas Higher Education Coordinating Board and the Texas Education Agency.

Receiving Your Score Report

A score report will be mailed to you about three weeks after the test date. Some scores may take longer to report, however, because of problems with examinee registration information or other matters affecting the score reporting process. You should receive your score report no later than five weeks after the test date. **Your score will not be released over the telephone or in person.**

For the March 4, 1989, test administration **only**, score reports will be mailed approximately **eleven** weeks following the test administration.

Format of Your Score Report

You will receive a separate score for each section of the TASP Test you take. Your score(s) will show whether you have passed each section of the test.

Your score report will include a description of your performance on the skills measured by each section of the test. This will provide valuable information for you to use in identifying your areas of strength and weakness. If you have failed a section of the test, this information will be particularly useful to you when you prepare to take that section again. Recommendations for books and other resources to use in addressing specific skills are provided in *The Official TASP Test Study Guide,* available from National Evaluation Systems. (If you are registering for the test, you may order the **study guide** by filling in the "Yes" oval in item 14 of the registration form. If you are not registering for the test but would like to order one or more study guide(s), complete the study guide request form on page 43.)

Score Verification Service

The multiple-choice questions of the TASP Test are scored by computer. If you have accurately followed directions and marked the answer sheets properly, the computer scoring process is virtually error free. However, if you believe that your score is incorrect and want it checked, you may request that this be done. It is not possible to rescore a paper written for the writing section of the TASP Test. All papers are scored according to standardized procedures during scoring sessions held immediately after each test administration. Scorers receive extensive training before the scoring session. As part of the process, papers are scored by more than one reader and, in essence, have been rescored.

The form to request verification of your answers on the multiple-choice section(s) of the TASP Test may be obtained from National Evaluation Systems. The score verification service is available **after** the individual score reports have been mailed and for the three-month period following the administration date. The fee for this service is $10.

12

About *The Official TASP Test Study Guide*

The Official TASP Test Study Guide is available from National Evaluation Systems to help you prepare for the TASP Test. The guide includes a description of the TASP and the TASP Test, strategies for preparing for the test, a complete description of the skills covered on the test, and a practice test.

Each tested skill is the subject of an instructional chapter designed to assist you in your review. The chapters have sample exercises similar to those on the test. The practice test results can provide you with an analysis of areas of potential weakness. You may order the study guide either as a part of the registration process or by submitting *The Official TASP Test Study Guide* request form on page 43.

Information About the Texas Academic Skills Program

Introduction

The major impetus for the development of the Texas Academic Skills Program has been *A Generation of Failure: The Case for Testing and Remediation in Texas Higher Education,* a report published by the Texas Higher Education Coordinating Board (THECB) in August 1985.

The legislative response to *A Generation of Failure* is an extension of existing requirements for students entering teacher preparation programs. Since 1984, education students have had to pass an academic skills test as a condition for admission to these programs. House Bill 2182, passed in spring 1987, extended this testing requirement to include all students entering Texas public colleges and universities and mandated (1) advisory programs on each campus to assist students early in their careers and (2) developmental education for students who do not meet the statewide standard.

The Texas Higher Education Coordinating Board and the Texas Education Agency (TEA) agreed to develop jointly a single test that would serve both as one of the criteria for admission to public and private teacher education programs and as the test mandated by House Bill 2182 for students entering public colleges and universities. In June 1987, a Request for Proposals was issued for this testing program. National Evaluation Systems, Inc. (NES), of Amherst, Massachusetts, was selected to develop and administer the testing component of the new academic skills program. Development of the TASP Test began in September 1987.

Test Development Process

The test development process for the Texas Academic Skills Program involved thousands of faculty members from Texas colleges and universities. Texas educators, working with National Evaluation Systems staff, performed the following:

- defined the skills to be measured on the test,

- developed the specific test instrument to measure these skills, and

- recommended performance standards for each section of the test.

Texas educators participated through a number of different committees. These included the following.

- **Content Advisory Committees.** The Coordinating Board and the TEA jointly established a Content Advisory Committee for each of the three basic skill areas. Each committee had approximately 30 members, all of whom were Texas college or university faculty members. Faculty were selected for their expertise in their content areas and to reflect the diversity of Texas colleges and universities.

- **Bias Review Committee.** A separate committee of 30 educators specifically addressed the issue of test fairness to students in Texas regardless of sex, ethnicity, race, or geographic region.

13

- **Regional Panels.** Nine regional panels of college and university educators reviewed test materials at various stages of development and made recommendations to the Content Advisory Committees. Approximately 300 Texas educators participated in these regional forums.

- **Coordinating Board Committees.** In addition to these committees and review panels, the Coordinating Board formed a number of committees that participated in the nontesting aspects of the program. For example, committees focused on developmental education and academic advising.

Identification of Skills to Be Tested

To gather empirical data on the appropriateness of the skills identified by the committees and to validate the content of the test, NES conducted a series of surveys of Texas educators and students to determine which skills they considered necessary for entering freshman-level students to have in order to perform effectively in undergraduate degree programs. The surveyed populations included college and university faculty, teacher education faculty, college and university students, public school educators, and teacher education students.

Combining the results of the validation surveys with their own professional judgments, the review committees of Texas educators recommended the final list of skills to be used in the TASP. The Coordinating Board and the State Board of Education adopted these skills.

Development of Test Questions

Test questions were written to match the defined skills for reading, mathematics, and writing. These questions were reviewed by the committees of Texas educators.

Conducting the Field Test

With the cooperation of colleges and universities throughout Texas, NES conducted a field test of the test questions. The purpose of the field test was to gather data on the statistical performance of the test questions and to identify any questions possibly requiring revision. The results of the field test were reviewed by Texas educators, who suggested any necessary revisions to questions.

Validation of Test Questions and Recommended Passing Standards

After NES completed its revision of the test questions, the various committees of Texas educators reviewed the questions again. Committees also recommended passing scores for each section of the TASP Test. The recommended passing scores were presented to both the Texas Higher Education Coordinating Board and the State Board of Education for final approval.

Test Fairness

The Texas Higher Education Coordinating Board, the Texas Education Agency, and National Evaluation Systems designed a test development process that would ensure that the TASP Test materials were fair to the diverse population involved in TASP. At each stage of the test development process, the Bias Review Committee examined materials explicitly for fairness. In addition, other participants in the process, including the Content Advisory Committees and members of the regional forums, dealt specifically with test fairness as a review criterion. Moreover, the field test results were analyzed for potential bias issues using statistical techniques.

Test Preparation Support Materials

The Official TASP Test Study Guide provides valuable assistance to individuals preparing for the test and to the faculty members who are working with them. The study guide provides general test-taking tips; information and practice questions about each of the tested skills; descriptions of test questions; and a review section of reading, mathematics, and writing skills.

Test Administration

In developing policies and procedures for test administration, the Coordinating Board, TEA, and NES established several general goals.

- **Standardized administrations.** The policies and procedures for administering the test would be the same at every test center. In this way, no examinee is either advantaged or disadvantaged by variation in administration procedures. It is important that the score on the test reflect only one's mastery of the tested skills and not factors related to testing conditions. Individuals administering the tests have been trained in, and are provided with instructions about, the procedures for test administration.

14

- **Convenience to examinees.** The dates and centers for administering the TASP Test were established for the convenience of examinees and institutions of higher education. Because the testing component is a requirement for students entering Texas public colleges and universities and teacher education candidates at either public or private institutions, it is important that examinees have reasonable access to the test administrations.

- **Test security.** It is important that no examinee gain an advantage by having unauthorized access to the TASP Test or by being able to cheat in any fashion during a test administration. As an examinee, you should be relatively unaffected by the various procedures used to prevent cheating and ensure the integrity of the test you will be taking. On the other hand, you should be confident that no examinee will gain an unfair advantage through unethical or unauthorized means.

- **Individualized treatment.** National Evaluation Systems believes that each examinee deserves professional service and attention. For this reason, the test is administered through an individualized registration process. In this way, examinees have an individual record of their performance on the test that is maintained, minimizing the possibility of any loss of information concerning their participation in the program.

- **Diagnostic reporting.** The score results that you will receive provide comprehensive and diagnostic information about your perfor-

mance on each section of the test. This information will help you focus on those skills that need improvement and will help college and university faculty provide appropriate advisement and academic assistance.

- **Preliminary TASP Test.** One feature of the TASP is the availability of a Preliminary TASP Test on college and university campuses. The Preliminary TASP Test provides students with an opportunity to take and receive diagnostic score reports based on a test similar to the official TASP Test. While these scores do not count toward completion of the TASP testing requirement, they do provide examinees an opportunity to discover areas of possible weakness before actually taking the official test. Knowing about potential problems in advance may help examinees to seek advice and support before taking the official TASP Test.

- **Customized policies and procedures.** Policies and procedures governing the development, administration, and score reporting for the TASP were developed jointly by the Texas Higher Education Coordinating Board, the Texas Education Agency, and National Evaluation Systems. These policies and procedures are reviewed on a regular basis by the staffs of these three organizations, with an eye toward continual improvement. Your comments are welcome. Please address them to National Evaluation Systems, TASP Program Manager, P.O. Box 140406, Austin, Texas 78714-0406.

Preparing for the TASP Test

This section of the registration bulletin provides suggestions on how you can prepare for the TASP Test. It presents a variety of study techniques and strategies that may help you to do your best on the day of testing.

General Study Methods

By the time they have completed high school or have begun college, many students have developed their own study methods. If you have used study methods that you have found to be effective, it may be best to continue to use them.

If you feel that your study methods should be changed, consider those presented below. The key to effective studying is to develop a study plan that works best for you and follow it throughout your test preparation. The following are some things that you can do to perform as well as possible on the TASP Test.

1. Review *The Official TASP Test Study Guide*

   One valuable resource to review is *The Official TASP Test Study Guide*, which can be purchased using the TASP registration form or the study guide request form. You may also review and use *The Official TASP Test Study Guide* at your college library or instructional resources center. It includes strategies for preparing for the test and a practice test.

You may also order the study guide either as part of the registration process or by submitting *The Official TASP Test Study Guide* request form.

2. Identify Resources

Identify resources that could help you master or review the required TASP Test skills. You may wish to use resources such as textbooks, self-instructional materials, remedial learning materials, and self-assessment materials. You may also ask college faculty who teach in the skill areas measured by the TASP Test (reading, mathematics, and writing) for suggested references and resources that could help you improve your skills. Your campus learning resources center may also suggest materials to help you.

3. Answer the Sample Questions

Sample reading, mathematics, and writing test questions are provided beginning on page 23. Read the directions and answer the sample test questions, including writing an essay.

NOTE: *Since examinees will* **not** *be allowed to use calculators, slide rules, or calculator watches during the test administration, you should not use them in answering the sample mathematics questions.*

4. Score the Sample Test Questions

After answering the sample multiple-choice questions, turn to the Sample Questions Answer Key on page 30 and score your answers. You may then wish to review any questions answered incorrectly in order to help you understand how each correct answer was obtained.

5. Evaluate Your Writing Sample

Evaluate the sample essay that you have written in response to the writing assignment. Since it is sometimes hard for individuals to evaluate their own writing, you may want to have your writing sample evaluated by someone who has experience in assessing

writing skills, such as a high school or college English teacher. Have the evaluator use the writing sample scoring criteria that are provided on page 22.

6. Assess Areas of Strength and Weakness

After reviewing *The Official TASP Test Study Guide,* identifying and reviewing resources related to the TASP Test skills, and answering and scoring the sample questions provided in this registration bulletin, you should have a fairly good idea of your areas of strength and weakness. Even if you cannot identify specific skill deficiencies, you may at least have a better idea of how much study time you need to set aside to prepare for each section of the test.

7. Take the Pre-TASP Test

Colleges and universities can provide you with an opportunity to take a version of the TASP Test. The Pre-TASP test is similar in difficulty and content coverage to the official TASP Test. While your score on the Pre-TASP test does not count toward the test requirement, you can use the Pre-TASP test as a way of practicing for the official version and to identify areas of potential weakness in the skill areas of reading, mathematics, and writing.

Ask your advisor or other placement counselor about making arrangements to take the Pre-TASP Test.

8. Prepare a Skills Development Plan

Based on steps 1–7 above, your determination of the areas in which you need skill development, and the time available to you before the day of testing, create a skill development plan. Included in this plan could be the following components:

- amount of study time planned for each test section and each skill within a test section,
- schedule for study activities,
- study resources to be used for each section,
- procedures for evaluating progress in developing the test skills, and
- identification of professional staff who can help you to develop these skills.

16

General Strategies to Use When Taking the TASP Test

The following are some general strategies that will help you take the test.

1. Follow Directions Exactly

   Many students make careless errors during a test because they do not follow directions carefully. Therefore, throughout the entire test, follow all spoken and written directions. In your test booklet there will be general directions for the whole test and specific directions for parts of the test. If you do not understand any part of the directions, you should raise your hand and ask your test administrator for assistance.

2. Pace Yourself

   The test schedule is designed to give you time to complete the test. You will have **four hours** to complete the test. If you need additional time, special arrangements can be made to provide you with one more hour of time. You can decide how much time you want to set aside for each section of the test (i.e., reading, mathematics, and writing). You may take one, two, or all three sections at a test administration. You do **not** need to take again any section you have already passed.

   Because you will decide when to move on to the next test section, you need to pace yourself during the entire test. There will be about 150 multiple-choice questions and one writing sample assignment, so you will have to establish a steady pace if you plan to complete all three sections at one administration. If you cannot answer a question right away, skip that question and move on. Make a mark in your test booklet beside the questions you skip so you can return to them later. **Be sure to leave a blank space on your answer sheet for any questions that you skip.**

   For most examinees, it would be a good idea to set aside one hour for the essay-writing part of the test. This probably will provide enough time for you to organize your writing, to write your response, and to review and revise it.

3. Read Carefully

   Read all test questions carefully. You need to select the best answer for each question. **Do not rush.** Choose the answer that seems most reasonable. Read all responses to a question before you choose one.

   The questions are written to be straightforward, not tricky.

4. Mark Answers Carefully

   Your answers for all multiple-choice questions will be scored by computer. For this reason, only one answer should be marked for each question. If you change an answer, erase the old answer completely. Do not make any marks or scribbles on your answer sheet. These marks could possibly alter your test score. You can make notes and marks in your test **booklet**, but your answers must be marked on your answer **sheet**.

   See Table 5 for sample answer sheet spaces and the correct way to record answers.

   Always check that the number of the question you are answering matches the number on your answer sheet.

5. Guess Wisely

   Do your best to choose the best answer for each question. If you have difficulty selecting the best answer, try to rule out responses that you think are clearly wrong, and guess from the remaining responses. You will not lose points for guessing wrong. Your score will be based on the number of questions you answer correctly.

6. Check Accuracy

   Use any time left at the end of the test session to check the accuracy of your answers. Go over the questions that were difficult for you and verify the answers you selected. Go over your answer sheet and make sure that you have marked your answers correctly.

17

Table 5

Sample Answer Sheet Spaces for Recording Answers to Multiple-Choice Test Questions

1 Ⓐ Ⓑ Ⓒ Ⓓ
2 Ⓐ Ⓑ Ⓒ Ⓓ
3 Ⓐ Ⓑ Ⓒ Ⓓ
4 Ⓐ Ⓑ Ⓒ Ⓓ

Incorrect Answer Sheet Marks

Wrong	**Wrong**	**Wrong**	**Wrong**
Ⓐ Ⓑ Ⓧ Ⓓ	Ⓐ Ⓑ ◉ Ⓓ	Ⓐ Ⓑ ✓ Ⓓ	Ⓐ Ⓑ ⊖ Ⓓ

CORRECT Answer Sheet Mark (The mark fills the circle completely)

Right

Ⓐ Ⓑ ● Ⓓ

Suggestions for Being Alert and Ready for the TASP Test

There are several things that you can do to prepare yourself both physically and mentally for taking the test, particularly on the days prior to the test and on the test administration day.

1. Get Adequate Rest

   During the two to three days before the test, try to get a proper amount of sleep. Examinees perform better on tests if they are well rested.

2. Avoid Cramming for the Test

   While it may be helpful to do some reviewing of the test skills during the week before the test, it will probably not help your test performance if you cram, particularly during the two to three days before the test. The tested skills generally represent those that you have learned over many years.

3. Avoid Alcohol or Drug Use

   The use of alcohol or nonprescription drugs during the days before the test may impair your test performance.

4. On the Morning of the Test

   Get up early the morning of the test. Eat a balanced meal before the test. Avoid an excessive intake of foods that could cause discomfort during the test (i.e., coffee). Be sure to gather all materials you will need for the test (i.e., admission ticket, several No. 2 pencils, two forms of identification). Plan to arrive at the testing room one half hour before the test begins so that you will be seated and ready to begin the test when you are instructed to do so.

18

TASP Skill Descriptions

The purpose of the test developed to support the goals of the Texas Academic Skills Program is to assess the reading, mathematics, and writing skills entering freshman-level students should have if they are to perform effectively in undergraduate certificate or degree programs in Texas public colleges or universities. The TASP Test is based on the skills listed below. Each skill is accompanied by a brief description of how the skill may be measured on the test.

TASP Reading Section

General Description

The reading section of the TASP Test consists of approximately ten to twelve reading selections of 300 to 750 words each. The selections represent a variety of subject areas and are similar to reading materials (e.g., textbooks. manuals) that students are likely to encounter during their first year of college. Students will be asked to answer several multiple-choice questions about each reading selection.

Skill Descriptions

The reading section of the TASP Test is based on the skills listed below. Each skill is accompanied by a description of the content that may be included on the test.

Skill: **Determine the meaning of words and phrases.**

Includes using the context of a passage to determine the meaning of words with multiple meanings, unfamiliar and uncommon words and phrases, and figurative expressions.

Skill: **Understand the main idea and supporting details in written material.**

Includes identifying explicit and implicit main ideas and recognizing ideas that support, illustrate, or elaborate the main idea of a passage.

Skill: **Identify a writer's purpose, point of view, and intended meaning.**

Includes recognizing a writer's expressed or implied purpose for writing; evaluating the appropriateness of written material for various purposes or audiences; recognizing the likely effect on an audience of a writer's choice of words; and using the content, word choice, and phrasing of a passage to determine a writer's opinion or point of view.

Skill: **Analyze the relationship among ideas in written material.**

Includes identifying the sequence of events or steps, identifying cause-effect relationships, analyzing relationships between ideas in opposition, identifying solutions to problems, and drawing conclusions inductively and deductively from information stated or implied in a passage.

Skill: **Use critical reasoning skills to evaluate written material.**

Includes evaluating the stated or implied assumptions on which the validity of a writer's argument depends; judging the relevance or importance of facts, examples, or graphic data to a writer's argument; evaluating the logic of a writer's argument; evaluating the validity of analogies; distinguishing between fact and opinion; and assessing the credibility or objectivity of the writer or source of written material.

19

Includes organizing and summarizing information for study purposes; following written instructions or directions; and interpreting information presented in charts, graphs, or tables.

TASP Mathematics Section

General Description

The mathematics section of the TASP Test consists of approximately 50 multiple-choice questions covering three general areas: fundamental mathematics, algebra, and geometry. The test questions focus on a student's ability to perform mathematical operations and solve problems. Appropriate formulas will be provided to help students perform some of the calculations required by the test questions.

Skill Descriptions

The mathematics section of the TASP Test is based on the skills listed below. Each skill is accompanied by a description of the content that may be included on the test.

FUNDAMENTAL MATHEMATICS

Skill: **Use number concepts and computation skills.**

Includes performing operations on fractions, decimals, and integers; using the order of operations to solve problems; solving problems involving percents; performing calculations using exponents and scientific notation; estimating solutions to problems; and using the concepts of "less than" and "greater than."

Skill: **Solve word problems involving integers, fractions, or decimals (including percents, ratios, and proportions).**

Includes determining the appropriate operations to solve word problems and solving word problems involving integers, fractions, decimals, percents, ratios, and proportions.

Skill: **Interpret information from a graph, table, or chart.**

Includes interpreting information in line graphs, bar graphs, pie graphs, pictographs, tables, charts, or graphs of functions.

ALGEBRA

Skill: **Graph numbers or number relationships.**

Includes identifying points from their coordinates, the coordinates of points, or graphs of sets of ordered pairs; identifying the graphs of equations or inequalities; finding the slope and intercept of lines; and recognizing direct and inverse variations presented graphically.

Skill: **Solve one- and two-variable equations.**

Includes finding the value of the unknown in one-variable equations, expressing one variable in terms of a second variable in two-variable equations, and solving a system of two linear equations in two variables.

20

Skill: **Solve word problems involving one and two variables.**

Includes solving word problems that can be translated into one-variable linear equations or pairs of two-variable linear equations and identifying the equation or equations that correctly represent the mathematical relationship(s) in word problems.

Skill: **Understand operations with algebraic expressions.**

Includes factoring quadratics and polynomials; adding, subtracting, and multiplying polynomial expressions; and performing basic operations on and simplifying rational expressions.

Skill: **Solve problems involving quadratic equations.**

Includes graphing quadratic equations, solving word problems involving quadratics, identifying the algebraic equivalent of stated relationships, and solving quadratic equations.

GEOMETRY

Skill: **Solve problems involving geometric figures.**

Includes identifying the appropriate formula for solving geometric problems, solving problems involving two- and three-dimensional geometric figures, and solving problems involving right triangles using the Pythagorean theorem.

Skill: **Apply reasoning skills.**

Includes drawing conclusions using the principles of similarity, congruence, parallelism, and perpendicularity; and using inductive and deductive reasoning.

TASP Writing Section

General Description

The writing section of the TASP Test consists of two parts: a multiple-choice part and a writing sample part. The multiple-choice part will include approximately 40 questions assessing a student's ability to recognize various elements of effective writing. The writing sample part will require students to demonstrate their ability to communicate effectively in writing on a given topic.

Skill Description: Multiple-Choice Part

The multiple-choice part of the writing section of the test is based on the skills listed below. Each skill is accompanied by a description of the content that may be included on the test.

Please note that the term "standard" as it appears below refers to language use that conforms to the conventions of edited American English.

ELEMENTS OF COMPOSITION

Skill: **Recognize purpose and audience.**

Includes recognizing the appropriate purpose, audience, or occasion for a piece of writing; and recognizing writing that is appropriate for various purposes, audiences, or occasions.

Skill: **Recognize unity, focus, and development in writing.**

Includes recognizing unnecessary shifts in point of view or distracting details that impair the development of the main idea in a piece of writing and recognizing revisions that improve the unity and focus of a piece of writing.

21

Skill: Recognize effective organization in writing.

Includes recognizing methods of paragraph organization and the appropriate use of transitional words or phrases to convey text structure, and reorganizing sentences to improve cohesion and the effective sequence of ideas.

SENTENCE STRUCTURE, USAGE, AND MECHANICS

Skill: Recognize effective sentences.

Includes recognizing ineffective repetition and inefficiency in sentence construction; identifying sentence fragments and run-on sentences; identifying standard subject-verb agreement; identifying standard placement of modifiers, parallel structure, and use of negatives in sentence formation; and recognizing imprecise and inappropriate word choice.

Skill: Recognize edited American English usage.

Includes recognizing the standard use of verb forms and pronouns; recognizing the standard formation and use of adverbs, adjectives, comparatives, superlatives, and plural and possessive forms of nouns; and recognizing standard punctuation.

Description: Writing Sample Part

The writing sample part of the TASP Test consists of one writing assignment. Students are asked to prepare a writing sample of about 300 to 600 words on an assigned topic. Students' writing samples are scored on the basis of how effectively they communicate a whole message to a specified audience for a stated purpose. The following characteristics may be considered in scoring the writing samples.

- APPROPRIATENESS—the extent to which the student addresses the topic and uses language and style appropriate to the given audience, purpose, and occasion.

- UNITY AND FOCUS—the clarity with which the student states and maintains a main idea or point of view.

- DEVELOPMENT—the amount, depth, and specificity of supporting detail the student provides.

- ORGANIZATION—the clarity of the student's writing and the logical sequence of the student's ideas.

- SENTENCE STRUCTURE—the effectiveness of the student's sentence structure and the extent to which the student's writing is free of errors in sentence structure.

- USAGE—the extent to which the student's writing is free of errors in usage and shows care and precision in word choice.

- MECHANICAL CONVENTIONS—the student's ability to spell common words and to use the conventions of capitalization and punctuation.

22

Sample Test Questions

Reading Section

DIRECTIONS: Read the passage below and answer the questions that follow.

The Development of Leisure Activities

1   The economic prosperity of the United States during the first hundred years of its history was due in large part to the popular notion that hard work leads to success and happiness. During the late 1800s, however, a number of changes in society, including the development of many laborsaving devices, greatly increased the free time of most workers. As a result Americans developed a new passion for inventing ways to enjoy their leisure time.

2   A wave of interest in organized sports and other athletic pursuits soon swept across the country. In 1876 the National League of Professional Baseball Clubs was founded, making professional baseball a popular spectator sport. Informal baseball games, played in backyards or vacant city lots, were also widely enjoyed. Young boys could even dream of careers as professional baseball players—an option that clearly did not exist before leisure time became a cultural phenomenon. Bicycling also became a fixture of the American recreation scene, especially after the unwieldy "high-wheeler," named for its huge front wheel and tall seat, was replaced by a safer model with two wheels of equal size. The emergence of bicycling as a pastime even eroded the prevailing belief that women were too delicate for strenuous exercise. As they took to their bicycles, women conveyed the message that their physical strength and endurance had long been underestimated.

3   During this period, numerous show business enterprises also became available to help Americans pass their leisure time. Traveling circuses, which had existed since the 1820s, became increasingly popular. Circus entrepreneurs responded to this new demand with sideshows and acts unlike anything circus audiences had seen before. Theater groups also sprung up in cities across the United States. The popular dramas of the day featured predictable plots in which heroes triumphed over villains and virtue was celebrated. Audiences also enjoyed lighthearted musical comedies, vaudeville acts, and comic operas. Although these forms of theatrical entertainment were relatively simple and unsophisticated by today's standards, they provided audiences with the welcome opportunity to escape from their worries and relish their free time.

4   Of all the forms of recreation introduced in the late 1800s, none has retained the broad-based appeal enjoyed by movies. Although the first moving pictures did not attempt to tell a story, the novelty of seeing moving images projected on a screen kept viewers spellbound. Eventually these simple moving pictures gave way to longer story films that used innovative camera techniques and featured professional actors. Movies became such a popular form of entertainment that even many small towns had at least one theater. Since going to a movie merely involved a stroll to the theater, many Americans developed the habit of seeing every movie that came to town. Indeed, the popularity of movies was unrivaled until the 1950s when television, an even more convenient form of entertainment, became widely available.

23

1. Which of the following statements best summarizes the main idea of this selection?

   A. The variety of recreational activities available in the United States is greater than that of any other country.

   B. The main categories of recreational activities in the United States are sports, theatrical performances, and movies.

   C. In response to the increased free time available to them, Americans of the late 1800s developed a variety of new leisure activities.

   D. The history of recreation in the United States indicates that most leisure activities go in and out of fashion rather quickly.

2. This selection suggests that movies have retained a broader base of appeal among Americans than other forms of entertainment because they:

   A. provide people with useful information as well as entertainment.

   B. are more convenient and readily available than many other forms of recreation.

   C. offer people the best form of escape from their worries and problems.

   D. are more likely to appeal to members of both sexes than are other forms of recreation.

3. In this selection, the author assumes that which of the following had to occur before the rapid development of leisure activities could take place in the late 1800s?

   A. People had to develop an interest in organized athletic pursuits.

   B. A number of laborsaving devices had to be developed.

   C. Moving pictures had to gain widespread popularity.

   D. Americans had to gain an appreciation for the value of hard work.

4. What does the word celebrated mean as it is used in the third paragraph of this selection?

   A. praised or extolled

   B. announced or proclaimed

   C. observed with festivities

   D. honored with solemn ceremony

24

Mathematics Section

DIRECTIONS: Choose the correct answer for questions 5 through 9. Do not use calculators or slide rules, as they will not be permitted at the actual test administration.

5. Perform the given operations.

$$\frac{1}{4} \left(\frac{3}{4} \div \frac{3}{5} \right)$$

A. $\frac{1}{5}$

B. $\frac{5}{16}$

C. $1\frac{1}{4}$

D. $1\frac{1}{2}$

6. Use the bar graph below to answer the question that follows.

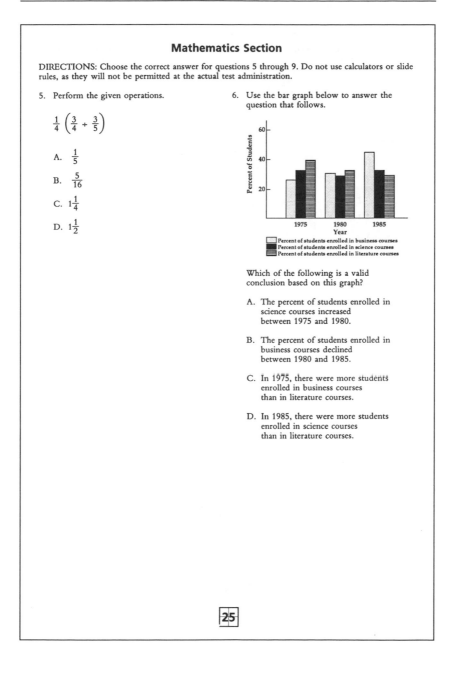

Which of the following is a valid conclusion based on this graph?

A. The percent of students enrolled in science courses increased between 1975 and 1980.

B. The percent of students enrolled in business courses declined between 1980 and 1985.

C. In 1975, there were more students enrolled in business courses than in literature courses.

D. In 1985, there were more students enrolled in science courses than in literature courses.

25

255

7. Use the graph below to answer the question that follows.

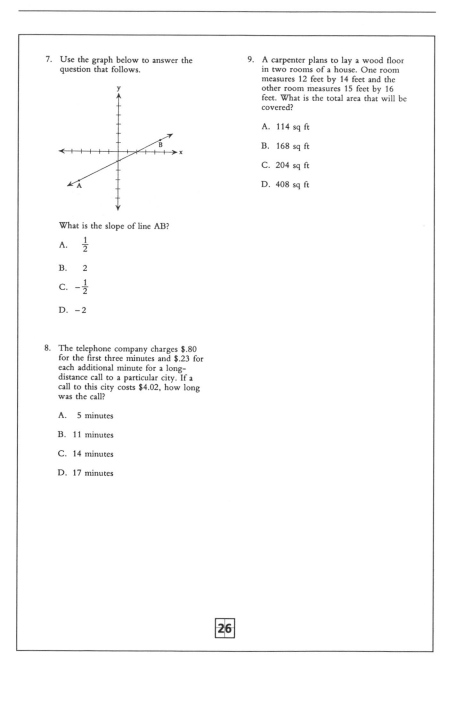

What is the slope of line AB?

A. $\frac{1}{2}$

B. 2

C. $-\frac{1}{2}$

D. -2

8. The telephone company charges $.80 for the first three minutes and $.23 for each additional minute for a long-distance call to a particular city. If a call to this city costs $4.02, how long was the call?

A. 5 minutes

B. 11 minutes

C. 14 minutes

D. 17 minutes

9. A carpenter plans to lay a wood floor in two rooms of a house. One room measures 12 feet by 14 feet and the other room measures 15 feet by 16 feet. What is the total area that will be covered?

A. 114 sq ft

B. 168 sq ft

C. 204 sq ft

D. 408 sq ft

26

Writing Section

Multiple-Choice Questions

DIRECTIONS: Use the passage below, taken from a college history textbook, to answer the questions that follow. The numbers at the beginning of each sentence indicate the parts of the passage referred to in the questions that follow.

[1]It is widely believed that the stock market crash of 1929 caused the Great Depression, but this is inaccurate. [2]Although the crash may have been the first sign of the crisis, the Depression had been building for years.

[3]In the 1920s, the U.S. economy depended on too few industries, mainly construction and automobiles. [4]When these industries began to decline, there was too little strength in other industries to support the economy. [5]Another problem was that purchasing power was not widely distributed among the population. [6]Manufacturers were left with large inventories of unsold goods in they're warehouses. [7]Banks also contributed to the economic crisis. [8]Many of them lent out a lot of money to farmers and other business people whose ability to repay depended on a healthy economy. [9]In addition, many banks had invested recklessly in the stock market during the boom years that preceded the crash. [10]Consequently, when the stock market crashed and, at the same time, their debtors defaulted on their loans, many banks failed.

[11]Thus, serious economic problems were growing beneath the surface of the prosperous 1920s. [12]Problems were building in Europe as well as in America, underlining the interdependence of nations in a world economy. [13]One product of these problems may have been the stock market crash. [14]The major effect was the Great Depression itself.

10. Which one, if any, of the following changes is needed in the above passage?

    A. Part 2: Change "had been building" to "has been building."

    B. Part 6: Change "they're" to "their."

    C. Part 8: Insert a comma after "farmers."

    D. None of these changes is needed.

27

11. Which of the following sentences, if added where indicated in the second paragraph, would be most consistent with the writer's purpose and intended audience?

   A. After Part 4: Such an improvident lack of economic diversification can place any economy, however vigorous initially, in grievous fiscal peril.

   B. After Part 5: More than half of American families were too poor to buy the cars and houses that the industrial economy was producing.

   C. After Part 7: Banks can be pretty greedy, of course, but in this case they got dumb as well and ended up in a real mess.

   D. After Part 10: I urge all American citizens to support measures that will make such a widespread, uncontrollable debt situation an impossibility in the future.

12. Which of the following numbered parts draws attention away from the main idea of the third paragraph?

   A. Part 14

   B. Part 13

   C. Part 12

   D. Part 11

28

Writing Assignment

DIRECTIONS: This part of the sample TASP Test consists of one writing assignment. You are asked to prepare a writing sample of about 300–600 words on an assigned topic. The assignment can be found below. Read the assignment carefully before you begin to write, and think about how you will organize what you plan to say.

Be sure to write about the assigned topic and use multiple paragraphs. Please write legibly. You may not use any reference materials during the test. Remember to review what you have written and make any changes you think will improve your writing.

Some people say modern machines have made our lives better, while others argue that machines are ruling our lives so much that it is hard to maintain our individuality. Write a brief essay to a group of educators, supporting one side of this argument. Use examples to support your argument. Your purpose is to persuade your readers either that machines are generally beneficial and serve humanity or that machines are basically dangerous and dehumanize us.

29

READING SECTION

Question Number	Correct Response	Skill Measured
1	C	Understand the main idea and supporting details in written material.
2	B	Analyze the relationship among ideas in written material.
3	B	Use critical reasoning skills to evaluate written material.
4	A	Determine the meaning of words and phrases.

MATHEMATICS SECTION

5	B	Use number concepts and computation skills.
6	D	Interpret information from a graph, table, or chart.
7	A	Graph numbers or number relationships.
8	D	Solve word problems involving one and two variables.
9	D	Solve problems involving geometric figures.

WRITING SECTION

10	B	Recognize edited American English usage.
11	B	Recognize purpose and audience.
12	C	Recognize unity, focus, and development in writing.

30

Table 6
Codes for Texas High Schools

This table lists all public high schools in Texas. Use this list for completing question number 8 on the registration form. Enter the four-digit number to the left of your high school in the box for number 8 on the registration form and then fill in the corresponding ovals.

The Independent School Districts are listed alphabetically. The Texas public high schools in that district are then listed alphabetically under the name of the district.

The codes for students from private high schools in Texas and from any out-of-state high school appear at the end of this table.

ABBOTT ISD	ANTON ISD	BARBERS HILL ISD	BORDEN COUNTY ISD
1001 Abbott School	1201 Anton HS	1406 Barbers Hill HS	1586 Borden School
ABERNATHY ISD	APPLE SPRINGS ISD	BARTLETT ISD	BORGER ISD
1006 Abernathy HS	1206 Apple Springs HS	1411 Bartlett HS	1591 Borger HS
ABILENE ISD	AQUILLA ISD	BASTROP ISD	BOSQUEVILLE ISD
1011 Abilene HS	1211 Aquilla HS	1416 Bastrop HS	1596 Bosqueville School
1016 Cooper HS	ARANSAS COUNTY ISD	BAY CITY ISD	BOVINA ISD
ACADEMY ISD	1216 Rockport-Fulton HS	1421 Bay City HS	1601 Bovina HS
1021 Academy HS	ARANSAS PASS ISD	BEAUMONT ISD	BOWIE ISD
ADRIAN ISD	1221 Aransas Pass HS	1426 Central Senior HS	1606 Bowie HS
1026 Adrian School	ARCHER CITY ISD	1431 West Brook Sr HS	BOYD ISD
AGUA DULCE ISD	1226 Archer City HS	BECKVILLE ISD	1611 Boyd HS
1031 Agua Dulce HS	ARLINGTON ISD	1436 Beckville HS	BOYS RANCH ISD
ALAMO HEIGHTS ISD	7001 Arlington HS	BEEVILLE ISD	1616 Boys Ranch HS
1036 Alamo Heights HS	1236 Houston HS	1441 Jones HS	BRACKETT ISD
ALBA-GOLDEN ISD	1241 Lamar HS	BELLEVUE ISD	1621 Brackett HS
1041 Alba-Golden HS	1246 Martin HS	1446 Bellevue School	BRADY ISD
ALBANY ISD	ARP ISD	BELLS ISD	1626 Brady HS
1046 Albany Jr-Sr HS	1251 Arp HS	1451 Bells HS	BRAZOSPORT ISD
ALDINE ISD	ASHERTON ISD	BELLVILLE ISD	1631 Brazosport HS
1051 Aldine Contemp Ed Ctr	1256 Asherton HS	1456 Bellville HS	1636 Brazoswood HS
1056 Aldine HS	ASPERMONT ISD	BELTON ISD	BRECKENRIDGE ISD
1061 Chester W. Nimitz HS	1261 Aspermont HS	1461 Belton HS	1641 Breckenridge HS
1066 Eisenhower HS	ATHENS ISD	BEN BOLT-PALITO BLANCO ISD	BREMOND ISD
1071 MacArthur HS	1266 Athens HS	1466 Ben Bolt-Palito Blanco HS	1646 Bremond HS
ALEDO ISD	ATLANTA ISD	BENAVIDES ISD	BRENHAM ISD
1076 Aledo HS	1271 Atlanta HS	1471 Benavides HS	1651 Brenham HS
ALICE ISD	AUBREY ISD	BENJAMIN ISD	BRIDGE CITY ISD
1081 Alice HS	1276 Aubrey HS	1476 Benjamin School	1656 Bridge City HS
ALIEF ISD	AUSTIN ISD	BIG SANDY ISD (Big Sandy)	BRIDGEPORT ISD
1086 Elsik HS-North House	1281 Anderson HS	1486 Big Sandy HS	1661 Bridgeport HS
1091 Elsik HS-South House	1286 Austin HS	BIG SANDY ISD (Livingston)	BRISCOE ISD
1096 Hastings HS North House	1291 Bowie HS	1487 Big Sandy School	1666 Briscoe School
1101 Hastings HS-South House	1296 Crockett HS	BIG SPRING ISD	BROADDUS ISD
ALLEN ISD	1301 F. R. Rice (Rosewood) HS	1491 Big Spring HS	1671 Broaddus School
1106 Allen HS	1306 LBJ HS	BIRDVILLE ISD	BROCK ISD
ALLISON ISD	1311 Johnston HS	1496 Haltom HS	1676 Brock School
1111 Allison HS	1312 Johnston Lib. Arts Mag.	1501 Richland HS	BRONTE ISD
ALPINE ISD	Prog.	BISHOP CONS ISD	1681 Bronte HS
1116 Alpine HS	1316 Lanier HS	1506 Bishop HS	BROOKELAND ISD
ALTO ISD	1321 McCallum HS	BLACKWELL CONS ISD	1686 Brookeland HS
1121 Alto HS	1326 Reagan HS	1511 Blackwell HS	BROOKESMITH ISD
ALVARADO ISD	1331 Science Academy	BLANCO ISD	1691 Brookesmith HS
1126 Alvarado HS	1336 Travis HS	1516 Blanco HS	BROOKS ISD
ALVIN ISD	1341 W. R. Robbins	BLAND ISD	1696 Falfurrias HS
1131 Alvin HS	AUSTWELL-TIVOLI ISD	1521 Bland HS	BROWNFIELD ISD
ALVORD ISD	1346 Austwell-Tivoli HS	BLANKET ISD	1701 Brownfield HS
1136 Alvord HS	AVALON ISD	1526 Blanket HS	BROWNSBORO ISD
AMARILLO ISD	1351 Avalon HS	BLEDSOE ISD	1706 Brownsboro HS
1141 Amarillo HS	AVERY ISD	1531 Bledsoe HS	BROWNSVILLE ISD
1146 Caprock HS	1356 Avery HS	BLOOMBURG ISD	1711 Brownsville-Hanna HS
1151 Palo Duro HS	AVINGER ISD	1536 Bloomburg HS	1716 Brownsville-Pace HS
1156 Tascosa HS	1361 Avinger HS	BLOOMING GROVE ISD	1721 Brownsville-Porter HS
AMHERST ISD	AXTELL ISD	1541 Blooming Grove HS	BROWNWOOD ISD
1161 Amherst HS	1366 Axtell HS	BLOOMINGTON ISD	1726 Brownwood HS
ANAHUAC ISD	AZLE ISD	1546 Bloomington HS	BRUCEVILLE-EDDY ISD
1166 Anahuac HS	1371 Azle HS	BLUE RIDGE ISD	1731 Bruceville-Eddy HS
ANDERSON-SHIRO CONS ISD	BAIRD ISD	1551 Blue Ridge HS	BRYAN ISD
1171 Anderson HS	1376 Baird HS	BLUM ISD	1736 Bryan HS
ANDREWS ISD	BALLINGER ISD	1556 Blum HS	BRYSON ISD
1176 Andrews HS	1381 Ballinger HS	BOERNE ISD	1741 Bryson HS
ANGLETON ISD	BALMORHEA ISD	1561 Boerne HS	BUCKHOLTS ISD
1181 Angleton HS	1386 Balmorhea School	BOLES HOME ISD	1746 Buckholts School
ANNA ISD	BANDERA ISD	1566 Boles Home HS	BUENA VISTA ISD
1186 Anna HS	1391 Bandera HS	BOLING ISD	1751 Buena Vista HS
ANSON ISD	BANGS ISD	1571 Boling HS	BUFFALO ISD
1191 Anson HS	1396 Bangs HS	BONHAM ISD	1756 Buffalo HS
ANTHONY ISD	BANQUETE ISD	1576 Bonham HS	BULLARD ISD
1196 Anthony School	1401 Banquete HS	BOOKER ISD	1761 Bullard HS
		1581 Booker HS	

BUNA ISD
  1766 Buna HS
BURKBURNETT ISD
  1771 Burkburnett HS
BURKEVILLE ISD
  1776 Burkeville Jr-Sr HS
BURLESON ISD
  1781 Burleson HS
BURNET CONS ISD
  1786 Burnet HS
BURTON ISD
  1791 Burton HS
BYERS ISD
  1796 Byers HS
BYNUM ISD
  1801 Bynum School
CADDO MILLS ISD
  1806 Caddo Mills HS
CALALLEN ISD
  1811 Calallen HS
CALDWELL ISD
  1816 Caldwell HS
CALHOUN CO ISD
  1821 Calhoun HS
CALLISBURG ISD
  1826 Callisburg HS
CALVERT ISD
  1831 Calvert HS
CAMERON ISD
  1836 Yoe HS
CAMPBELL ISD
  1841 Campbell HS
CANADIAN ISD
  1846 Canadian HS
CANTON ISD
  1851 Canton HS
CANUTILLO ISD
  1856 Canutillo HS
CANYON ISD
  1861 Canyon HS
  1862 Randall HS
CARBON ISD
  1866 Carbon School
CARLISLE ISD
  1871 Carlisle HS
CARRIZO SPRINGS ISD
  1876 Carrizo Springs HS
CARROLL ISD
  1881 Carroll HS
CARROLLTON-FARMERS BRANCH ISD
  1886 Newman Smith HS
  1891 Turner HS
  1896 Valley View Learning Ctr
CARTHAGE ISD
  1901 Carthage HS
CASTLEBERRY ISD
  1906 Castleberry HS
CAYUGA ISD
  1911 Cayuga HS
CEDAR HILL ISD
  1916 Cedar Hill HS
CELESTE ISD
  1921 Celeste HS
CELINA ISD
  1926 Celina HS
CENTER ISD
  1931 Center HS
CENTER POINT ISD
  1936 Center Point HS
CENTERVILLE ISD (Centerville)
  1941 Centerville Jr-Sr HS
CENTERVILLE ISD (Groveton)
  1946 Centerville HS
CENTRAL HEIGHTS ISD
  1951 Central Heights School
CENTRAL ISD
  1956 Central HS
CHANNELVIEW ISD
  1961 Channelview HS
CHANNING ISD
  1966 Channing HS

CHAPEL HILL ISD
  1971 Chapel Hill HS
CHARLOTTE ISD
  1976 Charlotte HS
CHEROKEE ISD
  1981 Cherokee HS
CHESTER ISD
  1986 Chester HS
CHICO ISD
  1991 Chico HS
CHILDRESS ISD
  1996 Childress HS
CHILLICOTHE ISD
  2001 Chillicothe HS
CHILTON ISD
  2006 Chilton School
CHINA SPRING ISD
  2011 China Spring HS
CHIRENO ISD
  2016 Chireno HS
CHISUM ISD
  2021 Chisum HS
CHRISTOVAL ISD
  2026 Christoval HS
CISCO ISD
  2031 Cisco HS
CLARENDON ISD
  2036 Clarendon HS
CLARKSVILLE ISD
  2041 Clarksville HS
CLAUDE ISD
  2046 Claude School
CLEAR CREEK ISD
  2050 Clear Brook HS
  2051 Clear Creek HS
  2056 Clear Lake HS
CLEBURNE ISD
  2061 Cleburne HS
CLEVELAND ISD
  2066 Cleveland HS
CLIFTON ISD
  2071 Clifton HS
CLINT ISD
  2076 Clint HS
CLYDE ISD
  2081 Clyde HS
COAHOMA ISD
  2086 Coahoma HS
COLDSPRING-OAKHURST ISD
  2091 Jones HS
COLEMAN ISD
  2096 Coleman HS
COLLEGE STATION ISD
  2101 A&M Cons HS
COLLINSVILLE ISD
  2106 Collinsville HS
COLMESNEIL ISD
  2111 Colmesneil HS
COLORADO ISD
  2116 Colorado HS
COLUMBIA-BRAZORIA ISD
  2121 Columbia HS
COLUMBUS ISD
  2126 Columbus HS
COMAL ISD
  2131 Canyon HS
  2136 Smithson Valley HS
COMANCHE ISD
  2141 Comanche HS
COMFORT ISD
  2146 Comfort HS
COMMERCE ISD
  2151 Commerce HS
COMMUNITY ISD
  2156 Community HS
COMO-PICKTON ISD
  2161 Como-Pickton School
COMSTOCK ISD
  2166 Comstock School
CONNALLY ISD
  7006 Connally HS

CONROE ISD
  2176 Conroe HS
  2181 Guidance & Placement Ctr
  2186 McCullough HS
  7011 Oak Ridge HS
COOLIDGE ISD
  2196 Coolidge Schools
COOPER ISD
  2201 Cooper HS
COPPELL ISD
  2206 Coppell HS
COPPERAS COVE ISD
  2211 Copperas Cove HS
CORPUS CHRISTI ISD
  2216 Carroll HS
  2221 King HS
  2226 Miller HS
  2231 Moody HS
  2236 Ray HS
CORRIGAN-CAMDEN ISD
  2241 Corrigan-Camden HS
CORSICANA ISD
  2246 Corsicana HS
COTTON CENTER ISD
  2251 Cotton Center School
COTULLA ISD
  2256 Cotulla HS
COVINGTON ISD
  7016 Covington School
CRANDALL ISD
  2266 Crandall HS
CRANE ISD
  2271 Crane HS
CRANFILLS GAP ISD
  2276 Cranfills Gap School
CRAWFORD ISD
  2281 Crawford HS
CROCKETT CO CONS CSD
  2286 Ozona HS
CROCKETT ISD
  2291 Crockett HS
CROSBY ISD
  2296 Crosby HS
CROSBYTON ISD
  2301 Crosbyton HS
CROSS PLAINS ISD
  2306 Cross Plains HS
CROSS ROADS ISD
  7021 Cross Roads HS
CROWELL ISD
  2316 Crowell HS
CROWLEY ISD
  2321 Crowley HS
CRYSTAL CITY ISD
  2326 Crystal City HS
CUERO ISD
  2331 Cuero HS
CULBERSON COUNTY ISD
  2336 Van Horn HS
CUMBY ISD
  7026 Cumby HS
CUSHING ISD
  2346 Cushing School
CYPRESS-FAIRBANKS ISD
  2351 Cy-Fair HS
  2356 Cypress Creek HS
  2361 Jersey Village HS
  2366 Langham Creek HS
D'HANIS ISD
  2371 D'Hanis School
DAINGERFIELD-LONE STAR ISD
  2376 Daingerfield HS
DALHART ISD
  2381 Dalhart HS
DALLAS ISD
  2391 Adams HS
  2396 Adamson HS
  2386 A. Maceo Smith HS
  2401 Arts Magnet HS
  2406 Business & Mgmt Center
  2411 Carter HS
  2416 Educ & Social Serv Magnet

DALLAS ISD (cont.)
  2421 Health Professions Magnet
  2426 Hillcrest HS
  2431 Hospital/Home-Bound
  2436 Jefferson HS
  2441 Kimball HS
  2446 Lincoln HS
  2447 Lincoln Hum./Comm.
       Magnet
  2451 Madison HS
  2456 Mag Ctr-Pub Serv:
       Govt/Law
  2461 Metropolitan HS
  2462 Multiple Careers Magnet
  2466 North Dallas HS
  2471 Pinkston HS
  2476 Roosevelt HS
  2477 Science Technology Magnet
  2481 Seagoville HS
  2486 Skyline HS
  2491 South Oak Cliff HS
  2496 Spruce HS
  2501 Sunset HS
  2506 Tag Magnet
  2511 W. W. Samuell HS
  2516 Walker Sp Ed Ctr
  2521 White HS
  2526 Wilson HS
DANBURY ISD
  2531 Danbury HS
DARROUZETT ISD
  2536 Darrouzett School
DAWSON ISD (DAWSON)
  2541 Dawson HS
DAWSON ISD (WELCH)
  2546 Dawson HS
DAYTON ISD
  2551 Dayton HS
DE LEON ISD
  2556 De Leon HS
DE SOTO ISD
  2561 De Soto HS
DECATUR ISD
  2566 Decatur HS
DEER PARK ISD
  2571 Deer Park HS
DEKALB ISD
  2576 Dekalb HS
DEL VALLE ISD
  2581 Del Valle HS
DELL CITY ISD
  2586 Dell City School
DENISON ISD
  2591 Denison HS
DENTON ISD
  2596 Denton HS
DENVER CITY ISD
  2601 Denver City HS
DETROIT ISD
  2606 Detroit Jr-Sr HS
DEVINE ISD
  2611 Devine HS
DEWEYVILLE ISD
  2616 Deweyville HS
DIBOLL ISD
  2621 Diboll HS
DICKINSON ISD
  2626 Dickinson HS
DILLEY ISD
  2631 Dilley HS
DIME BOX ISD
  2636 Dime Box School
DIMMITT ISD
  2641 Dimmitt HS
DODD CITY ISD
  2646 Dodd City School
DONNA ISD
  2651 Donna HS
DOUGLASS ISD
  2656 Douglass HS
DRIPPING SPRINGS ISD
  2661 Dripping Springs HS

DUBLIN ISD
  2666 Dublin HS
DUMAS ISD
  2671 Dumas HS
DUNCANVILLE ISD
  2676 Duncanville HS
EAGLE MT-SAGINAW ISD
  2681 Boswell HS
EAGLE PASS ISD
  2686 Eagle Pass HS
EANES ISD
  2691 Westlake HS
EARLY ISD
  2696 Early HS
EAST BERNARD ISD
  2701 East Bernard HS
EAST CENTRAL ISD
  2706 East Central HS
EAST CHAMBERS ISD
  2711 East Chambers HS
EASTLAND ISD
  2716 Eastland HS
ECTOR COUNTY ISD
  2721 Odessa HS
  2726 Permian HS
ECTOR ISD
  2731 Ector School
EDCOUCH-ELSA ISD
  2736 Edcouch-Elsa HS
EDEN CONS ISD
  2741 Eden School
EDGEWOOD ISD (Edgewood)
  2746 Edgewood HS
EDGEWOOD ISD (San Antonio)
  2751 Edgewood HS
  2756 Kennedy HS
  2761 Memorial HS
EDINBURG ISD
  2766 Edinburg HS
EDNA ISD
  2771 Edna HS
EL CAMPO ISD
  2776 El Campo HS
EL PASO ISD
  2781 Andress HS
  2786 Austin HS
  2791 Bowie HS
  2796 Burges HS
  2801 Coronado HS
  2806 El Paso HS
  2811 Irvin HS
  2816 Jefferson HS
ELECTRA ISD
  2821 Electra HS
ELGIN ISD
  2826 Elgin HS
ELKHART ISD
  2831 Elkhart HS
ELYSIAN FIELDS ISD
  2836 Elysian Fields HS
ENNIS ISD
  2841 Ennis HS
ERA ISD
  2846 Era School
EULA ISD
  2851 Eula HS
EUSTACE ISD
  2856 Eustace HS
EVADALE ISD
  2861 Evadale HS
EVANT ISD
  2866 Evant HS
EVERMAN ISD
  2871 Everman HS
FABENS ISD
  2876 Fabens HS
FAIRFIELD ISD
  2881 Fairfield HS
FALLS CITY ISD
  2886 Falls City HS
FANNINDEL ISD
  2891 Fannindel HS

FARMERSVILLE ISD
  2896 Farmersville HS
FARWELL ISD
  2901 Farwell HS
FAYETTEVILLE ISD
  2906 Fayetteville HS
FERRIS ISD
  2911 Ferris HS
FLATONIA ISD
  2916 Flatonia HS
FLORENCE ISD
  2921 Florence HS
FLORESVILLE ISD
  2926 Floresville HS
FLOUR BLUFF ISD
  2931 Flour Bluff HS
FLOYDADA ISD
  2936 Floydada HS
FOLLETT ISD
  2941 Follett School
FORESTBURG ISD
  2946 Forestburg HS
FORNEY ISD
  2951 Forney HS
FORSAN ISD
  2956 Forsan HS
FORT BEND ISD
  2961 Clements HS
  2966 Dulles HS
  2967 Kempner HS
  2971 Willowridge HS
FORT WORTH ISD
  2976 Arlington Heights HS
  2981 B. H. Carroll HS
  2986 Carter-Riverside HS
  2991 Diamond Hill HS
  2996 Dunbar HS
  3001 Eastern Hills HS
  3006 Metro Opportunity School
  3011 North Side HS
  3016 O. D. Wyatt HS
  3021 Paschal HS
  3026 Polytechnic HS
  3031 Southwest HS
  3036 Trimble Technical HS
  3041 Western Hills HS
FRANKLIN ISD
  3046 Franklin HS
FRANKSTON ISD
  3051 Frankston School
FREDERICKSBURG ISD
  3056 Fredericksburg HS
FREER ISD
  3061 Freer HS
FRENSHIP ISD
  3066 Frenship HS
FRIENDSWOOD ISD
  3071 Friendswood HS
FRIONA ISD
  3076 Friona HS
FRISCO ISD
  3081 Frisco HS
FROST ISD
  3086 Frost HS
FRUITVALE ISD
  3091 Fruitvale HS
FT DAVIS ISD
  3096 Ft Davis HS
  3101 High Frontier HS
FT HANCOCK ISD
  3106 Fort Hancock School
FT SAM HOUSTON ISD
  7031 Cole HS
FT STOCKTON ISD
  3116 Fort Stockton HS
GAINESVILLE ISD
  3121 Gainesville HS
GALENA PARK ISD
  3126 Galena Park HS
  7036 North Shore HS
GALVESTON ISD
  3136 Ball HS
  7041 Special Centers

GANADO ISD
  3146 Ganado HS
GARLAND ISD
  7046 GISD Evening School
  3156 Garland HS
  3161 Lakeview Centennial HS
  3166 N Garland HS
  3171 S Garland HS
GARRISON ISD
  3176 Garrison HS
GARY ISD
  3181 Gary School
GATESVILLE ISD
  3186 Gatesville HS
GEORGE WEST ISD
  3191 George West HS
GEORGETOWN ISD
  3196 Georgetown HS
GIDDINGS ISD
  3201 Giddings HS
GILMER ISD
  3206 Gilmer HS
GLADEWATER ISD
  7051 Gladewater HS
GLASSCOCK ISD
  3216 Glasscock County HS
GLEN ROSE ISD
  7056 Glen Rose HS
GODLEY ISD
  3226 Godley HS
GOLDBURG ISD
  3231 Stone Burg HS
GOLDTHWAITE ISD
  3236 Goldthwaite HS
GOLIAD ISD
  7061 Goliad HS
GONZALES ISD
  3246 Gonzales HS
GOODRICH ISD
  7066 Goodrich HS
GOOSE CREEK ISD
  3256 Lee HS
  3261 Sterling HS
GORDON ISD
  3266 Gordon HS
GOREE ISD
  3271 Goree School
GORMAN ISD
  3276 Gorman HS
GRADY ISD
  3281 Grady School
GRAFORD ISD
  3286 Graford School
GRAHAM ISD
  7071 Graham HS
GRANBURY ISD
  3296 Granbury HS
GRAND PRAIRIE ISD
  3301 Grand Prairie HS
  3306 So Grand Prairie HS
GRAND SALINE ISD
  3311 Grand Saline HS
GRANDFALLS-ROYALTY ISD
  3316 Grandfalls-Royalty HS
GRANDVIEW ISD
  3321 Grandview HS
GRANGER ISD
  3326 Granger HS
GRAPELAND ISD
  3331 Grapeland HS
GRAPEVINE-COLLEYVILLE ISD
  3336 Grapevine HS
GREENVILLE ISD
  3341 Greenville HS
GREENWOOD ISD
  3346 Greenwood School
GREGORY-PORTLAND ISD
  3351 Gregory-Portland HS
GROESBECK ISD
  3356 Groesbeck HS
GROOM ISD
  7076 Groom School

GROVETON ISD
  3366 Groveton JH-HS
GRUVER ISD
  7081 Gruver HS
GUNTER ISD
  3376 Gunter HS
GUSTINE ISD
  3381 Gustine School
GUTHRIE ISD
  3386 Guthrie School
HALE CENTER ISD
  3391 Hale Center HS
HALLETTSVILLE ISD
  3396 Hallettsville HS
HALLSVILLE ISD
  7086 Hallsville HS
HAMILTON ISD
  3406 Hamilton HS
HAMLIN ISD
  3411 Hamlin HS
HAMSHIRE-FANNETT ISD
  3416 Hamshire-Fannett HS
HAPPY ISD
  3421 Happy HS
HARDIN ISD
  3426 Hardin HS
HARDIN-JEFFERSON ISD
  3431 Hardin-Jefferson HS
HARLANDALE ISD
  3436 Harlandale HS
  3441 McCollum HS
HARLETON ISD
  3446 Harleton Jr-Sr HS
HARLINGEN ISD
  3451 Harlingen HS
HARMONY ISD
  3456 Harmony HS
HARPER ISD
  3461 Harper School
HARROLD ISD
  3466 Harrold School
HART ISD
  3471 Hart Jr-Sr HS
HARTLEY ISD
  3476 Hartley School
HASKELL ISD
  3481 Haskell HS
HAWKINS ISD
  3486 Hawkins HS
HAWLEY ISD
  3491 Hawley HS
HAYS CONS ISD
  3496 Jack C. Hays HS
HEARNE ISD
  3501 Hearne HS
HEDLEY ISD
  3506 Hedley School
HEMPHILL ISD
  3511 Hemphill HS
HEMPSTEAD ISD
  3516 Hempstead HS
HENDERSON ISD
  3521 Henderson HS
HENRIETTA ISD
  3526 Henrietta HS
HEREFORD ISD
  3531 Hereford HS
HERMLEIGH ISD
  3536 Hermleigh School
HICO ISD
  3541 Hico School
HIDALGO ISD
  3546 Hidalgo HS
HIGGINS ISD
  3551 Higgins School
HIGH ISLAND ISD
  3556 High Island HS
HIGHLAND ISD
  3561 Highland HS
HIGHLAND PARK ISD (Amarillo)
  3566 Highland Park HS

33

HIGHLAND PARK ISD (Dallas)	IOWA PARK CONS ISD	KINGSVILLE ISD	LEON ISD
3571 Highland Park HS	3851 Iowa Park HS	4071 King HS	4291 Leon HS
HILLSBORO ISD	IRA ISD	KIRBYVILLE ISD	LEONARD ISD
3576 Hillsboro HS	3856 Ira School	4076 Kirbyville HS	4296 Leonard HS
HITCHCOCK ISD	IRAAN-SHEFFIELD ISD	KLEIN ISD	LEVELLAND ISD
3581 Hitchcock HS	3861 Iraan HS	4081 Klein Forest HS	4301 Levelland HS
HOLLAND ISD	IREDELL ISD	4086 Klein HS	LEVERETTS CHAPEL ISD
3586 Holland HS	3866 Iredell School	4091 Klein Oak HS	4306 Leveretts Chapel School
HOLLIDAY ISD	IRION CO ISD	KLONDIKE ISD	LEWISVILLE ISD
3591 Holliday HS	3871 Irion HS	4096 Klondike HS	4311 Lewisville HS
HONDO ISD	IRVING ISD	KNIPPA ISD	4316 Marcus HS
3596 Hondo HS	3876 Irving HS	4101 Knippa School	4321 The Colony HS
HONEY GROVE CONSOLIDATED ISD	3881 MacArthur HS	KNOX CITY-O'BRIEN ISD	LEXINGTON ISD
3601 Honey Grove HS	3886 Mega HS	4106 Knox City HS	4326 Lexington HS
HOOKS ISD	3891 Nimitz HS	KOPPERL ISD	LIBERTY HILL ISD
3606 Hooks HS	ITALY ISD	4111 Kopperl School	4331 Liberty Hill HS
HOUSTON ISD	3896 Italy HS	KOUNTZE ISD	LIBERTY ISD
3611 Austin HS	ITASCA ISD	4116 Kountze HS	4336 Liberty HS
3616 Barbara Jordan HS	3901 Itasca HS	KRESS ISD	LIBERTY-EYLAU ISD
3621 Bellaire HS	JACKSBORO ISD	4121 Kress HS	4341 Liberty-Eylau HS
3626 Contemporary Lrn Cntr HS	3906 Jacksboro HS	KRUM ISD	LINDALE ISD
3627 Foley's Academy	JACKSONVILLE ISD	4126 Krum HS	4346 Lindale HS
3631 Davis HS	3911 Jacksonville HS	LA FERIA ISD	LINDEN-KILDARE ISD
3636 Furr HS	JARRELL ISD	4131 La Feria HS	4351 Linden-Kildare HS
3641 H. P. Carter	3916 Jarrell HS	LA GRANGE ISD	LINDSAY ISD
3646 Health Professions HS	JASPER ISD	4136 La Grange HS	4356 Lindsay HS
3651 Jones HS	3921 Jasper HS	LA JOYA ISD	LINGLEVILLE ISD
3656 Kashmere HS	JAYTON-GIRARD ISD	4141 La Joya HS	4361 Lingleville School
3661 Lamar HS	3926 Jayton HS	LA MARQUE ISD	LIPAN ISD
3666 Law Enfcrmt-Crim Just HS	JEFFERSON ISD	4146 La Marque HS	4366 Lipan School
3671 Lee HS	3931 Jefferson HS	LA PORTE ISD	LITTLE CYPRESS-MAURICEVILLE ISD
3676 Madison HS	JIM HOGG COUNTY ISD	4151 La Porte HS	4371 Little Cypress-
3681 Milby HS	3936 Hebbronville HS	LA POYNOR ISD	Mauriceville HS
3686 Night HS	JIM NED ISD	4156 La Poynor HS	LITTLE ELM ISD
3691 On-Going Education Ctr	3941 Jim Ned HS	LA PRYOR ISD	4376 Little Elm HS
3696 Perfor & Vis Arts HS	JOAQUIN ISD	7096 La Pryor HS	LITTLEFIELD ISD
3701 Reagan HS	3946 Joaquin HS	4166 Michelle HS	4381 Littlefield HS
3706 Sam Houston HS	JOHNSON CITY ISD	LA VEGA ISD	LIVINGSTON ISD
3711 Scarborough HS	3951 Johnson City HS	4171 La Vega HS	4386 Livingston HS
3716 Sharpstown HS	JONESBORO ISD	LA VERNIA ISD	LLANO ISD
3721 Sterling HS	3956 Jonesboro School	4176 La Vernia HS	4391 Llano HS
3726 Waltrip HS	JOSHUA ISD	LA VILLA ISD	LOCKHART ISD
3731 Washington B T H S	3961 Joshua HS	4181 La Villa HS	4396 Lockhart HS
3736 Westbury HS	JOURDANTON ISD	LACKLAND ISD	LOCKNEY ISD
3741 Wheatley HS	3966 Jourdanton HS	4186 Lackland Jr-Sr HS	4401 Lockney HS
3746 Worthing HS	JUDSON ISD	LAGO VISTA ISD	LOHN ISD
3751 Yates HS	3971 Judson HS	4191 Lago Vista HS	4406 Lohn HS
HOWE ISD	JUNCTION ISD	LAKE DALLAS ISD	LOMETA ISD
3756 Howe HS	3976 Junction HS	4196 Lake Dallas HS	4411 Lometa School
HUBBARD ISD (Hubbard)	KARNACK ISD	LAKE TRAVIS ISD	LONE OAK ISD
3761 Hubbard HS	3981 Karnack ISD	4201 Lake Travis HS	4416 Lone Oak HS
HUCKABAY ISD	KARNES CITY ISD	LAKE WORTH ISD	LONGVIEW ISD
3766 Huckabay HS	3986 Karnes City HS	4206 Lake Worth HS	4421 Longview HS
HUDSON ISD	KATY ISD	LAKEVIEW ISD	LOOP ISD
3771 Hudson HS	3991 Katy HS	4211 Lakeview HS	4426 Loop School
HUFFMAN ISD	3996 Mayde Creek HS	LAMAR CONSOLIDATED ISD	LORAINE ISD
3776 Hargrave HS	7091 Taylor HS	4216 Lamar Cons HS	4431 Loraine School
HUGHES SPRINGS ISD	KAUFMAN ISD	4221 Terry HS	LORENA ISD
3781 Hughes Springs HS	4006 Kaufman HS	LAMESA ISD	4436 Lorena HS
HULL-DAISETTA ISD	KELLER ISD	4226 Lamesa HS	LORENZO ISD
3786 Hull-Daisetta HS	4011 Keller HS	LAMPASAS ISD	4441 Lorenzo HS
HUMBLE ISD	KELTON ISD	4231 Lampasas HS	LOS FRESNOS CISD
3791 Humble HS	4016 Kelton School	LANCASTER ISD	4446 Los Fresnos HS
3796 Kingwood HS	KEMP ISD	4236 Lancaster HS	LOUISE ISD
HUNTINGTON ISD	4021 Kemp HS	LANEVILLE ISD	4451 Louise School
3801 Huntington HS	KENEDY ISD	4241 Laneville HS	LOVELADY ISD
HUNTSVILLE ISD	4026 Kenedy HS	LAREDO ISD	4456 Lovelady HS
3806 Huntsville HS	KENNARD ISD	4246 Dr. Leo Cigarroa HS	LUBBOCK ISD
HURST-EULESS-BEDFORD ISD	4031 Kennard HS	4251 Martin HS	4461 Coronado HS
3811 Bell HS	KENNEDALE ISD	4256 Nixon HS	4466 Dunbar-Struggs HS
3816 Trinity HS	4036 Kennedale HS	LATEXO ISD	4471 Estacado HS
HUTTO ISD	KERENS ISD	4261 Latexo HS	4476 Homebound
3821 Hutto HS	4041 Kerens School	LAZBUDDIE ISD	4481 Lubbock HS
IDALOU ISD	KERMIT ISD	4266 Lazbuddie School	4486 Monterey HS
3826 Idalou HS	4046 Kermit HS	LEAKEY ISD	4491 New Directions
INDUSTRIAL ISD	KERRVILLE ISD	4271 Leakey School	4496 Project Intercept School
3831 Industrial HS	4051 Tivy HS	LEANDER ISD	LUBBOCK-COOPER ISD
INGLESIDE ISD	KILGORE ISD	4276 Leander HS	4501 Cooper HS
3836 Ingleside HS	4056 Kilgore HS	LEFORS ISD	LUEDERS-AVOCA ISD
INGRAM ISD	KILLEEN ISD	4281 Lefors HS	4506 Avoca HS
3841 Ingram-Tom Moore HS	4061 Ellison HS	LEGGETT ISD	LUFKIN ISD
IOLA ISD	4066 Killeen HS	4286 Leggett HS	4511 Lufkin HS
3846 Iola HS			

34

LULING ISD
4516 Luling HS
LUMBERTON ISD
4521 Lumberton HS
LYFORD ISD
4526 Lyford HS
LYTLE ISD
4531 Lytle HS
MABANK ISD
4536 Mabank HS
MADISONVILLE CISD
4541 Madisonville HS
MAGNOLIA ISD
4546 Magnolia HS
MALAKOFF ISD
4551 Malakoff HS
MANOR ISD
4556 Manor HS
MANSFIELD ISD
4561 Mansfield HS
MARATHON ISD
4566 Marathon HS
MARBLE FALLS ISD
4571 Marble Falls HS
MARFA ISD
4576 Marfa HS
MARION ISD
4581 Marion HS
MARLIN ISD
4586 Marlin HS
MARSHALL ISD
4591 Marshall HS
4596 Pemberton HS
MART ISD
4601 Mart HS
MARTINS MILL ISD
4606 Martins Mill HS
MARTINSVILLE ISD
4611 Martinsville School
MASON ISD
4616 Mason HS
MASONIC HOME ISD
4621 Masonic Home School
MATHIS ISD
4626 Mathis HS
MAUD ISD
4631 Maud School
MAY ISD
4636 May HS
MAYDELLE ISD
4641 Maydelle HS
MAYPEARL ISD
4646 Maypearl Jr-Sr HS
MCALLEN ISD
4651 McAllen HS
4656 McAllen Memorial HS
MCCAMEY ISD
4661 McCamey HS
MCGREGOR ISD
4666 McGregor HS
MCKINNEY ISD
4671 McKinney HS
MCLEAN ISD
4676 McLean School
MCLEOD ISD
4681 McLeod HS
MCMULLEN ISD
4686 McMullen Co School
MEADOW ISD
4691 Meadow School
MEDINA ISD
4696 Medina School
MEDINA VALLEY ISD
4701 Medina Valley HS
MEGARGEL ISD
4706 Megargel HS
MEMPHIS ISD
4711 Memphis HS
MENARD ISD
4716 Menard HS
MERCEDES ISD
4721 Mercedes HS

MERIDIAN ISD
4726 Meridian School
MERKEL ISD
4731 Merkel HS
MESQUITE ISD
4736 Mesquite HS
4741 North Mesquite HS
4742 Ralph H. Poteet HS
4746 West Mesquite HS
MEXIA ISD
4751 Mexia HS
MIAMI ISD
4756 Miami School
MIDLAND ISD
4761 Lee HS
4766 Midland HS
MIDLOTHIAN ISD
4771 Midlothian HS
MIDWAY ISD (Henrietta)
4776 Midway School
MIDWAY ISD (Waco)
4781 Midway HS
MILANO ISD
4786 Milano HS
MILDRED ISD
4791 Mildred HS
MILES ISD
4796 Miles HS
MILFORD ISD
4801 Milford School
MILLER GROVE ISD
4806 Miller Grove School
MILLSAP ISD
4811 Millsap HS
MINEOLA ISD
4816 Mineola HS
MINERAL WELLS ISD
4821 Mineral Wells HS
MIRANDO CITY ISD
4826 Mirando HS
MISSION ISD
4831 Mission HS
MOBEETIE ISD
4836 Mobeetie School
MONAHANS-WICKETT-PYOTE ISD
4841 Monahans HS
MONTGOMERY ISD
4846 Montgomery HS
MOODY ISD
4851 Moody HS
MORAN ISD
4856 Moran HS
MORGAN ISD
4861 Morgan School
MORTON ISD
4866 Morton HS
MOTLEY COUNTY ISD
4871 Motley County HS
MOULTON ISD
4876 Moulton HS
MOUNT ENTERPRISE ISD
4881 Mount Enterprise HS
MOUNT PLEASANT ISD
4886 Mount Pleasant HS
MOUNT VERNON ISD
4891 Mt Vernon HS
MUENSTER ISD
4896 Muenster HS
MULESHOE ISD
4901 Muleshoe HS
MULLIN ISD
4906 Mullin School
MUNDAY ISD
4911 Munday HS
NACOGDOCHES ISD
4916 Nacogdoches HS
NATALIA ISD
4921 Natalia HS
NAVARRO ISD
4926 Navarro HS
NAVASOTA ISD
4931 Navasota HS

NAZARETH ISD
4936 Nazareth School
NECHES ISD
4941 Neches HS
NEDERLAND ISD
4946 Nederland HS
NEEDVILLE ISD
4951 Needville HS
NEW BOSTON ISD
4956 New Boston HS
NEW BRAUNFELS ISD
4961 New Braunfels HS
NEW CANEY ISD
4966 New Caney HS
NEW DEAL ISD
4971 New Deal HS
NEW DIANA ISD
4976 New Diana HS
NEW HOME ISD
4981 New Home HS
NEW SUMMERFIELD ISD
4986 New Summerfield School
NEW WAVERLY ISD
4991 New Waverly HS
NEWCASTLE ISD
4996 Newcastle HS
NEWTON ISD
5001 Newton HS
NIXON-SMILEY ISD
5006 Nixon-Smiley HS
NOCONA ISD
5011 Nocona HS
NORDHEIM ISD
5016 Nordheim School
NORMANGEE ISD
5021 Normangee HS
NORTH EAST ISD
5026 Churchill HS
5031 Lee HS
5036 MacArthur HS
5041 Madison HS
5046 Roosevelt HS
NORTH FOREST ISD
5051 Forest Brook HS
5056 Smiley HS
NORTH HOPKINS ISD
5061 North Hopkins HS
NORTH LAMAR ISD
5066 Frank Stone HS
NORTH ZULCH ISD
5071 North Zulch HS
NORTHSIDE ISD (San Antonio)
5076 Health Careers HS
5081 Holmes HS
5086 Jay HS
5091 Marshall HS
5101 Tom Clark HS
5106 William H. Taft HS
NORTHSIDE ISD (Vernon)
5105 Northside School
NORTHWEST ISD
5111 Northwest HS
NOVICE ISD
5116 Novice School
NUECES CANYON ISD
5121 Nueces Canyon HS
O'DONNELL ISD
5126 O'Donnell HS
OAKWOOD ISD
5131 Oakwood HS
ODEM-EDROY ISD
5136 Odem HS
OGLESBY ISD
5141 Oglesby HS
OLNEY ISD
5146 Olney HS
OLTON ISD
5151 Olton HS
ORANGE GROVE ISD
5156 Orange Grove HS
ORANGEFIELD ISD
5161 Orangefield HS

ORE CITY ISD
5166 Ore City HS
OVERTON ISD
5171 Overton HS
PADUCAH ISD
5176 Paducah HS
PAINT ROCK ISD
5181 Paint Rock School
PAINT CREEK ISD
5186 Paint Creek School
PALACIOS ISD
5191 Palacios HS
PALESTINE ISD
5196 Palestine HS
PALMER ISD
5201 Palmer HS
PAMPA ISD
5206 Pampa HS
PANHANDLE ISD
5211 Panhandle HS
PANTHER CREEK CONS ISD
5216 Panther Creek HS
PARADISE ISD
5221 Paradise HS
PARIS ISD
5226 Paris HS
PASADENA ISD
5231 Dobie HS
5236 Pasadena HS
5241 Rayburn HS
5246 South Houston HS
PATTON SPRINGS ISD
5251 Patton Springs HS
PEARLAND ISD
5256 Pearland HS
PEARSALL ISD
5261 Pearsall HS
PEASTER ISD
5266 Peaster School
PECOS-BARSTOW-TOYAH ISD
5271 Pecos HS
PENELOPE ISD
5276 Penelope School
PERRIN-WHITT CISD
5281 Perrin HS
PERRYTON ISD
5286 Perryton HS
PETERSBURG ISD
5291 Petersburg HS
PETROLIA ISD
5296 Petrolia School
PETTUS ISD
5301 Pettus HS
PEWITT ISD
5306 Pewitt HS
PFLUGERVILLE ISD
5311 Pflugerville HS
PHARR-SAN JUAN-ALAMO ISD
5316 Pharr-San Juan-Alamo HS
PILOT POINT ISD
5321 J. Earl Selz HS
PINE TREE ISD
5326 Pine Tree HS
PITTSBURG ISD
5331 Pittsburg HS
PLAINS ISD
5336 Plains HS
PLAINVIEW ISD
5341 Plainview HS
PLANO ISD
5346 Plano East Sr HS
5351 Plano Sr HS
PLEASANT GROVE ISD
5356 Pleasant Grove HS
PLEASANTON ISD
5361 Pleasanton HS
PLEMONS-STINNETT-PHILLIPS CISD
5366 West Texas HS
POINT ISABEL ISD
5371 Point Isabel HS
PONDER ISD
5376 Ponder HS

POOLVILLE ISD
  5381 Poolville School
PORT ARANSAS ISD
  5386 Port Aransas HS
PORT ARTHUR ISD
  5391 Austin HS
  5396 Jefferson HS
  5401 Lamar
  5406 Lincoln HS
  5411 Stilwell Technical Center
PORT NECHES ISD
  5416 Port Neches-Groves HS
POST ISD
  5421 Post HS
POTEET ISD
  5426 Poteet HS
POTH ISD
  5431 Poth HS
POTTSBORO ISD
  5436 Pottsboro HS
POTTSVILLE ISD
  5441 Pottsville School
PRAIRIE LEA ISD
  5446 Prairie Lea HS
PRAIRIE VALLEY ISD
  5451 Prairie Valley
PRAIRILAND ISD
  5456 Prairiland HS
PREMONT ISD
  5461 Premont HS
PRESIDIO ISD
  5466 Presidio HS
PRIDDY ISD
  5471 Priddy School
PRINCETON ISD
  5476 Princeton HS
PROGRESO ISD
  5481 Progreso HS
PROSPER ISD
  5486 Prosper HS
QUANAH ISD
  5491 Quanah HS
QUEEN CITY ISD
  5496 Queen City HS
QUINLAN ISD
  5501 Ford HS
QUITMAN ISD
  5506 Quitman HS
RAINS ISD
  5511 Rains HS
RALLS ISD
  5516 Ralls HS
RANDOLPH FIELD ISD
  5521 Randolph Jr-Sr HS
RANGER ISD
  5526 Ranger HS
RANKIN ISD
  5531 Rankin HS
RAYMONDVILLE ISD
  5536 Raymondville HS
REAGAN ISD
  5541 Reagan HS
RED OAK ISD
  5546 Red Oak HS
REDWATER ISD
  5551 Redwater HS
REFUGIO ISD
  5556 Refugio HS
RICE CONS ISD
  5561 Rice HS
RICHARDS ISD
  5566 Richards HS
RICHARDSON ISD
  5571 Berkner HS
  5572 District HS
  5576 Lake Highlands HS
  5581 Pearce HS
  5586 Richardson HS
RICHLAND SPRINGS ISD
  5591 Richland Springs School
RIESEL ISD
  5596 Riesel School

RIO GRANDE CITY ISD
  5601 Rio Grande City HS
RIO HONDO ISD
  5606 Rio Hondo HS
RIO VISTA ISD
  5611 Rio Vista HS
RISING STAR ISD
  5616 Rising Star HS
RIVER ROAD ISD
  5621 River Road Jr-Sr HS
RIVIERA ISD
  5626 Kaufer HS
ROBERT LEE ISD
  5631 Robert Lee School
ROBINSON ISD
  5636 Robinson HS
ROBSTOWN ISD
  5641 Robstown HS
ROBY ISD
  5646 Roby HS
ROCHELLE ISD
  5651 Rochelle School
ROCHESTER ISD
  5656 Rochester HS
ROCKDALE ISD
  5661 Rockdale HS
ROCKSPRINGS ISD
  5666 Rocksprings HS
ROCKWALL ISD
  5671 Rockwall HS
ROGERS ISD
  5676 Rogers HS
ROMA ISD
  5681 Roma HS
ROOSEVELT ISD
  5686 Roosevelt HS
ROPES ISD
  5691 Ropes HS
ROSCOE ISD
  5696 Roscoe HS
ROSEBUD-LOTT ISD
  5701 Rosebud-Lott HS
ROTAN ISD
  5706 Rotan HS
ROUND ROCK ISD
  5711 Round Rock HS
  5716 Westwood HS
ROUND TOP-CARMINE ISD
  5721 Carmine HS
ROXTON ISD
  5726 Roxton HS
ROYAL ISD
  5731 Royal HS
ROYSE CITY ISD
  5736 Royse City HS
RULE ISD
  5741 Rule School
RUNGE ISD
  5746 Runge HS
RUSK ISD
  5751 Rusk HS
S AND S CONS ISD
  5756 S and S Cons HS
SABINAL ISD
  5761 Sabinal School
SABINE ISD
  5766 Sabine HS
SABINE PASS ISD
  5771 Sabine Pass School
SAINT JO ISD
  5776 Saint Jo HS
SALADO ISD
  5781 Salado HS
SALTILLO ISD
  5786 Saltillo School
SAM RAYBURN ISD
  5791 Rayburn HS
SAMNORWOOD ISD
  5796 Samnorwood HS
SAN ANGELO ISD
  5801 Central HS
  5806 Lake View HS

SAN ANTONIO ISD
  5810 Brackenridge HS
  5811 Burbank HS
  5816 Cresthaven
  5821 Edison HS
  5826 Fox Technical HS
  5831 Healy-Murphy
  5836 Highlands HS
  5841 Houston HS
  5846 Jefferson HS
  5851 Lanier HS
  5856 Wheatley HS
SAN AUGUSTINE ISD
  5861 San Augustine HS
SAN BENITO CONS ISD
  5866 San Benito HS
SAN DIEGO ISD
  5871 San Diego HS
SAN ELIZARIO ISD
  5876 San Elizario HS
SAN FELIPE-DEL RIO C ISD
  5881 Del Rio HS
SAN ISIDRO ISD
  5886 San Isidro HS
SAN MARCOS ISD
  5891 San Marcos HS
SAN PERLITA ISD
  5896 San Perlita School
SAN SABA ISD
  5901 San Saba HS
SANDS ISD
  5906 Sands HS
SANFORD ISD
  5911 Sanford-Fritch HS
SANGER ISD
  5916 Sanger HS
SANTA ANNA ISD
  5921 Santa Anna HS
SANTA FE ISD
  5926 Santa Fe HS
SANTA ROSA ISD
  5931 Santa Rosa HS
  5936 So Texas HS—Hlth Prof
SANTO ISD
  5941 Santo HS
SAVOY ISD
  5946 Savoy School
SCHERTZ-CIBOLO-U CITY ISD
  5951 Samuel Clemens HS
SCHLEICHER ISD
  5955 Eldorado HS
  5956 Schleicher HS
SCHULENBURG ISD
  5961 Schulenburg HS
SCURRY-ROSSER ISD
  5966 Scurry-Rosser HS
SEAGRAVES ISD
  5971 Seagraves HS
SEALY ISD
  5976 Sealy HS
SEGUIN ISD
  5981 Seguin HS
SEMINOLE ISD
  5986 Seminole HS
SEYMOUR ISD
  5991 Seymour HS
SHALLOWATER ISD
  5996 Shallowater HS
SHAMROCK ISD
  6001 Shamrock HS
SHARYLAND ISD
  6006 Sharyland HS
SHELBYVILLE ISD
  6011 Shelbyville School
SHELDON ISD
  6016 King HS
SHEPHERD ISD
  6021 Shepherd HS
SHERMAN ISD
  6026 Sherman HS
SHINER ISD
  6031 Shiner HS

SIDNEY ISD
  6036 Sidney HS
SIERRA BLANCA ISD
  6041 Sierra Blanca HS
SILSBEE ISD
  6046 Silsbee HS
SILVERTON ISD
  6051 Silverton School
SIMMS ISD
  6056 James Bowie HS
SINTON ISD
  6061 Sinton HS
SKIDMORE-TYNAN ISD
  6066 Skidmore-Tynan HS
SLATON ISD
  6071 Slaton HS
SLIDELL ISD
  6076 Slidell School
SLOCUM ISD
  6081 Slocum School
SMITHVILLE ISD
  6086 Smithville HS
SMYER ISD
  6091 Smyer HS
SNOOK ISD
  6096 Snook School
SNYDER ISD
  6101 Snyder HS
SOCORRO ISD
  6106 Socorro HS
SOMERSET ISD
  6111 Somerset HS
SOMERVILLE ISD
  6116 Somerville HS
SONORA ISD
  8001 Sonora HS
SOUTH SAN ANTONIO ISD
  6126 South San Antonio HS
  6131 South San Antonio HS
       West
SOUTH TEXAS ISD
  6132 So. Texas HS
SOUTHLAND ISD
  6136 Southland HS
SOUTHSIDE ISD
  6141 Southside HS
SOUTHWEST ISD
  6146 Southwest HS
SPADE ISD
  6151 Spade HS
SPEARMAN ISD
  6156 Spearman HS
SPLENDORA ISD
  6161 Splendora HS
SPRING BRANCH ISD
  6166 Memorial HS
  6171 Northbrook HS
  6176 Spring Woods HS
  6181 Stratford HS
SPRING HILL ISD
  6186 Spring Hill HS
SPRING ISD
  6191 Spring HS
  6196 Westfield HS
SPRINGLAKE-EARTH ISD
  8006 Springlake HS
SPRINGTOWN ISD
  6206 Springtown HS
SPUR ISD
  6211 Spur Jr-Sr HS
SPURGER ISD
  6216 Spurger HS
STAFFORD ISD
  6221 Stafford HS
STAMFORD ISD
  6226 Stamford Jr-Sr HS
STANTON ISD
  6231 Stanton HS
STAR ISD
  6236 Star School
STEPHENVILLE ISD
  6241 Stephenville HS

36

STERLING CITY ISD
6246 Sterling City School
STOCKDALE ISD
8011 Stockdale HS
STRATFORD ISD
6256 Stratford HS
STRAWN ISD
6261 Strawn School
SUDAN ISD
6266 Sudan HS
SULPHUR BLUFF ISD
6271 Sulphur Bluff HS
SULPHUR SPRINGS ISD
6276 Sulphur Springs HS
SUNDOWN ISD
8016 Sundown HS
SUNRAY ISD
6286 Sunray HS
SWEENY ISD
6291 Sweeny HS
SWEETWATER ISD
6296 Sweetwater HS
TAFT ISD
8021 Taft HS
TAHOKA ISD
6306 Tahoka Jr-Sr HS
TALCO-BOGATA CONS ISD
6311 Rivercrest HS
TARKINGTON ISD
6316 Tarkington HS
TATUM ISD
8026 Tatum HS
TAYLOR ISD
6326 Taylor HS
TEAGUE ISD
6331 Teague Jr-Sr HS
TEMPLE ISD
6336 Temple HS
TENAHA ISD
6341 Tenaha HS
TERRELL COUNTY ISD
6346 Sanderson HS
TERRELL ISD
6351 Terrell HS
TEXARKANA ISD
6356 Texas HS
TEXAS CITY ISD
6361 Texas City HS
TEXAS SCHOOL FOR THE BLIND
6366 TX School for the Blind
TEXAS SCHOOL FOR THE DEAF
6371 TX School for the Deaf
Mid-HS
TEXLINE ISD
6376 Texline School
THORNDALE ISD
6381 Thorndale HS
THRALL ISD
6386 Thrall HS
THREE RIVERS ISD
6391 Three Rivers HS
THREE WAY ISD
6396 Three Way School
THROCKMORTON ISD
6401 Throckmorton HS
TIDEHAVEN ISD
6406 Tidehaven HS
TIMPSON ISD
6411 Timpson HS
TOLAR ISD
6416 Tolar HS
TOM BEAN ISD
6421 Tom Bean HS
TOMBALL ISD
6426 Tomball HS
TORNILLO ISD
6431 Tornillo HS
TRENT ISD
6436 Trent School
TRENTON ISD
6441 Trenton HS

TRINIDAD ISD
6446 Trinidad School
TRINITY ISD
6451 Trinity HS
TROUP ISD
6456 Troup HS
TROY ISD
6461 Troy HS
TULIA ISD
6466 Tulia HS
TULOSO-MIDWAY ISD
6471 Tuloso-Midway HS
TURKEY-QUITAQUE ISD
6476 Valley HS
TYLER ISD
6481 John Tyler HS
6486 Lee HS
6491 Roberts School
UNION GROVE ISD
6496 Union Grove HS
UNION HILL ISD
6501 Union Hill HS
UNION ISD
6506 Union School
UNITED ISD
6511 United HS
UTOPIA ISD
6516 Utopia School
UVALDE CONS ISD
6521 Uvalde HS
VALENTINE ISD
6526 Valentine HS
VALLEY MILLS ISD
6531 Valley Mills HS
VALLEY VIEW ISD
6536 Valley View School
VAN ALSTYNE ISD
6541 Van Alstyne HS
VAN ISD
6546 Van HS
VAN VLECK ISD
6551 Van Vleck HS
VEGA ISD
6556 Vega HS
VENUS ISD
6561 Venus HS
VERNON CONS ISD
6566 Vernon HS
VICTORIA ISD
6571 Stroman HS
6576 Victoria HS
VIDOR ISD
6581 Vidor HS
WACO ISD
6586 Metro Learning Ctr
6591 University HS
6596 Waco HS
WAELDER ISD
6601 Waelder HS
WALL ISD
6606 Wall HS
WALLER ISD
6611 Waller HS
WALLIS-ORCHARD ISD
6616 Brazos HS
WALNUT SPRINGS ISD
6621 Walnut Springs School
WARREN ISD
6626 Warren HS
WASKOM ISD
6631 Waskom HS
WATER VALLEY ISD
6636 Water Valley HS
WAXAHACHIE ISD
6641 Waxahachie HS
WEATHERFORD ISD
6646 Weatherford HS
WEBB CONS ISD
6651 Bruni HS
WEIMAR ISD
6656 Weimar HS

WEINERT ISD
6661 Weinert School
WELLINGTON ISD
6666 Wellington School
WELLMAN ISD
6671 Wellman HS
WELLS ISD
6676 Wells HS
WESLACO ISD
6681 Weslaco HS
WEST HARDIN ISD
6686 West Hardin HS
WEST ISD
6691 West HS
WEST ORANGE COVE CONS ISD
6695 West Orange—Stark
HS-East
6696 West Orange—Stark
HS-West
WEST OSO ISD
6701 West Oso HS
WEST RUSK ISD
6706 West Rusk HS
WEST SABINE ISD
6711 West Sabine HS
WESTBROOK ISD
6716 Westbrook School
WESTMINSTER ISD
6721 Westminster HS
WESTWOOD ISD
6726 Westwood HS
WHARTON ISD
6731 Wharton HS
WHEELER ISD
6736 Wheeler School
WHITE DEER ISD
6741 White Deer HS
WHITE OAK ISD
6746 White Oak HS
WHITE SETTLEMENT ISD
6751 Brewer HS
WHITEFACE CISD
6756 Whiteface HS
WHITEHOUSE ISD
6761 Whitehouse HS
WHITESBORO ISD
6766 Whitesboro HS
WHITEWRIGHT ISD
6771 Whitewright HS
WHITHARRAL ISD
6776 Whitharral School
WHITNEY ISD
6781 Whitney HS
WICHITA FALLS ISD
6786 Hirschi HS
6791 Rider HS
6796 Wichita Falls HS
WILLIS ISD
6801 Willis HS
WILLS POINT ISD
6806 Wills Point HS
WILMER-HUTCHINS ISD
6811 Wilmer-Hutchins HS
WILSON ISD
6816 Wilson HS
WIMBERLEY ISD
6821 Danforth HS
WINDHAM SCHOOLS
6826 Central (UN-GR)
WINDTHORST ISD
6831 Windthorst HS
WINK-LOVING ISD
6836 Wink HS
WINNSBORO ISD
6841 Winnsboro HS
WINONA ISD
6846 Winona HS
WINTERS ISD
6851 Winters HS
WODEN ISD
6856 Woden HS

WOLFE CITY ISD
6861 Wolfe City HS
WOODSBORO ISD
6866 Woodsboro HS
WOODSON ISD
6871 Woodson HS
WOODVILLE ISD
6876 Woodville HS
WORTHAM ISD
6881 Wortham HS
WYLIE ISD (ABILENE)
6886 Wylie HS
WYLIE ISD (WYLIE)
6891 Wylie HS
YANTIS ISD
6896 Yantis HS
YOAKUM ISD
6901 Yoakum HS
YORKTOWN ISD
6906 Yorktown HS
YSLETA ISD
6911 Bel Air HS
6912 Del Valle HS
6916 Eastwood HS
6921 J. M. Hanks HS
6926 Parkland HS
6931 Riverside HS
6936 Ysleta HS
ZAPATA ISD
6941 Zapata HS
ZAVALLA ISD
6946 Zavalla HS
ZEPHYR ISD
6951 Zephyr HS

ADDITIONAL CODES
9000 Any Texas private
high school
9050 Any out-of-state
high school
9060 Other Texas
public high school

37

TABLE 7
Codes for Texas Colleges and Universities

This table contains a list of Texas colleges and universities. Use this list to complete questions number 10 and number 13 on the registration form. The colleges and universities are listed alphabetically. Use the three-digit code to the left of the institution name to fill out questions number 10 and number 13.

Do not use this table to fill out question number 12. Use Table 8, TASP Test Centers, to fill out question number 12.

Code	Institution	Code	Institution	Code	Institution
101	Abilene Christian University	213	Northeast Texas Community College	301	Texas A&M University—College Station
103	Alvin Community College			303	Texas A&M University—Galveston
105	Amarillo College	215	North Harris County College—East		
106	Amber University			305	Texas Christian University
107	American Technological University	217	North Harris County College—South	307	Texas College
108	Angelina College			309	Texas Lutheran College
109	Angelo State University	219	North Harris County College—Tomball	311	Texas Southern University
111	Austin College			313	Texas Southmost College
113	Austin Community College	221	North Lake College	315	Texas State Technical Institute—Amarillo
115	Baylor University	223	Odessa College		
117	Bee County College	225	Our Lady of the Lake University	317	Texas State Technical Institute—Harlingen
119	Bishop College	227	Palo Alto College		
121	Blinn College	229	Pan American University—Brownsville	319	Texas State Technical Institute—Sweetwater
123	Brazosport College				
125	Brookhaven College	231	Pan American University—Edinburg	321	Texas State Technical Institute—Waco
127	Cedar Valley College				
129	Central Texas College	233	Panola Junior College	323	Texas Tech University
131	Cisco Junior College	235	Paris Junior College	324	Texas Tech University Health Sciences Center
133	Clarendon College	237	Paul Quinn College		
135	College of the Mainland	239	Prairie View A&M University	325	Texas Wesleyan College
137	Collin County Community College	241	Ranger Junior College	327	Texas Woman's University
139	Concordia Lutheran College	243	Rice University	329	Trinity University
141	Cooke County College	245	Richland College	331	Trinity Valley Community College
143	Corpus Christi State University	247	St. Edward's University	333	Tyler Junior College
145	Dallas Baptist University	249	St. Mary's University	335	University of Dallas
147	Del Mar College	251	St. Philip's College	337	University of Houston—Clear Lake
149	Eastfield College	253	Sam Houston State University		
151	East Texas Baptist University	255	San Antonio College	339	University of Houston—Downtown
153	East Texas State University—Commerce	257	San Jacinto College—Central		
		259	San Jacinto College—North	341	University of Houston—University Park
155	East Texas State University—Texarkana	261	San Jacinto College—South		
		263	Schreiner College	343	University of Houston—Victoria
157	El Centro College	265	Southern Methodist University		
159	El Paso Community College	267	South Plains College—Levelland	345	University of Mary Hardin—Baylor
161	Frank Phillips College	269	South Plains College—Lubbock		
163	Galveston College	271	Southwest Collegiate Institute for the Deaf	347	University of North Texas
165	Grayson County College			349	University of St. Thomas
167	Hardin-Simmons University	273	Southwest Texas Junior College	351	University of Texas at Arlington
169	Hill College	275	Southwest Texas State University	353	University of Texas at Austin
171	Houston Baptist University	277	Southwestern Adventist College	355	University of Texas at Dallas
173	Houston Community College	278	Southwestern Assemblies of God College	357	University of Texas at El Paso
175	Howard College			359	University of Texas at San Antonio
177	Howard Payne University	279	Southwestern Baptist Theological Seminary		
179	Huston-Tillotson College			361	University of Texas at Tyler
181	Incarnate Word College	280	Southwestern Christian College	362	University of Texas Health Science Center at Houston
182	Jacksonville College	281	Southwestern University		
183	Jarvis Christian College	282	Stephen F. Austin State University	363	University of Texas Health Science Center at San Antonio
185	Kilgore College				
187	Lamar University at Beaumont	283	Sul Ross State University—Alpine	364	University of Texas of the Permian Basin
189	Lamar University at Orange				
191	Lamar University at Port Arthur	285	Sul Ross State University—Uvalde Study Center	365	Vernon Regional Junior College
193	Laredo Junior College			367	Victoria College
195	Laredo State University	287	Tarleton State University	369	Wayland Baptist University
197	Lee College	289	Tarrant County Junior College—Northeast	371	Weatherford College
198	LeTourneau College			373	Western Texas College
199	Lon Morris College	291	Tarrant County Junior College—Northwest	375	West Texas State University
200	Lubbock Christian University			377	Wharton County Junior College
201	McLennan Community College	293	Tarrant County Junior College—South	379	Wiley College
203	McMurry College			381	Other Texas College/University
205	Midland College	295	Temple Junior College		
207	Midwestern State University	297	Texarkana College		
209	Mountain View College	299	Texas A&I University		
211	Navarro College				

38

TABLE 8
TASP Test Centers

Use this list to complete question number 12 on the registration form. Choose three test centers that would be convenient for you. Enter the four-digit code to the left of the test center in the boxes marked first choice, second choice, and third choice.

Test centers are listed alphabetically by city or town. If you register early, you are more likely to be assigned to the test center you list as your first choice. Your admission ticket will give the name of your test center and the testing location to which you should report.

City	Test Center Code	Institution	City	Test Center Code	Institution
Abilene	4101	Abilene Christian University	Keene	3277	Southwestern Adventist College
	4167	Hardin-Simmons University	Kerrville	6263	Schreiner College
	4203	McMurry College	Kilgore	3185	Kilgore College
Alpine	5283	Sul Ross State University	Killeen	6129	Central Texas College
Alvin	2103	Alvin Community College	Kingsville	1299	Texas A&I University
Amarillo	4105	Amarillo College	Lake Jackson	2123	Brazosport College
	4315	Texas State Technical Institute	Lancaster	3127	Cedar Valley College
Arlington	3351	University of Texas	Laredo	1193	Laredo Junior College
Athens	3401	Trinity Valley Community College	Levelland	4267	South Plains College
Austin	6113	Austin Community College	Lubbock	4200	Lubbock Christian University
	6353	University of Texas		4269	South Plains College
Baytown	2197	Lee College		4323	Texas Tech University
Beaumont	2187	Lamar University	Lufkin	2108	Angelina College
Beeville	1117	Bee County College	Marshall	3151	East Texas Baptist University
Big Spring	4175	Howard College		3379	Wiley College
Borger	4161	Frank Phillips College	McKinney	3407	Collin County Community College
Brenham	6121	Blinn College	Mesquite	3149	Eastfield College
Brownsville	1313	Texas Southmost College	Midland	5205	Midland College
Canyon	4375	West Texas State University	Mount Pleasant	3213	Northeast Texas Community College
Carthage	3233	Panola Junior College			
Cisco	3131	Cisco Junior College	Nacogdoches	2282	Stephen F. Austin State University
Clarendon	4133	Clarendon College			
College Station	6301	Texas A&M University	Odessa	5223	Odessa College
Commerce	3153	East Texas State University	Orange	2189	Lamar University
Corpus Christi	1147	Del Mar College	Palestine	3403	Trinity Valley Community College
Corsicana	3211	Navarro College	Paris	3235	Paris Junior College
Dallas	3125	Brookhaven College	Pasadena	2257	San Jacinto College—Central
	3145	Dallas Baptist University	Plainview	4369	Wayland Baptist University
	3157	El Centro College	Plano	3409	Collin County Community College
	3209	Mountain View College	Port Arthur	2191	Lamar University
	3245	Richland College	Prairie View	2239	Prairie View A&M University
	3265	Southern Methodist University	Ranger	3241	Ranger Junior College
Denison	3165	Grayson County College	San Angelo	6109	Angelo State University
Denton	3327	Texas Woman's University	San Antonio	6225	Our Lady of the Lake University
	3347	University of North Texas		6227	Palo Alto College
Edinburg	1231	Pan American University		6251	San Antonio College
El Paso	5159	El Paso Community College		6255	St. Philip's College
	5357	University of Texas		6359	University of Texas
Fort Worth	3291	Tarrant County Junior College	San Marcos	6275	Southwest Texas State University
	3325	Texas Wesleyan College	Seguin	6309	Texas Lutheran College
Gainesville	3141	Cooke County College	Sherman	3111	Austin College
Galveston	2163	Galveston College	Snyder	4373	Western Texas College
Georgetown	6281	Southwestern University	Stephenville	3287	Tarleton State University
Harlingen	1317	Texas State Technical Institute	Sweetwater	4319	Texas State Technical Institute
Hawkins	3183	Jarvis Christian College	Temple	6295	Temple Junior College
Hillsboro	3169	Hill College	Terrell	3405	Trinity Valley Community College
Houston	2171	Houston Baptist University	Texarkana	3297	Texarkana College
	2173	Houston Community College	Texas City	2135	College of the Mainland
	2215	North Harris County College—East	Tomball	2219	North Harris County College—Tomball
	2217	North Harris County College—South			
			Tyler	3307	Texas College
	2259	San Jacinto College—North		3333	Tyler Junior College
	2261	San Jacinto College—South	Uvalde	6373	Southwest Texas Junior College
	2311	Texas Southern University	Vernon	4365	Vernon Regional Junior College
	2337	University of Houston—Clear Lake	Victoria	2367	Victoria College
			Waco	6115	Baylor University
	2339	University of Houston—Downtown		6201	McLennan Community College
	2341	University of Houston—University Park		6237	Paul Quinn College
				6321	Texas State Technical Institute
	2349	University of St. Thomas	Weatherford	3371	Weatherford College
Huntsville	2253	Sam Houston State University	Wharton	2377	Wharton County Junior College
Irving	3221	North Lake College	Wichita Falls	3207	Midwestern State University

Texas Academic Skills Program
ADDITIONAL SCORE REPORT REQUEST FORM

DO NOT WRITE IN THIS SPACE

IMPORTANT: Use this form to request either a duplicate of your score report or that your score report be sent to the institution(s) you list.

Mail to: TASP Test
National Evaluation Systems, Inc.
P.O. Box 140347
Austin, TX 78714-0347

1. **Social Security Number:** ☐☐☐ - ☐☐ - ☐☐☐☐   2. **Date of Birth:** ☐☐☐☐☐☐
   Month Day Year

3. **Name:**

   Last   First   Middle Initial

4. **Address:** ☐ Check here if this is a change from the address you provided on your original registration form.

   Post Office Box or Street Address

   City or Town   State   Zip Code
                                           (see Table 2)

5. **Send Additional Score Report to Institution(s) Listed**

   PLEASE PRINT BELOW THE CODE OF THE INSTITUTION TO WHICH YOU WANT YOUR SCORE REPORT SENT.

   THREE-DIGIT INSTITUTION CODE (see Table ___)

   ☐☐☐ _____
                        Name of Institution

   ☐☐☐ _____
                        Name of Institution

   ☐☐☐ _____
                        Name of Institution

6. **Duplicate Score Report**

Please send me a duplicate of my score report (check one). (You may order only one [1])	☐ Yes	☐ No

7. **Payment**

Score Report	Number of Reports	Fee	Payment
Duplicate Score Report Sent to Me	one	X $12 each	= $
Additional Score Report Sent to Institution(s) Listed Above		X $ 5 each	= $
		Total Payment Enclosed	$

Please enclose a money order or personal check for the total amount payable to NES. Please include your social security number on the money order or check.

41

Texas Academic Skills Program
OFFICIAL TASP TEST STUDY GUIDE REQUEST FORM

DO NOT WRITE IN THIS SPACE

IMPORTANT: This form should be used to order a single study guide when you are not also registering for the TASP Test or for ordering more than one study guide.

Mail to: TASP Test Study Guide
National Evaluation Systems, Inc.
P.O. Box 140347
Austin, TX 78714-0347

1. **Name:**

Last   First   Middle Initial

2. **Address:**

Post Office Box or Street Address

City or Town   State (see Table 2)   Zip Code

3.

Number of Study Guides Ordered	Cost Per Copy*	Amount Due
_____	$15 each	$ _____

*Note: The cost per copy of $15 is a $12 price for each study guide plus $3 per copy for shipping and handling

Please enclose a money order or personal check for the amount due payable to NES. Please include your social security number on the money order or check.

-- Detach Here --

Texas Academic Skills Program
WITHDRAWAL REQUEST FORM

DO NOT WRITE IN THIS SPACE

IMPORTANT: Completion of this form signifies that you are withdrawing your registration for the TASP Test.

Mail to: TASP Test
National Evaluation Systems, Inc.
P.O. Box 140347
Austin, TX 78714-0347

1. **Social Security Number:**   2. **Date of Birth:**

Month   Day   Year

3. **Name:**

Last   First   Middle Initial

4. **Address:**

Post Office Box or Street Address

City or Town   State (see Table 2)   Zip Code

5. **Test date** for which you are requesting to withdraw:

_____ (1) March 4, 1989   _____ (3) July 29, 1989   _____ (5) Nov. 18, 1989
_____ (2) June 10, 1989   _____ (4) Sept. 30, 1989

6. I understand that this Withdrawal from the TASP Test Request Form must be **received** by National Evaluation Systems, Inc., no later than the Registration Deadline for the test administration date for which I am withdrawing in order for me to receive a refund.

Signature   Date

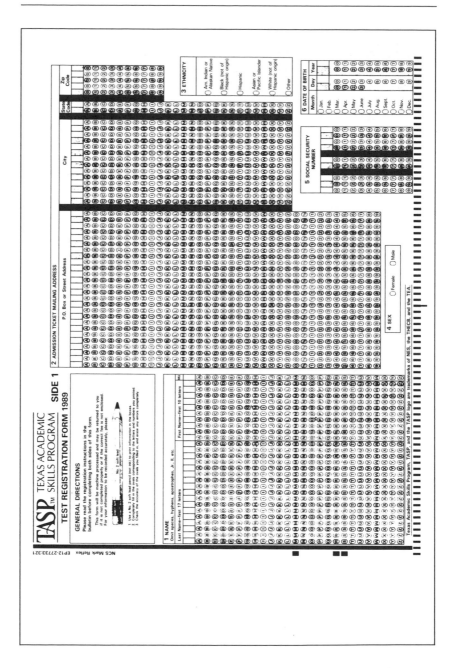

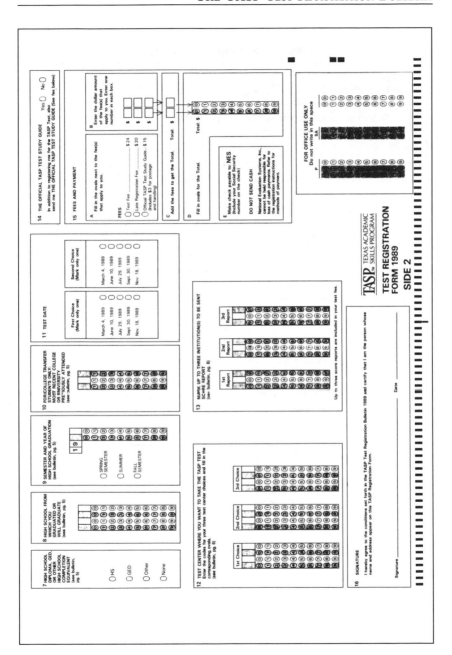

Registration Schedule for 1989

Test Date (Saturday Morning)	Postmark Deadline for Regular Registration	Late Registration Period
March 4, 1989	February 3, 1989	February 6, 1989–February 22, 1989
June 10, 1989	May 13, 1989	May 15, 1989–May 31, 1989
July 29, 1989	July 1, 1989	July 3, 1989–July 19, 1989
September 30, 1989	September 2, 1989	September 4, 1989–September 20, 1989
November 18, 1989	October 21, 1989	October 23, 1989–November 8, 1989

- For information about whether or not you have to take the TASP Test, see page X.
- Registration instructions appear on pages X–X.
- If you miss the Registration Deadline, see schedule for Late Registration Period.
- Requests for special administration procedures and alternate test dates must be made in writing. See page X.

TASP Test Registration and Other Fees

Fee for regular registration for all or any section of the TASP Test (fee includes sending score report to institution listed)	$24
Other Fees	
Change of Registration (test date, (test center)	$15
Late Registration	$20
Additional Score Report to Institution	$ 5
Duplicate Score Report	$12
Score Verification	$10
The Official TASP Test Study Guide	$12
Charge by NES for processing personal check returned by bank	$10